Kipling
Interviews and Recollections

Volume 2

KIPLING

Interviews and Recollections

Volume 2

Edited by

Harold Orel

Barnes & Noble Books
Totowa, New Jersey

First published in the U.S.A. 1983 by
BARNES & NOBLE BOOKS
81, Adams Drive, Totowa
New Jersey, 07512

ISBN 0-389-20276-2

Printed in Hong Kong

Library of Congress Cataloging in Publication Data

Main entry under title:

Kipling, interviews and recollections.

1. Kipling, Rudyard, 1865–1936—Interviews. 2. Authors,
English—19th century—Interviews. 3. Authors, English—20th
century—Interviews. I. Orel, Harold, 1926–
PR4856.K49   828'.809   82–1724
ISBN 0-389-20276-2   AACR2

Contents

v

PART VI TRAVELS

PART VII THE FINAL YEARS

Acknowledgements

Thanks are due to the American Philosophical Society for a grant-in-aid from the Primrose Fund; to Robert P. Cobb, Executive Vice-Chancellor of the University of Kansas, and to Gerhard Zuther, Chairman of the English Department, for encouragement on this project; to Frances D. Horowitz, Vice-Chancellor for Research, Graduate Studies and Public Service, and Dean of the Graduate School, and Robert C. Bearse, Associate Vice-Chancellor in the same office, for their support, provided through the General Research Fund; to Sankaran Ravindran for his help on some problems relating to Kipling's years in India; to Mary Davidson for assistance in solving a variety of annotation questions; and to the following individuals for responding helpfully to specific inquiries: Mrs T. P. Srinivasan, William Fletcher, George Jerkovich, Oliver C. Phillips, George J. Worth, L. E. James Helyar, Eleanor Symons and Helmut Huelsbergen. Nancy Kreighbaum, Peggy Wessel and Paula Oliver prepared the manuscript.

I am grateful to those who staff the Reference Desk and take care of Inter-Library Loan Services at the University of Kansas Library, and to Alexandra Mason, Director, and William Mitchell, of the Spencer Research Library.

Special thanks are due to Julia Steward and Valery Brooks of Macmillan for their thoughtful and helpful editorial assistance.

Kipling's writings are dated in terms of their first publication, to enable readers to relate a particular poem, short story, or book to a period in his life. The basic authority used for these identifications is *Rudyard Kipling: A Bibliographical Catalogue*, by James McG. Stewart, ed. A. W. Yeats (Toronto: Dalhousie University Press and University of Toronto Press, 1959). Difficult words, phrases, topical allusions, place-names and literary references are annotated whenever possible, and to the fullest extent within space limitations. While reviewing Kipling's own writings, I have found particularly helpful the 5672 pages of *The Reader's Guide to Rudyard Kipling's Work*, prepared by Roger Lancelyn Green, Alec Mason, and especially R. E. Harbord between 1961 and 1972 (Canterbury: Gibbs & Sons; later, Bournemouth: Boscombe Printers). All persons interested in Kipling are indebted to the contents of the *Kipling Journal*, published by the Kipling Society continuously since March

1927. A notable bibliography of secondary materials – of writings about Rudyard Kipling – was compiled and edited by Helmut E. Gerber and Edward Lauterbach, and published in *English Fiction in Transition*, III, nos 3–5 (1960), and VIII, nos 3–4 (1965). Three biographies of Kipling, based on intensive research and travel as well as first-hand information, are collectively indispensable: Charles Carrington's *Rudyard Kipling* (London: Macmillan, 1955, revised in 1978); Angus Wilson's *The Strange Ride of Rudyard Kipling* (London: Secker & Warburg, 1977); and Lord Birkenhead's *Rudyard Kipling* (London: Weidenfeld & Nicolson, 1978). I regret that the scope of this work prevents me from drawing more often on the surprisingly ample literature dealing with Rudyard Kipling's parents and family. They were colourful in their own right, and superb achievers of almost anything they set out to do; fascinating information about their lives and accomplishments turns up in many memoirs. But that is another story.

In addition, the editor and publishers wish to thank the following who have kindly given permission for the use of copyright material:

The Atlantic Monthly Co., for the extract from 'The Young Kipling' by Edmonia Hill, published in *The Atlantic Monthly*, April 1936, copyright 1936 by The Atlantic Monthly Co., Boston, Mass. The Earl Baldwin of Bewdley, for the extract from 'The Unfading Genius of Rudyard Kipling' by Arthur Windham Baldwin. Boydell & Brewer Ltd, for the extract from *The Cloak That I Left* by Lilias Rider Haggard. Curtis Brown Ltd, London, on behalf of Beverley Nichols, for the extract from *25: Being a Young Man's Candid Recollections of his Elders and Betters*. Faber & Faber Ltd, for the extract from *Listening for the Drums* by Sir Ian Hamilton. Hamish Hamilton Ltd, for the extracts from 'Kipling and Edgar Wallace' by Margaret Lane in *Edgar Wallace: The Biography of a Phenomenon*. Harper & Row, Publishers, Inc., for the extracts from *Mark Twain in Eruption*, edited by Bernard De Voto, copyright 1940 by the Mark Twain Co. Houghton Mifflin Co., for the extract from *A Golden Age of Authors* by William Webster Ellsworth. John Murray (Publishers) Ltd, for the extracts from *Francis Younghusband, Explorer and Mystic* by George Seaver, and from *The*

Lost Historian: A Memoir of Sir Sidney Low by Desmond Chapman-Huston.

Oxford University Press, for the extract from *Three Houses* by Angela Thirkell.

The executors of the Estate of Dorothy C. Ponton, for the extracts from her articles published in the *Kipling Journal*.

Charles Scribner's Sons, for the extracts from *These Many Years: Recollections of a New Yorker* by Brander Matthews, copyright 1917 by Charles Scribner's Sons, and renewed in 1945.

The Vermont Country Store, for the extract from *Rudyard Kipling's Vermont Feud* by Frederic F. Van De Water.

Whilst every effort has been made to locate owners of copyright in some cases this has been unsuccessful. The publishers apologise for any infringement of copyright or failure to acknowledge original sources and shall be glad to include any necessary corrections in subsequent printings.

Part V
Kipling and the United States

How Kipling Discovered America*

BAILEY MILLARD

That 'inglorious Columbus' of whom Mr Vining wrote so convincingly[1] discovered America while sailing over the blue Pacific from the Asiatic side of the world, and so did Rudyard Kipling. The maker of Mulvaney made his discovery of us in 1889, when he landed in San Francisco from the Pacific mail steamer *City of Peking*, and, like a true Britisher, walked all the way from the dock to the Palace Hotel.

Being the first American to welcome Mr Kipling to this country, and to assist him in its discovery, I feel that these jottings of mine, made after seventeen years of his glorious upward progress, may possess some interest to those younglings who have run wild with Mowgli in the jungle, and to those oldlings who have sat on the throne with 'The Man Who Would Be King'. When I speak of 'welcoming' Mr Kipling, I do not use the word in any special sense; San Francisco welcomes everybody. None of us had ever heard of Kipling, but he, with a few other Anglo-Indians, had heard of himself, and, being a very young writer, he was wondering why the whole world was not ready to rise and hail him. I am afraid, therefore, that I, at that time what he would call a 'pressman', did not approach him with becoming deference when, after seeing the entry, 'Rudyard Kipling, Allahabad, India', on the hotel register one evening, and firing a random card up at him, I met and proceeded to exploit him in the smoking-room. As I bore in those days the burden of 'covering' the hotels, this was all in the day's work, and the likelihood of getting anything worthwhile out of an obscure and doubtless barnacled Britisher was small; for, not being a Simla barrack-room man, to whom this local oracle had spoken

* *The Bookman* (New York) xxvi (Jan 1908) 484–8.

through his *Plain Tales*, how was I to know that the dark little moustached man with the eyeglasses and the Anglican air of indifference to everything was going to all the trouble of living the life of a distinguished literary personage? As I look back upon that first meeting of Kipling with a Californian who presumably knew how to read and yet had not read *him*, I can understand his prompt impatience for all things American, and his vast disappointment in the dozen or so lines which I wrote for my paper in celebration of his arrival.

Conceive me, then, all unknowing, in the presence of the great, asking the author of 'Without Benefit of Clergy' what they ate for breakfast in Allahabad, the kind of tricks the fakirs played, or some such simple questions, when I should have been breathlessly seeking information about his habits of literary composition and whether he wrote best before or after luncheon. It must have been about the time he had given me up as a hopeless case in a literary way, and had accepted San Francisco as the City Ignorant because it was not aware of him, that he fared forth into conversational fields of his own seeking, and began to talk of the native Press of India – curious little papers printed by hand and chronicling Hindu small beer. He also had something to tell about the way in which England maintained her supremacy in India, but what he offered on that subject is now dim to me, as are many other things he said during our talks, though the man made a cumulative and altogether extraordinary impression upon me.

'What do you think of San Francisco?' I asked. It was the stock question – the one that we reporters always put to overland tourists before they were out of their Pullman seats.

'Oh,' said he, his face lighting up, 'I have seen little of it, but it is hallowed ground to me because of Bret Harte.'[2]

'We Californians all venerate Harte', I said proudly. 'Our people nearly tore a fence to pieces up in Humboldt County[3] once for relics of his handiwork; and so greatly do they love him that even now, when it is known that it was not Harte, but Pat McCarren of Eureka, who built the fence, they still keep the bits of redwood on their mantelpieces.'

'I am glad to hear that', he laughed; 'but I have heard that your people resent Harte's expatriation.'

'They do', said I. 'The Californian of today hates to read in one of Mr Harte's stories that the Sacramento Valley is a naked plain, when, as a matter of fact, it is all covered with orchards, vineyards, and grain-fields. They feel that Mr Harte has been away from us too long, and that he should return and get acquainted with our prune-trees.'

'There may be something in that', he said; 'but a true artist can always paint very well at a long distance from his landscapes. Harte has done so well in England, and his work is so highly appreciated there, that I should think you might let him stay on our side and work out his own destiny.'

Mr Kipling continued to discuss Harte, waxing eloquent over 'The Luck of Roaring Camp', 'M'liss' and 'The Outcasts of Poker Flat', and he did not depart from the ground he had taken, nor acknowledge the point I had made when I told him that these stories, which were Harte's best work, and upon which his fame was based, were all written in California – he had done nothing in England to compare with them.

This talk led to an argument on the subject of English appreciation of American literature, and *vice versa*, and it was agreed that the home view of exotic writing was generally a very narrow one. It was characteristic of the Briton, however, that Kipling did not seem to care what view was taken of British literature by Americans.

Mr Kipling has celebrated our Bret Harte talk in his *American Notes*, throughout which he exhibits a positive genius for reporting the thing which was not. For some strange purpose he makes his interviewer say foolishly that 'Bret Harte claims California, but California doesn't claim Bret Harte' – a very handy hook upon which to hang his epigram: 'I never intended to curse the people with a provincialism so vast as this.'

Even to a man who knew nothing of his consummate genius, just then beginning to bud, there was something distinctive about Kipling, as there is about all men of marrow. Once his reserve was broken, one could not help being attracted by him and his conversation, and yet one was never convinced of his great culture. Over his brandy and soda he could be eloquent for five minutes at a time, but, on the whole, I remember him as a man more given to inquiry than ready to impart information. Indeed, it was only after several talks with him that I learned he was the correspondent of the Allahabad *Pioneer*, and that he intended to write his impressions of America for that paper.

On that first evening of his arrival he wanted someone to pilot him around town, which I readily volunteered to do. We walked up Market Street while the theatre crowds were pouring into that thoroughfare. He was plainly disappointed in all that he saw, for he was looking for something Western and raw. One thing that worried him was the rapid step of the crowd. He wanted to know if they always walked that way. The gorgeously lighted and lavishly spread shop-windows made him stare, and he said it was all vastly different from anything he had ever seen. The wonderfully decorated and bemirrored cafés, which were the boast of old San Francisco, were something amazing to him, and never failed to bring forth admiring comment. The prodigal free-lunch system of the town, by which you could buy a glass of wine and have a whole meal thrown in, appealed to him strongly.

I led him into the big newspaper building where I worked, and showed him the presses, the composition-room, and the editorial staff preparing the paper for the next morning. In these things he took much interest, and when I introduced him to some of the choice spirits of the press he talked with them in a friendly, though somewhat condescending, way. But we had always looked for this from Englishmen, and did not mind it. He made a strong impression upon the folk of the press, and, in fact, upon everyone to whom he was introduced. After his first brief pose of insular indifference, he revealed himself as a dynamic personality, readily conversable, strongly assertive, and as English as they make them.

I well remember our walk that night along Kearney Street, through which thoroughfare I was conducting him back to his hotel, that he might not get lost. He had much to say of literature, particularly of the big Frenchmen. He evinced a fondness for Maupassant[4] and Gautier,[5] and we talked of Taine's comparison between Alfred de Musset[6] and Tennyson, which was so much to the discredit of Tennyson. As I remember it, he did not greatly disagree with Taine in the salient points made in favour of De Musset's youthful warmth and his abounding love of life, on the one hand, and Tennyson's cool restraints on the other; but, being British and Tory, he must needs, after all, give Tennyson a much higher place than that of the great Frenchman.

On our way we picked up a late-wandering friend of mine, who, because he knew all about politics, greatly interested Mr Kipling. The conversation was a long and, to me, highly entertaining one. Kipling was the 'chiel amang us takin' notes'. I had never known a foreigner who asked so many and such strange questions about American affairs. Some of them seemed inspired, and touched the very heart of our economic system, but for the most part they were naïve enough. Boss methods in politics interested him greatly, and as my political friend, for the sake of drawing his fire, made bold to defend them, Kipling rushed hotly to the other end of the argument, and ventured such opinions upon our undemocratic democracy as would have won him the lifelong friendship of Mr Debs.[7]

During the fortnight or so of his stay in San Francisco I saw much of Kipling and heard more, for the rather convivial set of men-around-town who took him in tow seemed to revel in the novelty of him, and they recounted with delight the various ways in which they 'strung' him. They told him yarns – ancient, shrivelled ones, baggy at the knees; tales known everywhere except in Allahabad – and these he afterward solemnly related in his book as new stories. His innocence, as manifested by his artless questions, was a source of infinite joy to these reckless *raconteurs*, and inspired them to outdo themselves for his edification. But, on his own side, Kipling has told some yarns in his *Notes* that compare quite favourably with those told by the Californians, while they are almost as moss-grown. For examples, I should select the narratives of his experience with a bunco-steerer[8] and that of the Irish priest and the Chinaman as being purely apocryphal.

Please to remember that none of the club-folk, who rejoiced in getting hold of this young man fresh from India, had the slightest idea that he had literary greatness concealed about his person. We were used to the globe-trotters in San Francisco – the man who dared all sorts of things, even to the wearing of tweeds at formal dinners, and who puffed his pipe and wore his knee-breeches and long woollen hose down Market Street in defiance of the local ordinances in such case made and provided. Kipling was hardly of that sort, but he shared one trait with all his countrymen – that is to say, he regarded his visit to San Francisco as a sort of slumming tour, and was ready to go anywhere, in almost any company. Something is to be allowed for the youth of the man at that period and much for his curiosity, which seemed insatiable.

One of the men-about-town with whom he forgathered on more than one occasion was a festive club-chap named Bigelow, whom everybody called 'Petie'. 'Petie' endeared himself to Kipling by showing him through Chinatown and into all the worst dives of the Barbary Coast. Kipling seemed to be 'game' for whatever was forward. Even when he found that his new friend could embrace the flagon with more warmth and frequency than any other man on 'the route', and was, in fact, the bibulous prize of the town, he was not terrified.

It was 'Petie' who showed Kipling into the Barbary Coast resort where he found his 'dive girl with a Greek head', so rapturously set forth in his *Notes* as among the eight American maidens with whom he fell 'hopelessly in love'.

Item: A girl in a dive, blessed with a Greek head and eyes that seem to speak all that is best and sweetest in the world. But, woe is me! she has no ideas in this world or the next beyond the consumption of beer (a commission on each bottle), and protests that she sings the songs allotted to her nightly without more than the vaguest notion of their meaning.

After lauding the girls of England and France, Mr Kipling declares in his book that he found the American girls, as seen in California, 'above and beyond them all'. His dive beauty has in recent years been discovered by an enterprising newspaper-writer and exploited for a Sunday page, along with corroborative facts that seem substantial enough. But 'Petie' Bigelow, who introduced the Greek-headed damsel to the poet of *The Seven Seas*, is no more of earth. . . .

In the San Francisco Press Club they will tell you a story of how Kipling, who was anxious to raise money to meet his travelling expenses, offered two Mulvaney manuscripts to the Sunday editor of a local journal, and of how the editor, after reading them over, returned them to the author with his thanks and the comment that, while they were well written, they were not 'available', as there was no interest in East Indian tales in this country. I have heard this story repeated so many times that I am inclined to think it is true, though the editor, probably covered with confusion by the wonderful subsequent popularity of those very tales, would never admit the authenticity of the report. If it was true, as many believe and declare, here was another Kiplingian reason why San Francisco was 'a perfectly mad city'.

Well do I remember my last meeting with Kipling, on the occasion of his departure from town, after his inglorious discovery of us. It was at the Palace Hotel, where he was packing his trunk.

'Where are you bound?' I asked.

'For a journey through the States – Chicago, Buffalo, New York', he replied.

'And then?'

'To London.'

'What shall you do there?' I inquired. 'Journalism?'

'Literary work', was his brief reply.

'You are going to try to live by your pen?' I asked, and I remember that when he said 'Yes' I was full of grave apprehension for him. I had known other young men who had gone to London to live by their pens. Most of them had been starved out.

'Yes,' he replied, 'I am going to try for it.'

And he did 'try for it', working desperately hard, with very meagre encouragement at first, living in cheap London lodgings, content with small payment for his literary wares. Even when most discouraged he never entertained a thought of going back to journalism, but clung tenaciously to literature. Which reminds me of a story a man from India told me not long ago:

Once, when Kipling's father was aboard ship, and lying abed with that qualmy feeling, a passenger rushed into his cabin and cried, 'Mr Kipling! Mr Kipling! your boy is up on a yard-arm, and if he lets go he'll be drowned!'

'Don't worry', said Rudyard's father, smiling confidently through his qualms; 'he won't let go.'

So he clung to the precarious literary yard-arm, and was not gone from San Francisco a year before we were all avidly devouring the *Plain Tales*, *The Phantom 'Rickshaw* and *Soldiers Three*, and the whole country was ablaze with the fame of 'that fellow Kipling'. But the first harsh chapters of the *American Notes* tempered the literary pleasure of some of us.

It is to Mr Kipling's credit that in his revised edition he diluted his vitriol.

NOTES

Bailey Millard (1859–1941) was an editor of the *San Francisco Call* (1891–2) and of the *San Francisco Examiner* (1892–1902), *Cosmopolitan* (1905–7) and *Munsey's Magazine* (1913–14). He frequently wrote on agrarian reforms for California, and turned out a large number of short stories, articles, and novels.

1. Edward Payson Vining (b. 1847) published in 1885 *An Inglorious Columbus; or, Evidence that Hwui Shan and a Party of Buddhist Monks from Afghanistan Discovered America in the Fifth Century, AD*.

2. Harte (1836–1902) was a popular short-story writer, famous for his work on the *Overland Monthly* in California, dialect poems ('The Heathen Chinee'), and narratives such as 'The Luck of Roaring Camp' (1868) and 'The Outcasts of Poker Flat' (1869). He served as US Consul in Germany and Scotland (1878–85), and afterwards settled down near London.

3. On the Pacific Coast in north-western California. Mainly in the Coast Ranges, this county contains 400,000 acres of redwoods, or about 50 per cent of the world's total stand.

4. Guy de Maupassant (1850–93), French short-story writer and novelist.

Brilliant member of Émile Zola's circle. Noted for *Une vie* (1883), *Bel-ami* (1885), *Pierre et Jean* (1888), and *Notre coeur* (1890), as well as 300 short stories.

5. Théophile Gautier (1811–72), French poet and writer of prose, began as a Romantic and ended as a Parnassian. His most famous works are *Le Capitaine Fracasse* (1863), *Mademoiselle de Maupin* (1835), and *Voyage en Espagne* (1845). He argued eloquently the doctrine of art for art's sake.

6. Lord Charles Alfred de Musset (1810–54), French poet and playwright. Romantic by temperament, his works were strongly influenced by Byron. An unhappy love-affair with George Sand, described in *Confession d'un enfant du siècle* (1836), encapsulated the mood of an era.

7. Eugene Victor Debs (1855–1926), American labour leader; five times (1900–1920) Socialist candidate for president.

8. A person who persuades others to participate in a confidence game.

A Visit to the Bohemian Club of San Francisco*

ROBERT H. FLETCHER

Lieutenant Carlin was the executive officer of the *Vandalia*, which was totally wrecked with a loss of five officers and thirty-nine of the crew. And it was in this fearful chaos of wind and water and crashing timbers that Mr Carlin, who was a large and powerful man, did such effective service as to call forth the admiration of his no less heroic shipmates and of his fellow members of the Bohemian Club. And thus it was that the latter gave him a 'welcome home dinner' on 5 June 1889. As may be imagined, the Club was gorgeously decorated with national emblems, particularly of a nautical character; the Stars and Stripes, blocks and tackles, laurel wreaths, boat howitzers, stands of arms, anchors, ships' cutlasses and signal flags made up a glittering scene of military beauty, while the various stuffed owls of the Club gazed peacefully out upon this warlike show from various points of vantage. Many were the fine speeches that were made and inspiring were the songs. But perhaps

* *The Annals of the Bohemian Club*, ed. R. H. Fletcher (San Francisco: Hicks-Judd) [? 1909] III, pp. 84–91.

the most interesting description of the affair, if not the most accurate, is that given by an outsider, that outsider being no less a person than the distinguished author, Rudyard Kipling. Mr Kipling had only a few days before landed from the steamship that had brought him from India, and having a letter of introduction to one of the members, Mr George W. Spencer, was given a card to the Club and invited to this dinner. But the effulgent sun of Mr Kipling's fame had not yet risen above the literary horizon to dazzle the eyes of his associates, and so he sat throughout the dinner inconspicuous but nevertheless thoroughly enjoying himself, and from subsequent developments it appears that he took notes, mental notes, between the courses, and these are the comments as afterwards published in *American Notes*, New York, by M. J. Ivers and Co.:

Do you know the Bohemian Club of San Francisco? They say its fame extends over the world. It was created somewhat on the lines of the Savage by men who wrote or drew things, and has blossomed into most unrepublican luxury. The ruler of the place is an owl – an owl standing upon a skull and cross-bones, showing forth grimly the wisdom of the man of letters and the end of his hopes for immortality. The owl stands on the staircase, a statue 4 feet high; is carved in the woodwork, flutters on the frescoed ceiling, is stamped on the notepaper, and hangs on the walls. He is an ancient and honourable bird. Under his wings 'twas my privilege to meet with white men whose lives were not chained down to routine to toil, who wrote magazine articles instead of reading them hurriedly in the pauses of office work; who painted pictures instead of contenting themselves with cheap etchings picked up at another man's sale of effects. Mine were all the rights of social intercourse, craft by craft, that India, stony-hearted stepmother of collectors, has swindled us out of. Treading soft carpets and breathing the incense of superior cigars, I wandered from room to room studying the paintings in which the members of the club had caricatured themselves, their associates and their aims. There was a slick French audacity about the workmanship of these men of toil unbending that went straight to the heart of the beholder. And yet it was not altogether French. A dry grimness of treatment, almost Dutch, marked the difference. The men painted as they spoke – with certainty. The Club indulges in revelries which it calls 'jinks' – high and low – at intervals, and each of these gatherings is faithfully portrayed in oils by hands that know their business. In this club were no amateurs spoiling canvas, because they fancied they could handle oils without knowledge of shadows or anatomy – no gentleman of leisure ruining the temper of publishers and an already ruined market with attempts to write 'because everybody writes something these days'.

My hosts were working or had worked for their daily bread with pen or paint, and their talk for the most part was of the shop – shoppy – that is to say, delightful. They extended a large hand of welcome and were as brethren, and I did homage to the owl and listened to their talk.

They bore me to a banquet in honour of a brave lieutenant – Carlin, of the *Vandalia* – who stuck by his ship in the great cyclone at Apia and comported himself as an officer should. On that occasion – 'twas at the Bohemian Club – I heard oratory with the roundest of 'O's, and devoured dinner the memory of which will descend with me into the hungry grave.

There were about forty speeches delivered, and not one of them was average or ordinary. It was my first introduction to the American eagle, screaming for all it was worth. The lieutenant's heroism served as a peg from which the silver-tongued ones turned themselves loose and kicked.

They ransacked the clouds of sunset, the thunderbolts of heaven, the deeps of hell, and the splendour of the resurrection for tropes and metaphors, and hurled the result at the head of the guest of the evening. Never since the morning stars sung together for joy, I learned, had an amazed creation witnessed such superhuman bravery as that displayed by the American Navy in the Samoa cyclone. Till earth rotted in the phosphorescent star-and-stripe slime of a decayed universe that God-like gallantry would not be forgotten. I grieve that I cannot give the exact words. My attempts at reproducing their spirit is pale and inadequate. I sat bewildered on a coruscating Niagara of blatherumskite. It was magnificent – it was stupendous – and I was conscious of a wicked desire to hide my face in a napkin and grin. Then, according to rule, they produced their dead, and across the snowy tablecloths dragged the corpse of every man slain in the Civil War, and hurled defiance at 'our natural enemy' (England, so please you), 'with her chain of fortresses across the world'. Thereafter they glorified their nation afresh from the beginning, in case any detail should have been overlooked, and that made me uncomfortable for their sakes. How in the world can a white man, a sahib, of our blood, stand up and plaster praise on his own country? He can think as highly as he likes, but this open-mouthed vehemence of adoration struck me almost as indelicate. My hosts talked for rather more than three hours, and at the end seemed ready for three hours more.

But when the lieutenant – such a big, brave, gentle giant – rose to his feet he delivered what seemed to me as the speech of the evening. I remember nearly the whole of it, and it ran something in this way:

'Gentlemen – It's very good of you to give me this dinner and to tell me all these pretty things, but what I want you to understand – the fact is, what we want and what we ought to get at once, is a navy – more ships – lots of 'em – .'

Then we howled the top of the roof off, and I for one fell in love with Carlin on the spot. Wallah![1] He was a man.

The prince among merchants bade me take no heed to the warlike sentiments of some of the old generals. 'The sky-rockets are thrown in for effect,' quoth he, 'and whenever we get on our hind legs we always express a desire to chew up England. It's a sort of family affair.'

And, indeed, when you come to think of it, there is no other country for the American public speaker to trample upon. France has Germany, we have Russia, for Italy Austria is provided, and the humble Pathan possesses an ancestral enemy. Only America stands out of the racket, and therefore to be in fashion makes a sand-bag of the mother country and hangs her when occasion requires. 'The chain of fortresses' man, a fascinating talker, explained to me after the affair that he was compelled to blow off steam. Everybody expected it. When we had chanted 'The Star-Spangled Banner' not more than eight times, we adjourned.

Mr Kipling's impression of the number of orators speaks well for the Club's hospitality, but as a matter of fact there were not forty. General Barnes spoke, and Crittenden Thornton, and Colonel Stuart Taylor and Lieutenant Commander Chenery and the President,[2] and one or two others, maybe, whose names do not appear. Indeed, Mr Kipling privately offered to increase the number and if the Club had known him then as it has since, he undoubtedly would have been given ample opportunity. Perhaps some of the speeches in the matter of length may, under the circumstances, have seemed to Mr Kipling like five or six; then again, if some of them were inflammatory, others were charged with patriotic statistics of a cooling and soporific character calculated to allay all feverish symptoms. Nor was 'The Star-Spangled Banner' sung more than once. Mr Kipling's notes coruscate out of reason in this particular. But all this is of no importance. The bright and shining truth is that the Club gave Jim Carlin a dinner that night and it was a great dinner and the Club is glad that Mr Kipling was there.

One of the members of the Club, a young man, a very young man, was editor of the Sunday Supplement of one of the big daily papers at this time, and to him came the unlooked-for distinction of refusing a Kipling story. What one it was, whether 'The Incarnation of Krishna Mulvaney', 'The Courting of Dinah Shadd', or 'The City of Dreadful Night', is not known, but having just landed, as already stated, a stranger and almost unknown, Kipling sent a story to the editor of this Sunday Supplement who, glancing at it, replied, 'You say this man is just from India? Well, send this back and ask him to do us a snake-story.' Perhaps after all there was a journalistic instinct in this Sunday Supplemental youth's fatuity, for did not Kipling afterwards produce 'Kaa's Hunting', the greatest snake-story ever written? Kipling liked the Club, as his *Notes* amply testify, and frequented the big, sunny library a good deal during his stay, and before he went away he wrote some verses to the Owl. These lines, according to Mr Robertson, who received them, were very fine, and in an unusual spasm of prudence and caution they were not placed with the other archives of the Club, wherever that may have been, but locked up in the office safe. Then came a change of secretaries, a general clearing up, and much to everyone's regret the verses were lost.

NOTES

Robert Howe Fletcher (1850–1936), author and editor, began his career in the US Naval Academy, but transferred to the Army and served on the Indian frontier and in California before retiring in 1886. He directed the growth of the Mark Hopkins Institute of Art (1899–1915) and the San Francisco Institute of Art (1907–15). The Bohemian Club was founded in 1872 to bring together writers, painters, musicians, and actors in the San Francisco area. Its first meeting-place was on Pine Street, over the market. Its members were proud to sponsor the first production of Shakespeare out-of-doors in any country (*As You Like It*), circuses, and a number of cultural events. Nearly all its records were destroyed in the earthquake and fire of 1906.

1. An Anglo-Indian expression, meaning (roughly) 'What a man!' Lt. Carlin had survived the terrifying hurricane that destroyed six warships of the United States and German naval forces on 15–16 March 1889, at Apia, a seaport of western Samoa.

2. Peter Robertson (1847–1911), author of several comic operas and musical dramas.

An Inside Light on Rudyard Kipling*

MARGUERITE STABLER

When Kipling, through the mouth of the incorrigible small boy in his *Captains Courageous* says, 'Oh, I'm all right. I only feel as if my insides are too big for my outsides', he confides a large and personal truth to the reading public.

Kipling, as we know him in his *American Notes*, says many things, thinks many thoughts at our expense, and allows himself to be swayed by many whimsical whims. But Rudyard Kipling, as known by one American woman, at least shows an inside of appreciation and esteem somewhere larger than the public-known outside.

This American woman, the wife of an officer in the English army stationed in India, holds the distinction of having been 'guide, philosopher and friend' to young Kipling during his early war-correspondent days.

It was in answer to the laconic cable 'Kipling will do', from the War Department in India, that young Kipling, sick of his experiences in England, went back to India to *do*. And it was on the steamer *en route* that the friendship with the English officer and his American wife began and formed what he afterward refers to as 'the trio of tramps'.

At this time Kipling's one claim to distinction, if claim it could be called, was a thin, apologetic little volume entitled *Verses by Two Persons*,[1] done chiefly as a schoolboy, the other person representing Kipling *mater*. No one knows that volume now, few of Kipling's

* *Pacific Monthly* (Portland, Oregon), XVIII (Nov 1907) 560–2.

lovers have ever heard of it, the edition having been exceedingly modest; still less was it known then. It was, therefore, solely because of his boyish frankness and enthusiasm that the young chap interested the 'English–American honeymooners', as he called them.

Arrived in Poona,[2] the hospitable officer's home became the new war-correspondent's headquarters, where everything about the house, the grounds, even the gowns of his hostess soon bore the stamp of their guest's enthusiasms. Photographs representing the India home, show a charming little bamboo balcony jutting out with neither rhyme nor reference to the architectural scheme of the house – 'Rudyard did that' the hostess explains – 'he wanted a place where he could put his feet up when he was writing, so drew the design and had it put there himself.'

The walls on the inside bore the same impress of the man of fame-to-be. Pen-and-ink sketches of the Man and the 'Rickshaw', caricatures of the people who lived around them, quite regardless of the possibility of detection, a sketch with a skit scratched around the margin of 'Lieutenant-General Bangs, that most immoral man', and studies of 'Venus Anno Domini' covered the walls. And later, when things began to come his way, sketches for cover-designs began a line from door to door. The first cover-design for his *Soldiers Three* was done by Kipling senior. But, 'Mulvaney was straighter than that', Rudyard objected, 'Mulvaney doesn't slouch'; so the artist was kept at it until he evolved a Mulvaney with a 'soldierly bearing and informal manner'.

It was here, with his feet on the bamboo railing, the manuscript of his 'Baa Baa Black Sheep' was written and read aloud for encouragement and criticism. This being in the main the story of his own experiences at the English school to which he had been put accounts for his early impressions of English life and his grappling the natives of India to his soul as 'Mine Own People'. Often the floor was strewn with loose sheets in disgust at his singed muse, as the work on this first ambitious story progressed, but always as often gathered up by the American friend, who assured him he could do good things if he tried, and Rudyard was set to work again and told, 'You ought to be ashamed of yourself to get discouraged so easily.'

And it was with these good 'English–American honeymooners' the young author rejoiced uproariously when his manuscript was accepted by an English publisher for the munificent sum, as he put it, that would buy his clothes a whole year.

To these same kindest critics and severest friends often came the appeal, 'Do you think my work is coarse? So-an-So says it is.' And the sensitive young war-correspondent would then go over and over his work, arguing, 'How could my men have had a gentler treatment? They are not gentlemen. I'm not trying to set up any code of morals or immorals, I'm simply trying to give them life as they know it and I know it to be.'

This inside light that illumines the pages of many of his letters when his work called him off to the hill districts shows this sensitiveness of refinement on the part of the writer struggling with the love of portraying things for 'the God of Things as they are', and it is only those who knew both sides who appreciate how much too big for his outside respect of nice phraseology is his inside struggle for the truth for truth's sake, whether lovely or unlovely.

But it is because of this very delicacy – the delicate consideration of Rudyard Kipling for the reading public – that his verses entitled 'It' have never, so far, been published, although now in its rough form of pencil jotting on yellow block-paper it is one of the keenest and cleverest skits he has done. 'It', to the sea-sick steamer passenger, needs no explanation nor apology, and in the original manuscript, dashed off on deck under the inspiration of the moment, all the pathetic humour and humorous pathos of the romance of the sea-sick lovers, introduced by the sudden and common need of 'It' remains unpublished, even at so much *per* when he needed the money, and the delicate-minded public, in consequence thereof, remains unshocked.

It is after his early India career, however, that Kipling in this collection of letters in the hands of 'Miladi', as his American friend is called, takes his first 'ink-slings' at American institutions and the American people.

A letter written on the well-known letter-head 'Palace Hotel, San Francisco, California', runs as follows:

I might as well tell you that my head is getting swelled from the treatment I have received in 'Frisco. In the last day it has swelled to such an extent as to almost bury my left eye. It is a bad tooth! This morning by the aid of the other eye I managed to steer my way through the crowded streets into a firm of dentists, where one villain, after looking me over, passed me over to another, who, after an hour's work, hewed off the end of my toof. I 'quealed and 'quealed like anything and flung me down maimed and exhausted on a chair. They told me that if I would come back tomorrow they would put a crown on it, but I feel as if I already deserve a martyr's crown of suffering and go not back. You remember my mention of the Bohemian Club with the sign of the Owl? They have made me a sahib in their midst and the verses I enclose are on the Club and the Owl as you will see.

A pen-scratch here runs across the page with this sudden interruption: 'Have you gotten used, ever, to the use of the term *Mister*? I got a chit today from a young lady – first family too – addressing me *Mr* Rudyard Kipling. Ugh!'

Firm of dentists and young lady, whoever you are, arise and exclaim 'It is I!' You may be called villains and you may be said 'Ugh' at, but it is because of these same distinctions that you fasten your town in the memory of the callow young tourist.

The next page of the letter, in its fine, somewhat cramped hand, continues in the same bubbling, boyish vein, full of touch-and-go impressions of this wonderful Western world and references to the good old Poona days. But the second letter, dated the week later, strikes still more deeply at the San Francisco heart:

There is no place like it. Reckless and roaring like nothing you ever saw. The men make money and 'break up' with a rush that goes to your head. Everything is done on a large scale, even the coins are not small, two-bits is the smallest piece worthy the notice of a self-respecting citizen. But next to the ocean winds it is the reporter man that most takes you off your feet. Your soul is not your own, neither your secrets, your plans, your private ambitions, when they grapple you. It is knowing their Bohemian Club that makes you know San Francisco. High jinks and low jinks presided over by the Owl makes this body of men to hum. There was a 'blow-out' (know you the meaning of that?) given for a great sahib who had stuck by his ship – he was a fighting sahib, by the way – when there was a cyclone or something of unusual size. There were speeches and wittles and drink, twenty I should say, then more of both. Then the Man of the Cyclone rose up and said a few modest and harmless little words, whereupon we howls off the roof of the house. The man next me soothes me suddenly by saying, 'When we get on our hind legs we do like this. See?' I saw and if I could have induced wealth to rhyme with raiment my turn at a verse might have gone better, but I had to be satisfied with collars, dollars.

The letter ends with much anent the good-looking, expensively-clad women on the streets with the accent 'that would be cheap at 50 cents a word', who seem to have filled the Kipling eye during his few days of impression-gathering on the Pacific coast, with passing remarks on the Chinamen, negroes, cable-cars and police-force, ending with 'I wrote you Beatrice[3] is going to be married, I think.'

Many early unpublished efforts, corrected proofs, piles of letters, cartoons, first editions with marginal notes, dinner-cards of absurd jingles touching up each guest's peculiarities, tea-plates painted with rhymes about apples and plums no better than you or I could do, throw a vari-coloured inside light on the man behind the strenuous pen. And on the back of a bill of a little inn among the hills of India the youthful Kipling once scrawled this commentary on the depth of his heart and the shallowness of his pocket:

A coming May
To hills of green and shadows cool
We haste away.

A torrid June
With dance and mirth the circling days
Pass all too soon.

A gay July
A broken heart, a fond adieu, a little bill
And then we fly.

NOTES

Marguerite Stabler wrote light fiction for such periodicals as *St Nicholas* and *Overland Monthly* at the turn of the century.

1. Another title for *Echoes* (1884), a collection of thirty-nine poems written by Kipling and his sister Alice ('Trix'). Marguerite Stabler is mistaken in her identification of 'the other person' as Kipling's mother; it was, in fact, Kipling's sister Alice. Alice Macdonald Kipling contributed her own fiction and poetry to the contents of *Quartette*, the Christmas Annual for 1885 of the *Civil and Military Gazette* (as did Kipling himself and his father).

2. A division, district and city in Maharashtra, western India, on the tributary

of the Bhima River, 80 miles east-south-east of Bombay. Poona came under British rule in 1818, and was a military centre.

3. Most likely a reference to Trix, whose engagement to John Fleming was announced shortly before her brother left India to begin his travels through the United States to England. Trix used 'Beatrice Grange' as a pseudonym when she published her first novel in 1891.

An Unsuccessful Effort to Sell Short Stories*

GEORGE HAMLIN FITCH

It was in 1889 that *The Pioneer* sent him on a tour of the world and he wrote the series of letters afterwards reprinted under the title *From Sea to Sea*. Kipling, like Stevenson, had to have a story to tell to bring out all his powers; hence these letters are not among his best work.

Vividly do I recall Kipling's visit to San Francisco. He came into the *Chronicle* office and was keenly interested in the fine collections which made this newspaper's library before the fire the most valuable on this coast, if not in the country. He was also much impressed with the many devices for securing speed in typesetting and other mechanical work. The only feature of his swarthy face that impressed one was his brilliant black eyes, which behind his large glasses, seemed to note every detail. He talked very well, but although he made friends among local newspapermen, he was unsuccessful in selling any of his stories to the editors of the Sunday supplements. He soon went to New York, but there also he failed to dispose of his stories.

NOTE

Fitch (1852–1915) was a newspaperman, night city editor of the *New York Tribune* (1876–9), night and literary editor of the *San Francisco Chronicle* (1880–1915), and author of several books of literary criticism.

* *Modern English Books of Power* (San Francisco: Paul Elder, 1912) pp. 144–5.

When I Turned Down Rudyard Kipling*

FRANCIS L. H. NOBLE

In 1889, when Rudyard Kipling landed in San Francisco, fresh from India, his name was as utterly unknown in these United States as that of any other of the thousand and one globe-trotters who yearly ooze through the Golden Gate, unhonoured and unsung. Please recollect this in passing judgement on one who enjoys the doubtful distinction of being the first American editor to 'turn down' that literary meteor from India.

At that time I was the extremely youthful Sunday editor of the *San Francisco Examiner*, and as fearful of losing, as I was proud of, my job, in which I had barely had time to warm comfortably the editorial chair.

On the *Examiner* staff there was a very clever reporter, by the name of Coe, who 'did the hotels'. Daily prowling around the different hostelries, seeking unusual and 'queer' guests, who might furnish good copy in the shape of vivacious 'interviews', the odd name of 'Rudyard Kipling' caught his fancy and he promptly investigated the owner. Later in the day he came to my desk with a handful of pencilled sheets and a broad grin.

'That's a queer "bird" at the Palace', he said, 'from India. Says he's a grand little newspaperman, all right, and has written this for the paper. The city editor doesn't want it and told me to hand it to you. This Indian "bird" will take 10 a column for it, and there's about a column and a half of the stuff. Want it?'

I suppose Fame and Fortune were wiping their feet on my door-mat, but I failed to recognise either of the ladies.

The matter which Coe gave me has since been published by Kipling, though greatly extended and 'toned down' in his *American Notes*.

---

* *Boston Sunday Globe*, 27 Dec 1925, pp. 1, 5.

I read it over and observed, 'He's a cheerful sort of a liar, isn't he? It's pretty good stuff though and I guess I can use it, but he'll take one or two "raw" spots. He's got our prominent citizens killing each other with revolvers on every street-corner, using Bret Harte dialect, and here's an uncalled-for slap at the Roman Catholic Church.'

(In his *American Notes* Kipling subsequently 'used the soft pedal' on the shootings – there were four in one evening in the original manuscript given to me, and eliminated the anti-Catholic matter entirely.)

'He insists that not a line, word, or even a comma, be altered or omitted, or else you can't use it', said Coe cheerily.

'Can't use it is right', I replied and returned the article. 'Let him try it on the *Call* or the *Chronicle*.'

Whether Kipling took this advice or not, I do not know. At any rate the matter did not appear in either of these papers.

Here are some extracts from *American Notes* as written in the article offered me – only they were decidedly 'more so' in that manuscript – and which I naturally declined to publish 'verbatim', as they were simply ridiculous to any San Franciscan of ordinary intelligence:

A ponderous Irish gentleman, with priest's cords in his hat and a small nickel-plated badge on his fat bosom, emerged from the knot supporting a Chinaman who had been stabbed in the eye and was bleeding like a pig. The bystanders went their ways, and the Chinaman, assisted by the policeman, his own. Of course this was none of my business, but I rather wanted to know what had happened to the gentleman who had dealt the stab. It said a great deal for the excellence of the municipal arrangements of the town that a surging crowd did not at once block the street to see what was going forward. I was the sixth man and the last who assisted at the performance, and my curiosity was six times the greatest. Indeed, I felt ashamed of showing it. . . .

Originally the cliffs and their approaches must have been pretty, but they have been so carefully defiled with advertisements that they are now one big blistered abomination.

When a policeman, whose name I do not recollect, 'fatally shot Ed Harney' for attempting to escape arrest, I was in the next street. For these things I am thankful. It is enough to travel with a policeman in a tram-car, and, while he arranges his coat-tails as he sits down, to catch sight of a loaded revolver. It is enough to know that 50 per cent of the men in the public saloons carry pistols about them.

The Chinaman waylays his adversary, and methodically chops him to pieces with his hatchet. Then the Press roars about the brutal ferocity of the pagan.

The Italian reconstructs his friend with a long knife. The Press complains of the waywardness of the alien.

The Irishman and the native Californian in their hours of discontent use the revolver, not once, but six times. The Press records the fact and asks in the next column whether the world can parallel the progress of San Francisco. The American who loves his country will tell you that this sort of thing is confined to the lower classes. Just at present an ex-judge who was sent to jail by another judge (upon my word I cannot tell whether these titles mean anything) is breathing red-hot vengeance against his enemy. The papers have interviewed both parties, and confidently expect a fatal issue.

I have dwelt rather more fully on this incident, my first introduction to the writings of Mr Kipling, than perhaps the matter warrants, but I have a very just though personal reason. As often as old-time newspapermen gather together and Kipling comes up for discussion, someone arises and says, 'Did you ever hear of the "smart Alec" cub editor in San Francisco who refused to publish a story submitted to him by Kipling in person, and who told Rudyard that his "style" was not quite up to the standard of American journalism? Let me tell you about it. He was a fresh guy, just out of Harvard, one of Hearst's pets. Kipling offered him "The Reincarnation of Krishna Mulvaney" ' (or it may be the 'Strange Ride of Morrowbie Jukes', or 'The Man Who Would Be King', it all depends on the narrator's favourite story) 'and this "dumb-bell" threw it back at Kipling and said, "Not in a thousand years, my boy, that Indian drool is too amateurish for the columns of the *San Francisco Examiner*!' What do you think of that?'

I laughed at the story the first time I heard it myself, told at a Press Club dinner in New York, but oh, I am a-weary of it, a-weary of it, and would that it would die! It certainly has earned a peaceful tomb at last.

NOTE

Francis Noble (1867–1948) became Editor of the *San Francisco Examiner* in 1889, the year in which he countered Kipling's offer to sell him a 1½-column story for $10 with an offer of $7.5 (Kipling rejected it). Noble, who specialised in the writing of sea-stories, died at Kennebunkport, Maine, a famous coastal town.

Kipling before He Was Famous*

JOSEPH M. ROGERS

In the fall of 1889, as I remember, there came to my office – that of Managing Editor of the *Inquirer* (Philadelphia) – a short, well-built young man, who introduced himself as an Anglo-Indian travelling homeward via the 'States'. He said he was a newspaperman. At this I receded a trifle, for I expected an application for a position, and there were no vacancies. It appeared, however, that he was only after information, though my recollection is that he offered about ten short stories at a modest price. These were not accepted, much to my later regret. He spent the whole night in the office, and regaled me with many stories of India and Japan. He had just spent several months in the latter country, in which I was particularly interested, as I had some hope of making a journey thither myself. Upon my explaining this he became enthusiastic, and, sitting down, drew a rough map of Japan, indicating the places I ought to see, but which were not named in most of the guide-books.

Later on I expressed a desire to know of places in India I should visit when I got the chance. Most agreeably he drew another map, and jotted down the names of some particularly notable places in Benares which I should by no means miss. He was exceedingly modest, and never in the least intrusive. He displayed the same interest in the mechanical as in the editorial departments of the paper, and paid especial attention to the process of zinc etching, just

* *Book News Monthly*, xxv (Dec 1906) 209–10.

then coming into vogue, and to him entirely unfamiliar. That night I folded up the manuscript he had left, and placed it in my desk at home, among a lot of other papers. If I caught the name of my visitor it made no impression on me. In consequence when, a few years later, I was moving my household goods, and looking through my desk to sort out papers I found the maps and memoranda which until then I had completely forgotten, I was amazed to see at the bottom the now-familiar signature, 'Rudyard Kipling'.

Most unfortunately the papers were all destroyed by a fire which burned up many of my precious autographs and manuscripts.

This is the story of my introduction to Kipling. I have never met him since. But some years later, when on the editorial staff of *McClure's Magazine*, I had a good deal of correspondence with him, especially concerning his novel, *Kim*, which was published serially in the magazine, and for which, I believe, he was paid the largest sum ever given an author for serial rights. I was pleased to see in it references to some of those places which he had described to me so glowingly some years before.

There are those who suppose that Kipling writes easily, and changes nothing after it is once on paper. I know of no author who has a greater tendency to change and change again until it suits him. My recollection is that *Kim* was rewritten five times, three times after it was set in type. I think the most interesting manuscript I ever saw was that of the page-proofs of this book after it had been twice in type. It was filled with marginal corrections, some of minor and many of major importance. The author sought ever to get exactly the right word or phrase for his purpose, and that manuscript was a terror to compositors – all the more so because Kipling is extraordinarily particular about having every word and punctuation mark inserted just as he wrote it.

I believe that the people of America did not like *Kim* as well as was expected, and this was due to the fact that it told of things and had an atmosphere with which they were entirely unfamiliar. But the people of India, and all Britons who understood the situation, were enthralled with it because of its absolutely photographic accuracy. The skies of India, the heat, the passions, the people – all of that peculiar environment of the East – were described as never before or since. And at a cost to the author which it is difficult to estimate! When he lay sick in New York, in 1889, he spoke continually of this book, which was then well advanced in his mind, and which after so many changes was finally produced. It was about this time that I met William Archer, the well-known Scotch dramatic critic of London, in New York City. He said his first surprise on reaching America was while riding on a 'tram-car' to his hotel, when the motorman asked him the latest news of Kipling's condition.

Kipling's care in manuscript is shown by the fact that he once cabled a poem to this country for publication in *McClure's*. So careful was he in every punctuation point that when published he said there was not the slightest deviation from the original. At times, when a careless proof-reader or editor took the slightest liberty with his copy he would express his mind in no uncertain terms. I believe he was the first foreign author who hired permanently a copyright lawyer in this country to see that there was no violation of his rights. He has been accused of being rather close in money matters, but I am sure an author has as good a right to protection as a seller of a patented article, and Kipling's action has been good for authors on both sides of the Atlantic. During the Boer War I cabled Kipling's agent in London to know if he had any stories to sell. He answered that he had a certain number of stories containing so many words, at 25 cents a word. All of them were ordered. But before they were dispatched Kipling had worked them over and lengthened some of them so that they were a good deal longer than the original estimate, but he asked only the sum originally named. He was willing to stick to his bargain, but not to let anything leave his hands until it satisfied him.

NOTE

Joseph Morgan Rogers (1861–1922) was the Managing Editor of the *Philadelphia Inquirer* (1889–99), and briefly worked on the staff of *McClure's Magazine* before returning to the *Inquirer*. He wrote a number of books about the Civil War, Thomas Hart Benton, Henry Clay, and American presidents.

Still He Likes Us*

London, 29 June. Little more than a year ago a young man landed in San Francisco from an Indian steamship and almost immediately

* Unsigned article in *New York World*, 6 July 1890, p. 19.

began to write letters to the most important newspaper in India giving his impressions of our country. . . . Rudyard Kipling's name is Dennis[1] so far as personal popularity in the United States goes. He blazed away at us with a ferocity that throws far into the shade Mrs Trollope, Dickens and Max O'Rell[2] combined. After stopping four months in the United States, during which time he experienced a variety of sensations from a prayer-meeting at Chautauqua to an interview with Mark Twain, Rudyard Kipling came to London. He was comparatively unknown, though a few of his writings in India had been republished on this side of the water and had attracted attention. Today his books are piled deep on all the railway news-stands and conspicuously exhibited in shop-windows. Rudyard Kipling has leaped at a bound to the very top of the literary ladder. For a time he threatened to eclipse even the ubiquitous Stanley[3] as the lion of the London season. *The Times* took him up, and with a powerful column-shot landed him at once into the select symposium of 'literary fellers' who have been toiling here for years to establish reputations. Edmund Yates wrote him up as a 'celebrity' in *The World*, and while Labouchère[4] in *Truth* sneered at this as a rather unusual distinction for a 'week-old celebrity', still he admitted that the young novelist *was* a celebrity.

Following in the footsteps of Dickens, Wilkie Collins and Rider Haggard, Rudyard Kipling leaves the sale of his manuscripts and all other matters strictly pertaining to business to a literary agent, and he has the same agent as had the three novelists I have named – A. P. Watt. This agency plan may have its drawbacks, but it at least gives a man ample scope for uninterrupted work and saves him from innumerable petty annoyances to which he would otherwise be compelled to submit. At all events, it was through the intermediary kindness of Mr Watt that I was enabled to climb to the summit of a lofty building overlooking the Victoria Embankment and gain admittance to Rudyard Kipling's 'den' when I got there. The junior Kipling had not put in an appearance at the moment, so I had a chance to talk with his father, a thoroughly genial and com-panionable old gentleman, to whom I explained the object of my visit.

Rudyard Kipling's workroom has been described, with its soft-tinted Persian rugs, ancient prayer-carpets, dull green paper and pictures of military subjects.

In a few moments Rudyard Kipling entered – a short, broad-shouldered man, with dark-blue eyes. He is rapid of speech and active of movement.

'So you want to interview me about my travels in your country', he said, after extending a cordial greeting. 'Well, I like the people immensely, but in my letters to *The Pioneer*, in India, I hurled twelve-barrelled curses at the country. I don't think that Americans ever fully realise the discomforts that a civilised traveller who visits them for the first time is obliged to submit to. Doubtless it is all well enough when you are used to it. I want to go back to America this year if I can. Met some wonderfully nice people there. The Americans are nearer to my life than the English. They resemble our Anglo-Indians in square dealing and frankness of speech. When they have anything to say they say it. I was in America four months. I did not waste my time in trying to 'get acquainted', as you would call it, with celebrities, though of course I did not avoid any of them who came in my way, but I roamed about with the common people and studied all phases of American life. I went to ward meetings and caucuses, attended political conventions, went to camp meetings, attended classical lectures at Chautauqua, visited schools and colleges, interviewed Mark Twain, and in fact went everywhere that I possibly could and talked with everybody whom I thought had something interesting to tell me. I have written columns about what I saw, which the Indian papers printed. I am a newspaperman, so I wrote what I had to tell to the newspapers. They were my first impressions of the country, hurriedly written of course, but I mean to publish them in book form some day.'

Here Mr Kipling excused himself for a moment to get some letters ready for the Indian mail, and handed me his 'manifold book', which contained copies of his *Pioneer* letters about America, to while away the time. From the cursory examination I was able to make of it in the short time at my disposal I should advise Mr Kipling to defer publishing this correspondence until he has revisited America and left it with the intention of never going back there. Later on he very kindly allowed me to make some extracts from the scrap-book, which I give verbatim.

'What do you want me to talk about?' said Rudyard Kipling, when we had settled down to conversation. 'I cannot attempt to tell you what I think of each of the different cities I visited. I can speak only in a general way. Where shall I begin?'

'Suppose you begin with our women. How did they impress you?'

'I can safely refer you to my Indian correspondence on that topic', said Mr Kipling with a cheery smile. He handed over his scrap-book and I copied the following from one of his letters:

The American girls are pretty – very much so – with a piquancy, all of their own, impossible to describe as to resist. Sweet and comely are the maidens of Devonshire: delicate and of precious seeming those who live in the pleasant places of London: fascinating for all their demureness the damsels of France, clinging closely to their mothers and with large eyes wondering at the wicked world: excellent in her own place, and to those who understand her, is the Anglo-Indian 'Spin' in her second season: but the girls of America are above and beyond them all. They are clever, they can talk; yes, it is said they can think. Certainly they have an appearance of so doing which is delightfully deceptive. They are original and regard you with unabashed eyes as a sister might look at her brother. They are instructed, too, in the folly and vanity of the male mind for they have associated with boys from babyhood and can discerningly minister to both vices or pleasantly snub the possessor. They possess, moreover, a life among themselves, independent of any masculine associations. They have societies and clubs and unlimited tea-fights where all the guests are girls. They are self-possessed without parting with any tenderness that is their sex right. They understand. They can take care of themselves. They are superbly independent. When you ask them what makes them so charming they say, 'It is because we are better educated than your girls and we are more sensible in regard to men. We have a good time all around, but aren't taught to regard every man as a possible husband. Nor is he expected to marry the first girl he calls on regularly.' Yes, they have good times. Their freedom is large and they do not abuse it. They can go driving with young men and receive nods from young men to an extent that would make an English mother wink with horror; and neither driver nor drivee have a thought beyond the enjoyment of a good time.

But this freedom of the young girl has its drawbacks. She is – I say it with all reluctance – irreverent from her $40 bonnet to the buckles on her $18 shoes. She talks flippantly to her parents. She has a prescriptive right to the society of the man who arrives. The parents admit it. This is sometimes embarrassing, especially when you call on a man and his wife for the sake of information; the one being a merchant of varied knowledge, the other a woman of the world. In five minutes your host has vanished. In another five his wife has followed him and you are left alone with a very charming maiden doubtless, but certainly not the person you came to see.

The American of wealth is owned by his family. They exploit him for bullion, and sometimes it seems to me that his lot is a lonely one. Nothing is too good for an American's daughter. (I speak here of the moneyed classes.) The girls take every gift as a matter of course. And yet they develop greatly when a catastrophe arrives and the man of many millions goes up or goes down. His daughters take to stenography or typewriting. I have heard many tales of such heroism from the lips of girls who counted the principals among their friends.

'I noticed in looking over your letters', I remarked, 'that you made some unflattering observations on the American girl as she is seen at Chautauqua.'

'Yes,' said Mr Kipling. 'I was not very favourably impressed with Chautauqua, which is a sort of lawn-tennis academy of the arts and sciences. But the newspapers were all talking about it while I was there, so I went. I remember that during a short visit to Chautauqua I nearly got into trouble by remarking to a friend that the women's voices gave me the impression that they should be shut up and fed on oil for a year. I had a good opportunity at Chautauqua to study the average American woman out of doors, and I found myself wondering whether it was true, as the East had taught me, that women have no souls. The motions of their minds were like unto the jumpings of grasshoppers in a bait-box. They managed to invest everything they touched or talked about with a distressed air of unreality – these persons with "ideas", whose names were in the newspapers. Chautauqua seemed to me to be full of girls. The verandahs were alive with them; they filled the sinuous walks; they hurried from lecture to lecture, hatless, and three under one sunshade; they retailed little confidences, walking arm in arm, and rowed on the lake with their very young men.

'The lectures were arranged to suit all tastes. I got hold of one called "The Eschatology of Our Saviour". It set itself to prove the length, breadth and temperature of hell from information garnered from the New Testament. I read it in the sunshine under the trees with hundreds of pretty maidens pretending to be busy all around, and it did not seem to match the landscape. Then I studied the faces of the crowd. One-quarter were old and worn; the others were young, innocent, charming and frivolous. I wondered how much they really knew or cared for the art side of Greek or the Pope in the Middle Ages and how much for the young men who worked with them; also what their ideas of hell might be. I do not think much, as you say in America, of Chautauqua. People do not get an education that way. They must dig for it and cry for it and sit up o'nights for it, and when they have got it they must call it by another name or the struggle is of no avail.'

'What comments have you to offer on our young men?'

'The young men of America', he said, 'rejoice in the days of their youth. They gamble, yacht-race, enjoy prize-fights and cock-fights, the one openly, the other in secret; they establish luxurious clubs; they break themselves over horseflesh and other things and they are instant in quarrel. At twenty they are experienced in business; embark on vast enterprises; take partners as experienced as themselves, and go to pieces with as much splendour as their neighbours. Incidentally I may mention that nine American youths out of ten are heavily handicapped by the abnormal weakness of their heads. This is supposed to be due to a nervous and highly strung organisation, and in California, at least, the brilliant dryness of the air lends colour to the supposition. Phlegmatic and spiritual, however, they manage to get flushed, affable and drunk on astonishingly small quantities of liquor. The American nation gets drunk by easy stages. A man takes a nip here and a nip there in the morning until, by luncheon-time, while not really drunk, he is in a condition that no businessman ought to be until after dinner. I don't object to almost continuous beer-drinking as we see it in America. A man will die of dropsy rather than drunkenness if he drinks too much beer. But the American habit of taking mixed drinks at all hours of the day is a very bad one. In your climate a man can keep it up for a long time, till he suddenly drops off.'

'I notice that in your letters home you were particularly severe on our American newspapers.'

'That is because I am a newspaperman,' said Mr Kipling, 'and trained to deal with things as I find them. In most of the large cities I went to I made acquaintance with your newspapermen, and wonderfully good fellows most of them were. I enjoyed nothing better than to go around with the boys. But my first experience with an American reporter in San Francisco was not encouraging. One of them grappled with me before I had left the ship. What he wanted to know was the area of India in square miles. I referred him to Whitaker.[5] He had never heard of Whitaker. He wanted it from my own mouth, and I would not tell him. Then he swerved off to details of journalism in the country. When I ventured to suggest that the interior economy of a paper most concerned the people who worked it, he protested.

' "That's the very thing that interests us", he said. "Have you got reporters anything like our reporters, or Indian newspapers?"

' "We have not", I said, and suppressed the "Thank God!" that was rising to my lips.

' "Why haven't you?" said he.

' "Because they would die", I said.

'It was exactly like talking to a child – a very rude little child. He would begin almost every sentence with "Now tell me something about India", and would turn aimlessly from one question to the other without the least continuity. I was not angry, but keenly interested. The man was a revelation to me. To his questions I returned answers mendacious and evasive. After all it really did not matter what I said. He could not understand. I can only hope and pray that one of my readers in India will never see that portentous interview. The man made me out to be an idiot several sizes more drivelling than my destiny intended, and through the rankness of his ignorance managed to distort the few poor facts with which I supplied him into large and elaborate lies. "Then," thought I, "the matter of American journalism shall be looked into later on. At present I will enjoy myself." '

Later on Mr Kipling did write about American newspapers with a vengeance. Here is what he said from Chicago during the Cronin trial:[6]

Within the past few weeks I have learned what it is to be ashamed of my profession. To their credit be it said that the average American journalist disdains any idea of teaching or elevating his public. Not one, but scores of newspapermen have said to me: 'We aren't responsible for the morals of the people. We give 'em what they want.' Gentlemen not in the profession have bade me watch the papers in the hand of the crowd, and note how a cheap press was elevating the people. I prefer to believe the journalists. They are responsible for publications which are a lively and perfect image of a purposeless Hell. With infinite pains and the expenditure of a vast amount of money, they produce day by day newspapers that ought to move a man to despair.

And yet they are amusing when one gets over the recurrent thrill of horror. The 'direction' of a leading San Francisco journal afloat on the boundless sea of Continental politics has lately been

moving me to tears of graceless merriment. They were grappling
with a European crisis and naturally spoke of 'old Bismarck',
'Young William', and so forth in the true Republican spirit and
the way in which the royalties and diplomats of effete Europe
were banged and jumbled about was amazing. The writer was
going to have Europe fixed to rights somehow, though he wasted
half a column over it. If in the setting he ignored not more than
three of the conditions under which Europe lies, and showed as
all-embracing ignorance of the history of the past five years, the
defaults did not weight his radiant spirit. A man does not know
what genuine American humour means till he watches a journal
sailing out upon the vast profound of 'Russia and the Balkan
States', 'The Outlook in France', or something similar. But mirth
dies in face of their studies. It is not amusing to read again and
again at breakfast in the papers from Chicago, Cincinnati, New
York, and the rest, coarse and ill-considered attacks on England,
her Queen, her Court, her customs and everything that is here.
Were the expressions of dislike genuine and prompted let us say
by the unquenched hate of a hundred years, they would be
laudable enough, though hardly wise. But both those who write
and those who read are at pains to assure you that the outpouring
is nothing more than a daily performance gone through for the
purpose of catching the Irish eye. Here, then, we find a nation
descended from Anglo-Saxon stock compelled to swear so many
times per annum at the land of her birth by order of an alien who
does not happen to approve of the aforesaid land. The vituperat-
ive skittles may or may not find its way to England, where it does
no harm beyond helping to still further corrupt over-decaying
speech; but what is the effect on the average American citizen?
Does he without exception know that it is all play – ugly play
because it is compulsory, but play none the less – or does he
believe in it and mould his notions accordingly? I should very
much like to find out. At present I cannot understand.

From the first to the tenth-rate journal this note of uneasiness
runs without break. The leading journals of New York will devote
time and space that is presumably valuable to rebuking a
President's son for being 'overcome by monarchial influences',
the said son on a European tour merely having made himself
pleasant as every man of the world should do to his hosts. This is
provincialism, rank, untamed, contemptible, but pathetic. Some
day circumstances will call these journals to account for making

fools of their clientele. It is not useful in season and out of season to pander to every form of pride that grows in the breast of a nation – to tell the town that there was never finer city on the sod, the village that there was never sturdier commune, the man that there was never better citizen, or the author and poet that they excel their brethren throughout the earth. Because the earth is a very big place, stocked with some remarkably large men, and the end of these dreamings is an uncomfortable awakening, or, if not, at least the lowering of self-respect.

'Which of our principal cities impressed you most?'
'New York, of course. The city of San Francisco itself seemed to me to be pitched down on the sand bunkers of the Bikiner desert.[7] About one-fourth of it is ground reclaimed from the sea, and the remainder is a ragged, unthrifty sand-hill, held down by the houses. From an English point of view there has not been the least attempt at grading those hills. And, indeed, you might as well try to grade the hillocks of Scinde. Cable cars have, for all practical purposes, made San Francisco a dead level. I particularly watched Young California, and saw that it was at least expensively dressed, cheerful in manner and self-asserting in conversation. The maidens were of generous build, large and well-groomed. Kearney Street at nine o'clock seemed to my strange eyes to level all distinctions of rank as emphatically as the grave. I had an experience of course, with your bunco-steerer – one of the true old California style. He did not secure me for his prey, but after an hour or two conversation with him I readily understood how it is that year after year, week after week the American bunco-steerer (who is the confidence, trick and the card-sharper man of other climes) secures his prey. . . . I also met, of course, some of your rich Western millionaires. I found these persons harmless in their earliest stages. That is to say a man worth $3 or 4 million may be a good talker, clever, amusing, and of the world. A man with twice that amount is to be avoided. And a 20 million man is – just 20 million.'
'In the East everybody asked me what I thought of the West. Often I dared not answer that it was as far from their notions and motives as Hindustan is from Hoboken, and the West, to my poor thinking, is an America which has no kinship with its neighbour. In the East I learned also of yet another America – that of the South – alien and distinct. Into the third America, alas, I had no time to penetrate. The newspapers and oratory of the day told me that all ill

feeling between North and South was extinct. None the less, it impressed me that the Northerner, outside of his newspapers and big men, had a contempt for the Southerner, which the latter repays by what seems very like a deep-rooted aversion to the Northerner. I learned what the sentiments of the great American nation mean. The North speaks in the name of the country. The West is busy developing its own resources. The Southerner sulks in his tent. His notions do not count, but his girls are very beautiful. Several Southern ladies that I met had the soft, sweet voice of their English sisters. Americans can hardly imagine how the harsh, sonorous voices of some of the Northern women grate on the ears of a stranger to their country.'

'I was not so much impressed by your universal suffrage after I had looked into it a little as it is understood in San Francisco. A citizen may not know how to run his own business, control his wife, or instill reverence into his children; he may be pauper, half-crazed with drink, bankrupt, desolate, or merely a born fool; but he has his vote. If he likes he can be voting most of his time for Governor, municipality officers, local option, sewage contracts, or anything else of which he has no special knowledge. Once every four years he votes for a new President. In his spare moments he votes for his own judges – the men who shall give him justice. These are dependent on popular favour for re-election every two or three years. He talks much of his time about a thing called the tariff, which he does not understand, but which he conceives to be the bulwark of the country, or else the surest power for its destruction, according to his politics. Naturally wherever a man has a vote and may vote about every conceivable thing, there exist certain men who understand the art of buying up votes retail and selling them wholesale to whoever wants them.'

'The three American centres, San Francisco, Chicago and New York, are administered by the alien for the alien; by the Irishman for his own interests, and by the German for those of the Germans, and the rule of the democracy is a rule of iron.'

'I spent some delightful days in Buffalo and some of her sister cities in the northern part of New York. In all the Eastern cities I was impressed by the deep fringe of elegance, as you might say, with which Americans surround the business-quarters of their towns. The American will go to the bad place because he cannot speak English, and is proud of it. But he knows how to build a home for himself and his mate, knows how to keep the grass green in front of his verandah, and knows how to use the mechanism of life – hot water, gas and bell-ropes, telephones, etc. He is encumbranced with all manner of labour-saving appliances, though this does not seem to prevent his wife and daughter slaving themselves to death over household drudgery. When you have seen the outsides of a few hundred thousand American homes and the insides of a few more, you begin to understand why the American (the respectable one) does not take a deep interest in what they call politics, and why he is so generally proud of the country that enables him to be so comfortable.'

Mr Kipling devoted a separate letter to Chicago. It is brisk and breezy. The first few lines are sufficient to give a general idea of his impressions. Here they are: 'I have struck a city – a real city – and they call it Chicago. . . . Having seen it, I urgently desired never to see it again. It is inhabited by savages. Its water is the water of the Hugh[8] and its air is dirt. . . . I do not believe that it has anything to do with this country. . . . I spent ten hours in that huge wilderness, wandering through miles of those terrible streets and jostling some few hundred thousand of these terrible people who talked *paisa-bai*[9] through their noses.'

NOTES

1. Possibly a reference to the hangman in Dickens's *Barnaby Rudge*.

2. Léon Paul Blouet (1848–1903) served in the Franco-German War as a cavalry officer, and was wounded. From 1872 on he was a correspondent in England for several French papers, and a keen observer of English eccentricities. Under the pen-name 'Max O'Rell' he wrote *John Bull et son île* (1887), and became a popular teacher, writer and lecturer.

3. Sir Henry Morton Stanley (1841–1904), journalist and empire-builder, made his last African journey in 1887–9 to find Emin Pasha, and thus helped to put Uganda within the British sphere of influence. Stanley, born in Wales, had become a naturalised American citizen; but in 1892 he became a British citizen again, and served in Parliament from 1895 to 1900. He was knighted in 1899.

4. Henry Du Pré Labouchère (1831–1912) wrote for the *Daily News* and *World*; founded the weekly journal *Truth*; was a powerful radical in the House of Commons; and worked for the reorganisation of the Liberal Party.

5. *Whitaker's Almanack*, published annually, supplied vital statistics about the Empire, other countries, remarkable occurrences, 'places of interest and amusement', and so on.

6. A famous murder in the 1890s. Sherwood Anderson, in *Winesburg, Ohio* (1919), describes it thus in the chapter 'The Philosopher': 'Some men murdered him and put him in a trunk. In the early morning they hauled the trunk across the city. It sat on the back of an express wagon and they were on the seat as

unconcerned as anything. Along they went through quiet streets where everyone was asleep. The sun was just coming up over the lake.'

7. A desolate tract, part of the Thar Desert in Rajasthan, North-western India, without a single stream. Often spelled 'Bikaner'.

8. The Hooghly, or Hugli River, most westerly and commercially the most important channel of the Ganges River in the Ganges Delta, West Bengal, India.

9. Money-matters.

Rudyard Kipling at Naulakha*

CHARLES WARREN STODDARD

It was a pretty climb up at Brattleboro and the day was passing fair. At the station I looked in vain for Rudyard Kipling, who had bidden me to be his guest at Naulakha. I searched in some anxiety for the young man who was all my fancy painted and more, too, before I had ever laid eyes on him; there was no Rudyard in the flesh within my horizon and I was almost in despair when a good Samaritan said softly, 'Are you looking for Mr Kipling? There is his trap.' There it was, to be sure, as English as English: a handsomely groomed cob, a smart cart, a smarter British coachman in livery on the high seat and all at my service, if you please.

We scattered H's by the way and were the observed of all observers until we got out of the hilly town and were well on the road to Naulakha.

A pretty land that, gloriously green, and with hill and dale well wooded and a rushing river that is choked with logs in springtime.

Of course I might have known that a busy author has no time to meet an idle one at a way station – if I had only thought of it in season. I might have known, as well, that the fittest turnout in all Vermont could belong to none other than the gentleman farmer, who was so little understood by his neighbours on the other side of the fence that there came a crisis in his life and adventures, and like

* *National Magazine*, XXII (June 1905) 259–68.

the Arab of the uncrowned American laureate, he silently stole away.

Perhaps no one knows just why affairs turned out as they did. Surely he never intruded upon the Brattleboronians, unless it were a small piece of his mind – and that more in sorrow than in anger – when they permitted a tiresome and tireless trolley to profane the most aristocratic and exclusive of their streets in the high and mighty residence quarter. Who that has a free soul would not chafe at such an innovation? Perhaps they gloried in their disgrace after they discovered that it pained the young man's pride in them. At any rate the breech widened and there was no rest for his soul or the sole of his foot until there was another post-office on the railway map, and a time-table that hung upon the hem of his garment, as it were, down yonder in the lap of his meadows. He had only to wave his hand now and the steam-horse reared on its hind legs and stood panting while it waited for him to mount and alight.

His hail-fellows wanted the impromptu station to be called Kipling, as indeed it should have been, for it was his inspiration and resulted through his individual efforts; but he was too modest to lend his noble name to this mote in the eye of Brattleboro, and so the post-office is called Waite – only this and nothing more.

As we went bowling over the country road on our way to Naulakha, I thought of the little note in my pocket – so very unlike the notes in other keys that have been attributed to him:

Naulakha, Brattleboro,

Vermont

21 June 1895

You have but to let us know about when you are coming; to name the day, when you know it, a week or so in advance; and give us the NY hour of departure of your train from the Grand Central, and welcome shall you be. I mention these homely details at length that when you find you can get away you may not say, 'They don't expect me and my coming suddenly might throw 'em out.'

Remember now not to go wandering by up the Massachusetts shore or playing in Beverly Farms[1] or otherwise giving us the slip. I am concerned truly about the Californian business but I cannot say truthfully I shall be so sorry if it brings you here.

How very good all this seemed to me at that moment; I felt almost as
if I were 'on the road to Mandalay', where 'the sun comes up like
thunder, out of China 'cross the way'.

The road climbed up the hill and dropped into little hollows
beyond it. We passed the country school-house – how still it was in
vacation time – and the comfortable farm-house where the Kiplings
lived while Naulakha was being built; we threaded musical groves
and came out upon a hill-top that was as good as a mountain-height
for the great and glorious view that it commanded. Suddenly we
turned an airy corner and dashed down the road between a villa
and a stable, both trim and handsome and, best of all, very
hospitable-looking and home-like.

This was Naulakha!

In the doorway waving a welcome stood Mr and Mrs Kipling,
radiant with good cheer. The home was an ideal one, the realisation
of a cherished dream. The house has a wholesome, English air. It is
ingeniously planned. The master's Den is upon the lower left above
the basement. A door opens upon the verandah in the picture. From
the verandah one descends into a terraced enclosure, where every
sweet and homely flower was in blossom when I arrived, and where
the butterflies and bees were evidently enjoying a garden party. A
high wall upon the upper side of the garden shut it off from prying
eyes; the road lay just beyond it; the garden sloped to the sunshine
and lay open to all the winds of heaven; from its paths one could look
upon wide vales and distant hills and bits of wildwood and acres and
acres of grain; it was a lovely, restful and inviting view. Now the art
of it all is, and the charm of it, that the Den cannot be approached
save through a great living-room, and there was always someone
there to head off intruders. Mrs Kipling was usually the guardian
angel of the house. It was not unfrequently her unpleasant duty to
refuse admittance to persistent interviewers. They did not, I believe,
ever scale the wall, nor enter the garden, otherwise, and so the Den,
while it seemed as careless of intrusion as all-out-of-doors, was in
reality inviolate. It was my happiness to be ushered at once into the
Den and to be offered its freedom so long as I remained a guest at
Naulakha.

'You must not mind me', said RK, wheeling about in his chair at
the writing desk; 'I shall not mind you. Help yourself to books.
When I am not writing, I shall chat with you.'

That is just what he did. I found the originals of all those booklets
he published in India, which are now so rare and bring such

extravagant prices. I read while he wrote. From time to time I could hear him humming a little tune to himself and presently he would wheel round and read me the couplet he had just written in that rhythm. Or perchance it was a bit of prose he read me. He seemed to have no fixed hours for composition but to be in the writing mood at almost any time, or even all the time. I think he was not easily disturbed; that he could write anywhere, at any time; that silence and solitude, and the fine frenzy were not necessary to him. I know he has written some of his ringing lyrics going at the rate of sixty miles an hour on the Limited Express.

Then why does he so carefully guard himself against intruders? Because intruders are not necessarily interesting; they are apt to be a distraction, if nothing worse; and they rob him of time that is very precious to him. Every little while he would take a turn in the garden; this rested him after a spurt; or, if his spirit flagged a little, he would talk for a while and always delightfully. He never wasted words; whatever he said was said with neatness and dispatch.

Why did the reading public get the impression that he was discourteous and even boorish, especially in the treatment of the interviewer? He did not need the assistance of any interview to make his work known to the world; he, personally, chose not to be known. He felt that if an Englishman's house is his castle, his American home should serve him in the same stead; and that he had the right to privacy even if he were a transient guest at some hotel in town or country.

Here is a brief chapter in the new Calamities of Authors: A blizzard was furiously raging in the Green Mountains. Naulakha was snowbound; no one thought of ploughing through the mile-long drifts that lay between Kipling and Brattleboro. No one? Yes, someone, just one only, did, and that one a woman. At the height of the storm there was a cry for help at the door of Naulakha. A half-frozen woman, young if not beautiful, was dug out of the buffalo robes in the depths of a livery sleigh and placed within a safe distance of the great fireplace in the living-room. Restoratives were applied; the reviving cup of tea thawed the tears upon her icy cheeks. Icy cheek? I should say so! The Lady of Naulakha was filled with pity, anxiety and surprise. To her questions the stranger answered, 'I have come to interview Rudyard Kipling!'

Then followed the following:

'But you cannot interview Mr Kipling.'

'I must interview him. I have been sent all the way from New

York to interview him for "The Largest Circulation"; I insist upon interviewing him.'

'It is quite impossible. He is engaged upon an important piece of work and shall not be interrupted.'

'But I have come all the way from Brattleboro through this awful storm, and I insist upon seeing him.'

'If you had telephoned me from Brattleboro, I might have spared you the journey.'

'I cannot leave without seeing him!'

Mrs Kipling touches the button. Enter butler. Mrs K to butler – 'Johnson, see that this lady's conveyance is at the door at once. Permit me, madam, to escort you to the waiting-room. I am sorry you have had your trouble in vain. Good day!'

There was no alternative; the journalist departed speechless with rage. In due season a full-page interview with Rudyard Kipling appeared in the daily represented by the unwelcome visitor, and in it RK was made to say everything utterable or unutterable that was calculated to put him in the most unfavourable light before the public. I suppose the moral is that one should welcome one's interviewer with open arms and fill her with milk and honey. Surely this little note could not have been written by a man who is as brusque and bitter as Kipling has by some been thought to be:

Now I've been wondering where that telegram of mine went to. Your note caught me in the midst of a midsummer's whirl and I wired you at a venture to catch you on the hop. 'What did an acre of maniacs matter?' [I feared to find him in a crowd at a watering-place and abandoned my visit to him.] I am grieved that you came not. Anyhow we could have shunted the bores into a cranberry bog while we confabulated. Your complete, not to say careful, silence heretofore persuaded me that you must have taken a trip to Mars or the moon. Now I rejoice to know you are within hail and trust we see each other in New York sometime before spring. I think of going there and you may recollect an engagement, too.

The papers – I'm grateful to 'em – lied about my wife and her accident. It might have been a bad smash, but as it was, nothing happened beyond a mental disturbance – quite bad enough without desperate cables from Europe and consequent explanations. I'm very busy and this must be my excuse for a scratchy note; but, ere I send, get, steal if needful, Lafcadio

Hearn's *Unfamiliar Japan*. It's all you feel about the South Seas, but large.

One day when we were talking, Kipling suddenly said to me, 'Why don't you write a novel?'

'I have written one', replied I.

'By Jove! I'd like to see it.'

'You can if you wish to.'

'When?'

'Now!'

'Where is it?'

'Upstairs in my room.'

'Bring it to me at once!'

I brought it. He opened it upon the desk before him and dipped into it here and there. We sat for some time in silence; he reading and occasionally grunting a little grunt; I, with my heart in my throat, waiting for the verdict. The longer I waited the less hope I had that he might find something in my manuscript worth commending. The story was a story that lay hatching in my brain for twenty years before I put the first word of it on paper. When I at last began it, one summer at York Harbor during the long vacation, it reeled itself off without effort and the writing of it was a joy. Once finished, I sealed my manuscript without rereading it, resolved that I would forget it for a year. At the end of the year I read a page or two with no visible emotion; sealed it again and returned it to the safety vault for another year of solitary confinement. When it was two years old I had it typewritten and was utterly at a loss as to its worth or unworth. I was on my way to California for the summer, revisiting the old home after an absence of a dozen years. I resolved to take the story with me and submit it to the judgement of critical friends. On my way to the Pacific coast I swung off the track in order to visit Kipling at Naulakha, and that is why I was able to produce the manuscript on the instant.

I broke the anxious silence by saying, 'I am sure you see nothing in it.'

Still turning the leaves, he said, 'My dear fellow, I can't tell you how much I see in it; but' – I had symptoms of heart failure – 'It should be written all over again.'

The amateur novelist is perhaps unduly sensitive. I know that at that moment I felt that if the thing must be rewritten, it was perhaps not worth rewriting; and that in any case I could not possibly rewrite it. I said as much and was laughed at; and then he gave me much judicious criticism, all of which I deeply appreciated, and made suggestions that were enlightening and which kindled a spark of hope within me. For my title, which now strikes me as having been quite idiotic, to wit, *So Pleased to Have Met You*, he substituted *For the Pleasure of His Company*. My alleged hero's name, Paul Westoner, he objected to, and suggested another, which I gladly accepted. His local habitation, Galesborough, indicative of the climatic activity of San Francisco, was pronounced unfit, and for a sub-title Mr Kipling proposed 'An Affair of the Misty City'. So the title page is his, and I am very grateful to him for it. I speak of this here because he did not lose interest in the story after I had taken it away with me; but wrote me so freely and fairly and so wisely that I wish to quote from these letters – they being, it seems to me, a kind of school-for-novelists, and throwing much light upon his interesting method of work.

I had returned from California to my Bungalow in Washington, DC, and announced the fact to my friend. Busy as he was, he yet took time to write me often and such letters as anyone might be proud and happy to receive. Do they not show a vital interest in my poor efforts?

All right. The trip to California gave you just the shake-up you needed and it would be absurd to expect a man to take in and give out at the same time. Now, *ere the stimulus dies out*, get you to work quietly on that novel. I've paved the way in London and my agent has been writing to me to know about it, and I've told two or three men who are not likely to forget, I think, that there is a book called *For the Pleasure of His Company* somewhere in the background. I haven't lost my faith in you, for you are only as I am, damned lazy, and I propose to stir you up with a stick from time to time. This is the first warning. Send it along to me *chapter by chapter* and I will pour on your head such insults and outrages as shall make you work ferociously. Remember you've got to do it because you can do it splendidly. Wherefore lament not about coming to naught, but 'preserve a cheerful countenance, and a good exertion'. Let's have the first chapter, typewritten, in one month please.

It was very slow work, for me, undoing in cold blood what I had done in a rush of enthusiasm. I found that my story, what there was of it, was like a braid of three strands; I unbraided it and made each strand comparatively independent of the other, like a separate book; in each book the same story was told, but from a different point of view.

I was writing him with violet ink and in a rather blind hand, so I have been told. He says,

> Do not waste time in analine hieroglyphics, but send along the first chapter and we'll get to business.
>
> There is nothing wrong with Paul Westoner (my hero's original name), but on the other hand there is nothing catching about it. Here are a few names that may come in handy sometime when you are naming characters. (Twenty names, all uncommon.) All these are fairly good; they are all at your service.
>
> I don't like *So Pleased to Have Met You* for the title of a whole novel. It's too long; but it would do exceedingly well for a chapter heading; why not use it for that and stick – as far as the name of the novel goes – to *For the Pleasure of His Company*.
>
> RK

He suggested a new conclusion to my tale – a conclusion with a yacht in it. Here are some data he forwarded to aid me:

> *For the Pleasure of His Company.* Knock out second chapter and scatter contents broadcast. Change Galesborough to 'The Misty City', and Flaneur to something decent. Also revise names carefully so as to believe in names' reality. Do not, if possible, create a complete new set of characters to fill yacht in last chapter, but gather in people mentioned incidentally all along the book; thus the reader has not to meet new people late in the day. Get good name for yacht. This is especially important. Yacht names – Amity, Pathfinder, St Agnes – late Ventnor. Names for characters – Julian, Gratton, Otis, Wardlow, Arthur, Braye, Lambert, Pycroft, Gregory R. Clitheroe. Big 500-ton ocean-going, screw, triple expansion engines, with complete installation electric lights, mahogany deck-house, varnished deck, three masts.

Somewhat later he was to visit England and wrote me thus:

Now let us talk Biz. I go across (the sea) I believe, for four or five weeks in July, returning at the end of August. Towards the end of September I expect you to ascend these hills joyously with *For the Pleasure of His Company*, well and truly typewritten, under your left arm. I hope and believe all good things will ensue in due course, but buckle thee down to the tale in the place where it was conceived and be of great good courage; for, as I have said, there is meat and marrow in the yarn.

Probably I should have accomplished nothing without the stimulus of his breezy letters; they filled my sails every time and I took a fresh start, full of new hope and courage.

I was puzzled upon some point and appealed to him. He hastened to reply:

Your note just in. No, go straight ahead and put in the last chapter and send it along. I think the best title is *For the Pleasure of His Company*; and below, as sub-title, 'An Affair of the Misty City'. When I get the last chapter and your assurance that you don't want the stuff back to touch up again, I'll see if I can put the machinery in motion. But hurry with the last chapter.

RK

When my new version of the story was completed I sent it to Mr. Kipling and awaited his criticism with what patience I could. I feared the manuscript had gone astray, for I heard nothing from him until this arrived:

Forgive my inexcusable delay in acknowledging your favour, but the Lord sent me a little daughter last Monday and since then things have been somewhat upside-down here. As soon as I get settled I'll give you my noble verdict. Glad to hear you like your bungalow.

RK

Later came the following:

We've been down to Lakewood[2] and the wife hasn't been well and I've been jogging at the tail end of a yarn to be illustrated. In addition I've been reading your tale many times – about thirty. It's rummy, queer, original, fascinating; and in places damn badly written, but I think something ought to come of it. Now are you willing I should send it over the water to be sold to publishers? If so, kindly let me know if you want the book back for one last polish, title, etc., and what you would take in the way of terms. I can't tell you how attractive the wild thing is.

RK

Sometime afterward he wrote me thus:

There is no accounting for publishers. One firm I've tried the tale on kick because the thing lacks form and cohesion. That is a matter which, it seems to me, you could easily give it. Now if I send the typed copy back so soon as it returns won't you go over it again and whack it into more connected shape for the base needs of the market? I haven't tried it in England yet, but this experiment in the American market shows us, I think, what buyers want.

Don't you be in any way discouraged. It's merely a question of making the thing more of a story with less description, and that you ought to be able to do in a month. It may put the check on, but it will be, I think, only a temporary one and we must have horses shot under us if we expect to go anywhere.

Doubtless I felt disheartened and showed it in my letter to him. He replied,

Your last letter was a sad one – and truly I am nearly as sad as you are; but I beg you to reconsider your first decision about throwing up the sponge, and tackle the job anew. The man who wrote *South Sea Idyls* could write nearly anything he put his mind to. Take a big pull on yourself and solemnly walk through the novel anew. There's heaps and heaps in it, as I have always maintained: the only thing needed is to throw it into somewhat closer-knit shape.

RK

That I never did. I felt that I could not do it. The book was a part of myself, my very being, and, as I cannot alter myself, I could not alter the book. He had done what he could for it and for me; doubtless he believed in me, and hoped that I might better the book and make a success of it. I laid it aside and endeavoured to forget it, but it would not go out of my mind; there is so much of me in it that I felt obsessed so long as it lay unpublished.

To save myself, to have the path cleared before me so that I might be free to do something else, I gave it to Robertson of San Francisco, and he brought it out in a pretty volume that excited some diversity of opinion among the critics, and this is perhaps the pleasantest and most profitable fate that can befall an author.

Before we met I wrote and asked Kipling if he had a copy of *South Sea Idyls*, and, if not, might I have the pleasure of sending him one. He replied,

> I've heard and seen much of *South Sea Idyls* and a copy from the author is a gift indeed. This summer I missed – for the second time – taking a trip through that fairyland. Now I'll be dependent on your eyes and will probably have a better time than if I'd ploughed the South Pacific in a schooner to Apia.

I was glad of the privilege of sending him the *Idyls*, and waited rather anxiously to hear if they had succeeded in interesting one to whom the world is his oyster. The answer came,

> Your book has come, been read and read aloud. I don't think it was quite kind of you to send it. I'm settled down for a New England winter in a grey land, among an austere people, 200 miles away from the blue water, and
>
> *Here you come with your old music* and give me as bad an attack of *go-fever* as I've had for a long time past. The mischief of it is that this time last year I was wandering around Auckland way[3] and missed my steamer to those Islands of the Blessed. I had got over the disappointment but you've stirred me up again. It's too bad. You should keep your Orient liquor for sober-headed folk instead of making a poor fellow who has 'drunk delight of travel' to the lees hanker after fresh draughts.
>
> Go to! Your book is highly improper, and I doubt not immoral. What has the Hula-hula – or the John Kino, for the matter of that – to do with New England? There are no such things as coconut palms in the world, and the *lomi-lomi*[4] – which we call *molish* in India – is a pure invention. A land where people do nothing, if such a land there be, is clearly a wicked land, and it is sinful beyond telling that a man should wear no clothes. Therefore you will see it follows that the South Seas never existed; and if they did, or do exist, I for one daren't believe in them just now. You have broken the peace of an ordered household and set

two folks who are gypsies by birth or inheritance longing to take ship again and GET OUT.

In return please to accept as an example my sober and continent verses [*Barrack-Room Ballads*] which have nothing to do with roving and roystering or racketing on far-away beaches.

Yours hungrily, admiringly and upsettedly,

Rudyard Kipling

It is thus the fond author casts his bread, even though it be but a crust, upon the waters, and it sometimes returns to him not water-logged, but spread thick with honey.

In the book of *Barrack-Room Ballads* he sent me I find these lines quoted upon the title-page:

> I ploughed the land with Horses
> But my Heart was ill at ease
> For the old sea-faring men
> Came to me now and then
> With their Sagas of the Seas.

That Kipling dearly loved Naulakha goes without saying. It was a house built to his taste and planted upon a height of his own choosing. Together we climbed the wooden slopes about the place – he and she and I, and sometimes the delightfully old-fashioned little daughter, his eldest, who died unknown to him while he, himself, lay at death's door and all the world was hoping and praying for his recovery; we lay among the tall grass and talked and dreamed and schemed, with that glorious summer sky above us and the 'Sunshine on the hills asleep'.

I was piloted through the house by host and hostess, and perhaps the happiest hour of all was that we passed in quite the most delightful attic it was ever my privilege to explore. It was the whole top of the house, lit by sunny gable-windows, and had a certain Gothic atmosphere that added a romantic charm. Many odds and ends were there, though the house was not an old one, but the object that first caught my eye and caused me to return to it again and again, as if the spell of its fascination were not to be resisted, was an old desk, black with age and no doubt rheumatic in every joint. Its lid was a solid panel but curved in the fashion of a roll-top desk.

Across the length of it, cut deep in large letters such as schoolboys love to carve, was this legend: 'OFT WAS I WEARY WHEN I TOILED AT THEE'.[5] So sang the galley-slave in a faultless verse; and so, in the hour of triumph, Rudyard Kipling graved upon the cover of the desk at which he won his fame.

He went to London a stranger from India; alone, unknown, discouraged, miserably ill; it was the brother of his bride-to-be who found and nourished his fainting spirit. Perhaps there never was a more beautiful fellowship than theirs, or a sadder one, for young Wolcott Balestier, Jr, who wrote with him that admirable picture of life in the far East and far West, *Naulahka*, died all too soon.

It was with real regret that I turned away from that bungalow – it is built on the East Indian plan – and the bungalow life we led there together for a few days. They said to me when I arrived, 'You are not to dress for dinner – unless you prefer to. You must not mind if we do; we have to in order to retain the respect of our British-bred servants.' And then Kipling, under his breath, 'I wish I needn't!'

They went abroad presently; they were always going or coming, having, as he said, 'the go-fever'. By and by came a letter from England, the last I shall take the liberty of quoting.

Is it not the letter of one in perfect health and spirits and whose heart is in the right place?

Arundel House, Tisbury, Wilts, England

I rejoice to see your hand-writing again, *but* the company that have defaced and defiled the make-up of your book [*Lazy Letters from Low Latitudes*] should be killed by slow fires and fish-bones and things. Knowing what manner of stuff would be inside it the flagrant covers made me very wroth. I have stripped off the hide and am sending the carcass in to a man I know on the PMG [*Pall Mall Gazette*] to see if he doesn't like it too. Yes, it's a very tropic of colour and fragrance. Much do I wish, too, that you were here. Our wet and slobbering spring has suddenly taken a brace and the last three whole days have been really warm – even hot in places; with a faint blue-grey sky and the hay smelling like all England since the Conquest. My stays in England had been so short that I find I know very little of my own country outside London, and it's very amusing to go about.

We had an excursion the other day as wild as anything in a dream. Went down seaward through a flat and fatted country and suddenly found ourselves in the middle of Macbeth's blasted heath, half heather, half burned grass, with a low mist rolling in from the sea and an enchanted castle bobbing in and out of the haze and, somewhere out to the seaward, HMS *Thunderer,* creeping to and fro and firing titanic guns.

England's a fine land, if she would only stop raining thrice a week. The wet and the damp make me want to be back in Vermont. When shall we see you in that place?

Alas! Never again, for it has passed into other hands.

NOTES

Charles Stoddard (1843–1909) wrote his most popular book, *South Sea Idyls*, in 1873. He taught English at the University of Notre Dame (1885–6) and at the Catholic University of America (1889–1902). He was Mark Twain's secretary for several years. A number of his books deal with Hawaii.

1. A resort village, part of a residential city in Essex County, north-east Massachusetts, on the coast just north of Salem. Oliver Wendell Holmes and his son, the Associate Justice of the Supreme Court, lived here.

2. At 'The Laurel House', a small private hotel in Lakewood, New Jersey, Rudyard Kipling recovered slowly from the shock of Josephine's death in 1899.

3. New Zealand's principal port in North Island; replaced by Wellington as the capital in 1865.

4. Hawaiian *lomi-lomi*, reduplication of *lomi*, to rub with the hand; the shampooing practised among the Hawaiians (*OED*).

5. See p. 117, n. 6.

Rudyard Kipling's Vermont Feud*

FREDERIC F. VAN DE WATER

Beatty had horses and cattle, a hired man and a hired girl, a daughter, his first wife and a mighty thirst when he welcomed the

(Weston, Vt: Countryman Press, 1937) pp. 85–119.

Kiplings to Vermont. One by one in the years that followed, he lost them all but the last. He was well on his way through the first fortune he had inherited by the time Naulakha was completed. By then, the feud whose seed had been planted, no man knows how or when, already was sprouting.

Beatty's family and the Kiplings lived within eye and earshot of each other. Month by month, incompatibility bred heat. The Kiplings were remote; Beatty, gregarious. The Kiplings chose to be intimate with only the best people. Beatty was hail-fellow with all men. The Kiplings were formal and temperate and increasingly prosperous. Beatty was none of these.

Small, persistent frictions bred grievances. Grievances swelled into quarrels, trivial at first and then larger. Beatty's conduct was wilful, riotous, defiant, definitely un-English. There was trouble over that and Caroline Kipling, the ardent Anglican, was bitterly reproachful.

And there was greater trouble over the Kipling's effort to be charitably helpful to their erring kinsman. Beatty had been his brother-in-law's bailiff. He had superintended the construction of Naulakha, he had bought coal and wood and other bulk supplies for the establishment. He had engaged craftsmen. The salary Kipling had paid him had been his chief source of income.

The Kiplings felt that their relative's haphazard and rowdy manner of life in Vermont was doing him no good. They strove to mend his spendthrift ways. Beatty, they decided, without consulting him, really needed the corrective discipline of a steady job. Wherefore, they schemed to save him from himself. They overlooked in their charitable and helpful spirit the obvious fact that himself was the last person in the world from whom Beatty had the least desire to be saved.

Kipling went to his brother-in-law and laid before him a well-meant offer. If Beatty would go to work, if he would leave his cronies and Vermont and go elsewhere and devote himself to honest toil, Kipling would support Beatty's wife and child for a year while the scapegrace was absolving himself of his rowdy ways and finding his feet.

Perhaps the would-be benefactor expected contrition, or at least gratitude. What he got was a dazzling and blasting display of Balestier rage that left him gasping. Beatty told Kipling explicitly what he could do with his charity. The two households saw less of each other from then on but the final and open break came later.

'We had a fight over property', Beatty told me. 'And by God, I still think I was right about it. You know that mowing right across the road from Naulakha? I owned it then. Rud and Caroline wanted it. They were afraid that sometime it would get into other hands and someone would build a house there that would block their view. I told Rud I'd sell it to him for a dollar. I said to him, "Hell, I don't care about the property as a building-site. All I want off it is the hay for my stock. You agree to let me keep on mowing it, and you can have it." '

He stirred in his chair and the rasp of long-cherished grievance came into his voice.

'And then, by God, I heard that Caroline had had a landscape architect up and was going to turn that mowing into a formal garden. I didn't believe it but when they came one night to dinner at my house, I asked about it and Caroline said it was true. I told her, "You're in my house; you're my guest but by Christ, once you've left it, I'll never speak to you again as long as I live."

'We had a quarrel then, Caroline and I. Rud didn't say anything. He just sat there.'

For a full year thereafter, there was grim and boding silence between the households, and Beatty was no longer bailiff to the Kipling establishment. Thus, his own fortunes sank steadily lower while his brother-in-law's soared. This did not tend to soothe him, but if Kipling had held his tongue, if he had adhered more stoutly to British reticence and had not gossiped about Beatty, he might have lived and died in Dummerston[1] and his heirs might still be occupying the grey-green house above the Connecticut. But he did talk and, since all rural regions are whispering galleries, his opinion of Beatty, not diminished by repetition, found its way back to his kinsman's ears.

Anger, born thirty-nine years earlier, heated and sharpened Beatty's voice as he repeated that disastrous, faintly comic insult.

'Rud stopped in the Brooks House for a drink. Colonel Goodhue was there and they got to talking about me. Rud said, "Oh, Beatty is his own worst enemy. I've been obliged to carry him for the last year; to hold him up by the seat of his breeches."'

Someone snickered and Beatty broke off his recital to glare.

'By God, that's what he said. "By the seat of his breeches."'

That was the precipitating affront, the fulminate that set Balestier on fire when he met Kipling, riding his bicycle on the Pine Hill road.

Beatty's harsh, hooked features had been younger then but the rage that had fired him thirty-nine years before when he had shouted defamation at his brother-in-law still glowed in his voice as he told me the tale.

Kipling had stood and endured it, sucking the cut on his wrist. When Beatty paused for breath, the other had asked, 'Let's get this straight. Do you mean personal violence?'

For a genius, he seemed at that moment to be singularly dense. He testified that Beatty replied, 'Yes, by God. I'll give you one week to retract the lies you've been telling and if you don't, I'll blow out your Goddamned brains.'

So Kipling testified. So it may have been, though those who knew Beatty best doubt it. A gun would have been too impersonal, too chill a weapon for so ardent a lover of physical strife. Beatty insisted in court; he swore to me, that all he ever promised his brother-in-law was the licking of his life.

Mulvaney, or Learoyd of the mighty fists, or Crook O'Neill of the Black Tyrone or any of the many valiant men whom Kipling sired would have dragged his traducer from the buckboard and have done his earnest best to beat his head off. Beatty would have understood and respected such a retort but Kipling answered, 'You will have only yourself to blame for the consequences', nor could Beatty's further insults drive him beyond that mild counter-attack. It may be that authors of the most virile prose or verse are at heart the meekest of men.

'In the course of the conversation,' Kipling testified, 'he also called me a liar, a coward and a cheat.'

Beatty at last ran out of invective. He turned his team and drove home. Kipling mounted his bicycle and pedalled back to Naulakha to consult his wife.

On the following Sunday, while Beatty was in Brattleboro with his own wife and little daughter, Sheriff Starkey arrested him on a warrant charging 'assault with indecent and opprobrious names and epithets and threatening to kill' against Rudyard Kipling.

These were 'the consequences' to which Kipling had referred darkly. This was a law-revering Britisher's reprisal. It is possible that he hoped merely to frighten his brother-in-law into contrition. It was, as Kipling shortly learned, dangerous to try to frighten Beatty.

The man's insurgent mind ever worked most brilliantly under the drive of strong stimulant – anger, danger, alcohol. In the fell clutch of the 200-pound sheriff, he did not weep or cry aloud. Kipling may have been encouraged by the meekness with which Beatty submitted to arrest. Presently, as the drama that rocked the Balestier family and thrilled the neighbourhood and amused the English-speaking world unfolded, Kipling felt anything but heartened. He had joined battle with an antagonist too crafty, too heavily armoured. Beatty did not mind scandal. He liked publicity. He doted on battle and he had no morbid craving for privacy. In these and in many other matters he was the direct opposite of his brother-in-law. Gradually Beatty's purpose grew plain, even to those less astute than Rudyard Kipling.

There is a saying in this region: 'Give a calf enough rope and he'll hang himself.' Beatty supplied plenty of rope.

Defendant and plaintiff faced each other before William S. Newton, justice of the peace and Brattleboro's town clerk, who had issued the warrant. Kipling was ill at ease. He got no comfort at all from his brother-in-law's calm. Beatty's answer to 'Uncle Billy' Newton's questions were quiet and malign.

Had he threatened the distinguished author, Mr Rudyard Kipling? He had indeed. With a licking.

Had he called Mr Kipling this and that and the other? Beatty admitted this, too, and supplied several epithets Mr Kipling seemed to have forgotten.

Then, Justice Newton would be obliged to hold Mr Balestier, pending further hearing. Mr Balestier, no doubt, was ready to furnish bond. Mr Balestier grinned and shook his head. He was not ready to furnish any such thing.

Did Mr Balestier understand that if bail were not forthcoming, he could be committed to jail? Mr Balestier replied that he understood that entirely. He was ready – he looked even eager – to go to jail. Might he first have a single hour's stay to take his wife and baby home?

The plaintiff was beginning to suffer now. He, too, had a quick and vivid mind. He could see where the apparently safe course he had taken now was leading. He, the rich and famous man, was about to cast his poor, obscure brother-in-law into prison. Kipling had been a newspaperman. He remembered too the animosity he had sown among men of his own former calling. He could imagine the witches' sabbath reporters would delight to hold over such a plight as this into which he had thrust himself. He saw in all its ghastly splendour what Beatty had discerned from the first. Kipling had a bear by the tail.

The plaintiff flourished a cheque-book. He babbled to Justice Newton, 'I shall be glad to supply the defendant's bail myself.'

Uncle Billy did not have to weigh the legal merit of this Gilbert and Sullivan proposal. Beatty promptly refused to accept his brother-in-law's aid. He seemed poisonously willing to go to jail. At length, he was released on his own recognisance to appear in court again the following Tuesday.

The hearing was adjourned. Kipling fled. Beatty drove home in triumph. Local correspondents of the metropolitan newspapers sprinted for the telegraph office.

When the hearing was reopened on Tuesday, Beatty's cup was full and Kipling's misery complete. Reporters had arrived by the dozens. Most of the region, likewise, had declared an impromptu holiday. The whole world was to be audience to the quarrel two men had begun on a hill road and Kipling, who loathed newspaper intrusion upon his affairs, who detested the invasion of his privacy by any save a few sanctified, had brought this down upon his own head. The crowd overwhelmed Uncle Billy's office. The hearing was adjourned to the town hall where it played to a capacity audience.

Meanwhile, between Sunday and Tuesday, there had been turmoil and anguish in the Balestier clan. Beatty alone had remained direly calm. He was having a fine time. He was deaf to all attempts at compromise. Other members of the family were summoned from New York and elsewhere when the feverish efforts of local relatives had failed to get the lid back on the scandal.

Joseph Balestier, Beatty's favourite uncle, came post-haste. He sought out his recalcitrant nephew and pled with him. If he would only apologise to Kipling, even at this late date, the whole ghastly affair might blow over, unpublicised. The warrant could be withdrawn, the thing could be hushed up.

'He said', Beatty told me, ' "Beatty, you can't go on with this. You mustn't. Think of your family." '

'I told him: "Go on with it? What the hell can I do? Goddamn it, who's arrested, anyway?" '

The hearing was all that Beatty had hoped and Kipling had

feared. C. C. Fitts, state's attorney, conducted the prosecution. Colonel Kittredge Haskins appeared for the plaintiff and Beatty was represented by George B. Hitt. The town hall was packed and in the forefront of the crowd were the maliciously gleeful representatives of the Press.

They enjoyed themselves. So did Beatty. So, too, did the rest of the audience that for four years had endured thwarted curiosity concerning the celebrated and reticent owner of the mansion on the Dummerston hillside. It was a good show and it lasted all day. Justice Newton, contemporary press reports say, 'allowed wide latitude in examination and cross-examination'. He had a good time, too. Everyone had a good time save the wretched plaintiff who sweated and twisted and suffered.

The audience saw reticence ripped from Kipling by Hitt's ironical cross-examination. They were thrilled by the intimate details of the family row that questions dragged forth. They enjoyed the sufferer's occasionally savage retorts.

The direct examination of Kipling by Fitts went smoothly and glibly enough. Kipling gave his version of the hill-road encounter with Beatty. He admitted that Beatty had made no attempt to get out of his buckboard but had waved his arms and shouted a good deal.

The witness also testified that he and Beatty had not spoken for a year before the preceding Wednesday. He insisted that he believed himself in danger of his life at Beatty's hands.

'I honestly think he will kill me sometime,' he told the court, 'if he loses his head again.'

He added that, at the time of the encounter, he thought Beatty insane. He 'was shaking all over, raving mad'.

Hitt's cross-examination lasted the rest of the morning and part of the afternoon. It was caustic, intrusive and excessively painful to a man who wished all of his life, save his published works, to remain inviolably private.

Kipling admitted that his trouble with Beatty had begun in May the year before at a visit to Beatty's home. Thereafter, he testified, he had gone twice to Beatty's farm to see him but had failed both times. He confirmed in substance the 'seat of his breeches' conversation with Colonel Goodhue, but insisted that he had not talked to many persons of his relations with his brother-in-law.

'I suppose', Hitt sneered, 'that you haven't discussed it with reporters', and Kipling snapped, 'The assumption is correct.'

Hitt pounced on the allegation that Kipling was supporting Beatty and shook it like a terrier. He forced the witness to admit that for the last year he had not been carrying his brother-in-law. Kipling also testified that the many loans he had made Balestier always had been paid in full. He professed to have held, until the recent assault, only the kindliest feelings for his kinsman. Was it, Hitt asked, out of his kindliness that he had sworn out this warrant? 'No. I have a distinct aversion to being shot at.'

Hitt delved into the more distant past. Under his goading questions, the suffering witness was prodded into an implausibly great-hearted pose. He testified that he had promised the late Wolcott Balestier to watch over and guide his friend's younger brother. He spoke of Beatty, who was four years his junior, as 'this poor boy' and hinted that the prime reason that had moved him to settle in Vermont was concern for Beatty's welfare.

'Then', Hitt asked, 'taking care of Mr Balestier has been your chief occupation?'

'I have also', the witness answered, 'written a thing or two.'

Attorney for the defendant then took up the actual encounter of the preceding Wednesday. Kipling reiterated his belief that Beatty had been crazy. He said his kinsman had been 'blue with fury'.

'Not red?' Hitt asked, 'Not white?'

'No', Kipling replied. 'Blue', and Justice Newton rapped to check the courtroom titter.

'If you think that Mr Balestier was crazy, why don't you have him examined and adjudged insane?'

'That', Kipling retorted, 'would probably keep my brains in my head.'

Further grilling brought out that Kipling had seen no gun on Wednesday and that he had never known Beatty to go about armed, but the witness clung to his earlier statement that he had felt himself, during the quarrel, in danger of being shot.

'You shared that quarrel with Mr Balestier, didn't you? You made no attempt to smooth it out?'

The harried witness retorted, 'This was the first time I had had my life threatened. I did not know the precise etiquette in such cases.'

'But you made no acknowledgment that you might just possibly be in the wrong?'

Kipling raised his voice: 'I would not retract a word under threat of death from any living man.'

At last the ordeal was over. The hearing ended. Beatty was held in $400 bail for the September Grand Jury. He was bound over in $400 more to keep the peace. Technically, the victory was Kipling's. He found small ground for satisfaction. The worst was not yet.

The comic feud brightened the pages of the American Press. It was featured, twisted into all manner of shapes, served up with a variety of sauces. The newspapermen were not merciful. One reported the hearing under a by-line 'By Terrence Mulvaney'. Even the Brattleboro *Reformer* published inept parody, beginning,

> 'What's that a-loping down the lane?' said the copper-ready-made.
> 'It's Rudyard, running for his life', the first selectman said.
> 'Who's pawing up the dust behind?' said the copper-ready-made.
> 'It's Beatty, seeking Brother-in-Law', the first selectman said.

Heretofore, Kipling had been pestered. The seclusion he longed for had been marred, but most of the earlier intruders had been pilgrims, approaching with awe and worship the threshold of the Master. Now all was changed. The spotlight was on him and the world was laughing. It was no comfort to feel that he had turned that bitter radiance on himself.

Even in his study at Naulakha, more fiercely guarded than ever before, he could hear that enduring, distant, galling mirth. Where once an occasional reporter had tried to see him, a dozen now haunted his gates. A group of Brattleboro worthies came as a deputation to assure him he had the sympathy and the support of all the best people in the region, but he thought they stifled mirth while they said it.

Beatty and the newspapermen liked each other. He drank and yarned and roistered with them. He took some of them fishing. He and they enjoyed themselves. He knew that, despite the outcome of the hearing, he actually had won.

His diabolical mind, once the sheriff had arrested him, had laid hold upon a plan of vengeance more blighting, more comically scathing than any physical assault. And the end of his triumph was yet a long way off. The case would come before the Grand Jury. Perhaps Beatty would be indicted. He hoped most earnestly that he would be, for if he were, Kipling still raw and bleeding from his last ordeal would have to appear as a witness not once but twice more. Beatty had solid ground for his vindictive glee.

The Grand Jury was to meet in September. In August the Kiplings left Vermont for ever. Theirs was the haste of headlong flight. They took only their most personal belongings with them. They sailed from Hoboken, 2 September, on the liner *Lahn*.

'I expect to come back', Kipling told reporters coldly, 'when I get ready. I haven't the least idea when that will be.'

'He never has come back to Vermont. He never will while I'm alive', Beatty told me almost forty years later.

The Kiplings returned to New York in February 1899. Newspapers said they planned to reopen their Vermont home in the spring. The eminent and reputable of Brattleboro and Dummerston hailed the news with solemn joy. They set about preparing a round robin to Kipling, urging him to come and live among them once more. This promised, among other things, a reception and a dinner of state upon his arrival. It is questionable whether the recluse author or his vengeful brother-in-law regarded this proposal with the greatest horror.

'By God,' Beatty told me, 'I wasn't going to let him come back into my country again. It would have blackened my face. I'd have had to get out myself.'

He chuckled. The fiendish expedient still had a pleasant flavour.

'He didn't come back, because I scared him off again. I knew Rud's weakness. He'd had a hell of a time on the witness-stand. I knew he'd run if he thought he'd have to appear in court again.'

New York papers for 12 February 1899 announced that Beatty Balestier was bringing action for $50,000 damages against Rudyard Kipling for 'malicious persecution, false arrest and defamation of character'.

The World said Beatty had come to New York to institute the suit. *The Times* said he would arrive in Manhattan in a few days. Actually no suit ever was brought at all. There was scant ground on which such an action might stand. It was the hollowest of bluffs, but it worked. The Kiplings stayed away from Vermont. After the author's own grave illness in New York and the death of his elder daughter, Josephine, they went back to England never to set foot on American soil again. Matthew Howard, their coachman, who had been left as caretaker at Naulakha, made a special trip across the Atlantic to take his employers some cherished keepsakes from their Vermont home, among them an oil-portrait of the dead daughter.

Kipling visited Canada in 1906. That was his nearest subsequent approach to his first home. He found in the dominion, so his autobiography says, 'Safety, Law, Honour, Obedience', and on the other side of the line 'frank, brutal decivilisation'. In the framing of this judgement, Beatty no doubt had his share. By then Naulakha had been sold to Miss Mary Cabot.

Indian draperies that Caroline Kipling first hung still adorn the mansion's windows. The stranded ark watches Wantastiquet and Brattleboro's far roofs and the long vista of the Connecticut valley down which its builder and first owner fled.

In the once carefully guarded study still stands the desk on which Kipling wrote much of his best work, and on which he carved the legend his Greek galley slave scratched on his oar: 'Oft was I weary as I toiled at thee'.[2] Caroline Kipling sent back orders from England that this carving should be erased before the place was sold. No one knows why.

Over the mantel is the text that Lockwood Kipling carved for his son: 'For the night cometh when no man can work.'[3] That night has come for both the principals in a childish, serio-comic feud. Only a few months after Rudyard Kipling's ashes were laid in Westminster Abbey, Beatty Balestier followed his kinsman and enduring enemy up a straighter and steeper way than the Pine Hill road.

NOTES

An American journalist and author, Van De Water (1890–1968) was a reporter, night editor and book critic on various New York newspapers. He worked on the staff of the *Ladies' Home Journal* from 1922 to 1928. Among numerous books he wrote are *Grey Riders* (1921) and *The Real McCoy* (1931).

1. Town in Windham County, south-east Vermont, just north of Brattleboro.
2. See p. 117, n. 6.
3. John 9: 4

Why Kipling Did Not Become an American Citizen*

GEORGE CALVIN CARTER

Brattleboro, Vermont, is unique in many ways and has a charm all its own, not comparable with any other place in the world. The lordly Connecticut rolls majestically by, and Vermont, whose state line is the west bank of the river, cares not one whit that New Hampshire owns the whole stream.

The West River, with its lovely string of small towns, flows from the very heart of the Green Mountains, joining the larger river at Brattleboro. Whetstone Brook comes bouncing right through the business section of the town and in the spring laughingly sprays its cold flood over all who may be crossing the bridge.

On the New Hampshire side, there rises immediately from the edge of the Connecticut, majestic Mount Wantastiquet, 5 miles long and 1335 feet above sea level, a splendid wind-break against east and north-east storms.

A few miles southerly, is that mythical and mysterious point where New Hampshire, Vermont and Massachusetts come together in pin-point precision. Having once stood in the Coos County wilderness of New Hampshire, where I could have my right foot in New Hampshire, my left in Vermont, and leaning over, placing both hands in Canada, I thought it would be nice to do the same thing at the three-state intersection below Brattleboro.

Here I learned something that I had not previously known and the tourists do not know today. There is a three-state monument visible from the highway, but a close examination of the lettering on the monument states that the actual three-state intersection is so many feet easterly.

One day, after a long drive in the hills west of Brattleboro, where

* *Kipling Journal*, XXXII (Dec 1965) 48–52.

I enjoyed the crisp October air, and that 'orderly riot of the hills' which goes by the name of 'fall foliage' I decided that whatever the risks or impediments I would stand where the three states met.

I proceeded by car across the field and over a gully or two, walking the rest of the way to the river. There was no marker on the river-bank, which was quite disconcerting. While I pondered the sunlight penetrated the ripples on the water and I saw my marker very clearly. It was the top of a granite hitching post, set in the sloping sides of the river-bank, definitely under water, and about 8 feet from the edge of the bank.

Ordinarily what I did could not be done, but in this case fortune favoured the brave. Workmen had been repairing a telephone line and there was an ample supply of waste wire in the grass. I fashioned this into a strong four strand rope, tied one end securely to a tree, doffed coat, hat, shoes and stockings, and rolled my trousers up as far as they would go.

Winding the surplus wire around my waist I proceeded down the bank. It was terribly slippery. It was almost impossible to stand up, but I held tightly to the wire, dug my toes into the bank to keep from being swept down the river.

Carefully and gingerly, like stepping on holy ground, I gained the top of the stone and found that lines had been cut across the top, a copper spike being deeply inserted at the intersection. Initials 'NH' 'Vt' and 'Ms' were in their proper places. I spent the next few minutes paddling around in Vermont, New Hampshire and Massachusetts.

Gaining the bank again after quite a struggle with its wet, slippery slope, I had time to survey the dangers of the trip and one of the famous phrases of Shakespeare came to mind – 'What fools these mortals be.'[1]

To this Elysian vale in Vermont came Kipling and his family, in February 1892, fresh from India. Writing a friend, he said, 'The countryside here is beautiful beyond expression.' During the winter he learned to use snow-shoes, and in the spring he visited the maple-sugar camps. He was captivated by his environment and all that pertained to it.

Joseph Balestier was a native of Martinique, but had bought land in the Brattleboro area. His son Wolcott collaborated with Kipling in England and Wolcott's sister became Mrs Kipling. Wolcott died in Dresden in 1891. Caroline, the sister, began to feel the pull of her Vermont home and Kipling was eager to go.

A home site was selected on a hill plateau just over the

Brattleboro line in the little town of Dummerston. Here he built what he often spoke of as 'The only real home I ever knew' and planned to spend the rest of his life there.

For the Kiplings, their new home and its environment constituted an ideal situation. A certain amount of privacy was necessary and this mountain plateau gave them just what they wanted. The stores and culture of Brattleboro were close at hand and there were beautiful drives everywhere.

In addition to the main home of adequate proportions and specially arranged for Kipling's work, there was a barn for the cows and a stable for the horses. There was a vegetable-garden and a flower-garden, both special projects of Caroline.

The basket phaeton, with its side seats, the light vehicle being drawn sometimes by one pony and sometimes by two in tandem, made a beautiful sight on the streets of Brattleboro as well as on the inter-vale roads.

They had their own post-office called 'Waite, Windham County, Vermont' and their own railroad station, 'Naulakha'. There were instructions to add 'Windham County' to mail addressed to Waite, as this name would not be found in the last postal guide. Mrs Waite was the post-mistress, the office being in her home.

Beatty Balestier, brother of Caroline, who already had a farm of his own, was engaged to do the work. At first it went well for Beatty was capable. No one dared tell Kipling what the townspeople already knew, that Beatty was really lazy, a heavy drinker, a tempestuous character, who seemed to revel in making trouble, creating scenes and always blaming the other fellow.

At first Beatty did well, but when Kipling or Caroline wanted this or that thing done, the risibles began to rise and Beatty would explode. It finally became necessary for Kipling to have it finished by someone else, and the so-called 'Kipling–Balestier Feud' began, a rift never to be healed.

This battle was going strong when I made my first trip to Brattleboro as a reporter for what is now Dun and Bradstreet Inc. I stopped at the famous Brooks House and under a special arrangement made that my headquarters, off and on for some time.

There were no room phones in those days, messages being written on yellow slips and tucked into the door. Returning to the room one evening I found a yellow slip reading 'Mr Rudyard Kipling wishes to see Mr Carter at the earliest possible moment. Speak with desk clerk at office at once.'

The clerk sent for the author and we spent the evening together.

From that time on I saw Kipling fairly often and twice was a guest at his home, Naulakha. He always dressed for dinner but well knew I did not own any evening clothes, and laughingly said he would not like it if I did.

Why did he wish to see me? Beatty had been riding him hard and blaming him for not lending him more money. He had options on timber-lands, water-rights and all sorts of things. Kipling had inquired of the banks and others and they all said, 'See the Dun and Bradstreet man. He has the real facts.'

I did, because I had been over his financial affairs with Beatty and up to that time I had never seen anything like the financial situation in which he was floundering. His statements were wild, far from the truth and his values based on what he imagined he could sell the items for. Most of his options as he called them were not options at all but were merely unconsummated deals about which he had talked with somebody. He did not know how much he owed and did not care. Someday his ship would come in and he would clean up everything.

When Kipling outlined to me what he had done for Beatty I was perfectly astounded. At first there were outright gifts, then loans on notes, and lastly endorsement on Beatty's notes to banks both in Brattleboro and elsewhere. Kipling gave me a complete list of them and then I saw how Beatty based the claim that he always paid Kip back, for when pressed he would give a new note, forgetting to add the accumulated interest.

In abbreviating the conversational name of the author, Beatty always called him 'Rud' while the bankers and tradesmen spoke of him as 'Kip' and I followed this precedent. Kip, at the suggestion of the banks, sought my help in two ways. First, to determine Beatty's financial condition as well as to check his claims, and secondly, to see if I could straighten him out financially as well as to stop his constant insults and threats of bodily harm.

I rounded up all of Beatty's liabilities, including some he had forgotten about and reported to Kip that his brother-in-law was hopelessly insolvent but did not know it, and that in business matters, because he was a dreamer instead of a realist, he would end up in bankruptcy. I told Kipling that in my judgement, he was stuck for every note he had endorsed.

As to Beatty, while he was 'friendly' with me, and wanted me to call on him whenever I was in Brattleboro, I could do nothing with him to stop his war on his benefactor. I found him increasingly loud and noisy, explosive, sarcastic, bombastic and brutal. In spite of Caroline's apologies for him and her attempts to bring him to his senses, I predicted he would grow worse rather than better.

I had already had several talks with Kipling about his plans for American citizenship. He had made no public announcement and said he had talked to no one but me and Caroline about it. Caroline was as enthusiastic as her husband. Both were happy in their environment. Due to the nature of Kipling's work they could not be part of everything that was going on or mix freely with the common herd, but they were a part of the little coterie which constituted the best of Brattleboro. Both very sincerely wanted to spend the rest of their lives here and become an integral part of the community.

Kip asked me how Brattleboro would take it and I said the people would be delighted, and would continue to respect his desire and necessity for privacy, but I knew it could never be and finally had to tell him so, and considering the way Beatty was behaving, the sooner Kip returned to England the safer he would be. Beatty was getting completely out of hand.

Beatty was unbelievably beastly. He seized upon every bit of trivia he could find or make up, enlarged it, and then sailed into the fray with sadistic fury. He accused Kipling of saying things the latter never said, and demanded retraction with an apology within a week or he would knock Kipling's block off. Several times Beatty said to me, 'If that s.o.b. does not come clean, with a public written apology and a retraction, I will kill him as sure as fate.' I told the authorities something must be done and done quickly.

Beatty was arrested, placed under $400 bonds to keep the peace, and under bonds of $400 more to appear before the September Grand Jury. This was done in a session of the municipal court held in the town hall, which could not contain all the townspeople who wanted to get in. In the meantime Beatty had a friend tip off the New York papers that Beatty had sued Kipling for defamation of character in the sum of $50,000. No such suit was ever brought. It was simply a final thrust from a man whose greatest delight was to see a great man squirm.

Kipling called me to Naulakha for a brief farewell. Both husband and wife were visibly shaken. Their dream of American citizenship, for creature comforts, agreeable companionships, and still greater novels from the pen of the master-craftsman were all shattered beyond recall.

Both thanked me several times for what I had done for them and invited me to visit them in England. As soon as the three of us had recovered from the emotion of the decision, Kipling said, 'Mr Carter, do you personally think Beatty would actually kill me, or is that his beastly boasting?'

I replied, 'Who can understand the working of the human mind? Personally I think you are in real danger and I think you should depart at once, secretly and quietly, like getting away safely from a conflagration. Your coachman can bring your personal things to you in England.'

28 August, just before the opening of the September term of court, Kipling and Caroline, with their two little girls, slipped quietly and unnoticed away from their beloved Naulakha and never came back to Vermont. The charges of assault and battery and threat to kill, were never pressed against Beatty.

In this quiet but determined departure, perished the fondest dream of one of the world's great – that of American citizenship. The household was pledged to the strictest secrecy and it was some time before Brattleboro was convinced that Kipling would not return.

A meeting of leading citizens was quickly arranged in the parlour of the Brooks House and I was asked to attend as they knew I had been the confidant of both Beatty and Kipling.

In this meeting I was closely questioned for details. Since these were now a matter of public knowledge I could talk frankly and freely which I did, telling them that all efforts to get him to return would be fruitless, but I kept faith with Kipling by saying nothing about his intention to become an American citizen. He had not told anyone in Brattleboro for obvious reasons.

Convinced that further effort would be useless, the meeting was adjourned by the chairman with the following words: 'Mr Carter, this is a real tragedy. We had hoped he would become one of us.'

NOTES

George Carter (b. 1876) worked for Dun and Bradstreet from 1893 on. A member of various historical societies in New Hampshire, he wrote and lectured on colonial and American Indian history.

1. *A Midsummer Night's Dream*, III. ii. 115.

Teaching Kipling How to Golf*

ARTHUR CONAN DOYLE

Rudyard Kipling I know far less than I should, considering how deeply I admire his writings, and that we live in the same country; but we are both absorbed in work, and both much away from home, which may explain it. I can well remember how eagerly I bought his first book, *Plain Tales*, in the old South Sea days, when buying a book was a rare strain upon my exchequer. I read it with delight, and realised not only that a new force had arisen in literature, but that a new method of story-writing had appeared which was very different from my own adherence to the careful plot artfully developed. This was go-as-you-please take-it-or-leave-it work, which glowed suddenly up into an incandescent phrase or paragraph, which was the more effective for its sudden advent. In form his stories were crude, and yet in effect – which, after all, is everything – they were superb. It showed me that methods could not be stereotyped, and that there was a more excellent way, even if it were beyond my reach. I loved the *Barrack-Room Ballads* also, and such poems as 'The Bolivar', 'East and West', and above all the badly named 'L'Envoi' became part of my very self. I always read the last one aloud to my little circle before we start on any fresh expedition, because it contains the very essence of travel, romance, and high adventure.

I saw Kipling most nearly in his very early days when he lived at Brattleboro, a little village in Vermont, in a chivalrous desire to keep his newly married wife in touch with her own circle. In 1894, as I have recorded, there was a good deal of tail-twisting going on in the States, and Kipling pulled a few feathers out of the Eagle's tail in retaliation, which caused many screams of protest, for the American

* *Memories and Adventures* (Boston, Mass.: Little, Brown, 1924) pp. 245–6.

was far more sensitive to such things than the case-hardened Briton. I say 'was', for I think as a nation with an increased assurance of their own worth and strength they are now more careless of criticism. The result at the time was to add oil to flames, and I, as a passionate believer in Anglo-American union, wrote to Kipling to remonstrate. He received my protest very good-humouredly, and it led to my visit to his country home. As a matter of fact, the concern shown in America, when the poet lay at death's door a few years later, showed that the rancour was not very deep. Perhaps he was better known at that time in America than in England, for I remember sitting beside a busman in London, who bowed his red face to my ear and said, 'Beg your pardon, sir, but 'oo is this 'ere Kiplin?'

I had two great days in Vermont, and have a greateful remembrance of Mrs Kipling's hospitality. The poet read me 'M'Andrew's Hymn', which he had just done, and surprised me by his dramatic power which enabled him to sustain the Glasgow accent throughout, so that the angular Scottish greaser simply walked the room. I had brought up my golf-clubs and gave him lessons in a field while the New England rustics watched us from afar, wondering what on earth we were at, for golf was unknown in America at that time. We parted good friends, and the visit was an oasis in my rather dreary pilgrimage as a lecturer.

My glimpses of Kipling since then have been few and scattered, but I had the pleasure several times of meeting his old father, a most delightful and lovable person, who told a story quite as well as his famous son. As the mother was also a very remarkable woman, it is no wonder that he carried such a cargo.

NOTE

Conan Doyle (1859–1930), English writer of historical romances and various historical studies, is best remembered for having created the figures of Sherlock Holmes and Dr Watson, beginning with *A Study in Scarlet* in 1887.

A Chat with Rudyard Kipling*

CYRIL CLEMENS

'You're just in time for tea. Unfortunately my wife is away at present, so it will be only you and me', said Rudyard Kipling as he stood at his front-door with hand outstretched to welcome me. I will always remember the author's ancient brick home, named 'Bateman's', protected by a high thick hedge from the nearby, white-surfaced roadway. Equally unforgettable was Kipling with his bald head, heavy eyebrows, and friendly quiet smile.

Over delicious scones, buttered toast, and fragrant China tea, my host was soon recalling his first visit to America away back in the year 1889, and his stop-off at Elmira, New York, where Mark Twain was summering.

'I was determined to meet the great American whose *Roughing It, Innocents Abroad* and *Tom Sawyer* had given me such keen pleasure. So after sending in my card,

RUDYARD KIPLING

ALLAHABAD

I was admitted to a big, darkened room, a huge chair, a man with large luminous eyes, a brown moustache, a strong, square hand shaking mine, and the slowest, calmest, levellest voice in all the world saying, 'Well, you think you owe me something, and you've come all the way from India to tell me so. That is' what I call squaring a debt handsomely!'

At first Kipling felt he was meeting an elderly man, but within a very few minutes he 'knew otherwise and perceived how youthful

* *Dalhousie Review*, XXI (1941) 325–30.

were the eyes looking at me and that the grey hair was merely a
trivial accident'. 'He was really and essentially quite young.
Reading his books in distant India, I had endeavoured to get an
idea of his personality, but all preconceived notions proved
erroneous. No illusion whatsoever awaited me in being brought face
to face with my favourite author.'

'The first thing we discussed was the copyright question. I told
Clemens that I had just received a letter from Grant Allen, which
said,

> Use your personal influence in favour of international copyright,
> and prevent the organised robbery of English authors by the
> American people. Work like mine brings me in a bare pittance in
> England: the only reading public that cares for it – the
> American – steals it and pays the author nothing!

'After Mark had talked a good deal about copyright, I asked,
"You feel then that all the world has no commercial sense? But the
book that will live forever can't be artificially kept up at inflated
prices. There will always be very expensive editions of it, and cheap
ones issuing side by side."'

'"I remember one unprincipled publisher", continued Mark.
"He used to take my short stories – I can't call it steal or pirate them.
It was beyond these things altogether. He took my stories one at a
time and made a book of it. If I wrote an essay on dentistry,
orthoëpy, or any little thing of that kind – that publisher would
amend and improve my essay. He would then get another man to
write some more to it, or cut it about exactly as his needs required.
Then he would publish a book called *Dentistry, by Mark Twain*, that
little essay and some other things not mine added. Theology would
make another book, and so on. I do not think that fair. It's an insult.
But he's dead now. I didn't kill him."'

'I then asked Twain some questions about his books, and wanted
to know whether Tom Sawyer married Judge Thatcher's daughter,
and whether we were ever going to hear of Tom Sawyer as a man.'

'"I haven't decided", returned Mark. "I have thought of writing
the sequel to *Tom Sawyer* in two ways. In one I would make him rise
to great honour and go to Congress, and in the other I should hang
him. Then the friends and enemies of the book could take their
choice."'

Kipling said that when he objected to any such theory as this, because to him and to hundreds of thousands of others Tom was real, Mark continued, 'Oh, he is real, very real to me also. He's all the boy that I have known or recollect; but that alternative will probably never present itself, as I do not expect to take Tom into manhood.'

When I mentioned that I had recently enjoyed a pleasant conversation with Marconi in Rome, Kipling said, 'In 1899, when Mrs Kipling and I were living at the Elms, Rottingdean, our friend Mr H. H. McClure[1] wrote asking if he could bring Marconi[2] to see us. They graciously accepted my invitation to lunch at one o'clock. I got Marconi to talk about wireless, and at the end of an hour I felt that I knew as much about wireless as it was possible for a layman to learn. During the talk I consciously or unconsciously was gathering much material for my story, "Wireless",[3] in which I carried the idea of etheric vibrations into the possibilities of thought transference.'

Although he was much too modest to say so, it was evident that Kipling had remembered every word that Marconi had spoken during his long and rather complicated exposition, and that his story reflected all the exact technicalities required.

Speaking of truth and the like in literature, Mark declared that an autobiography was the one work in which a man, against his own will and in spite of his utmost striving to the contrary, revealed himself in his true light to the world.

'A good deal of your life on the Mississippi is autobiographical, isn't it?' Kipling asked.

'As near as it can be,' replied Mark, 'when a man is writing a book about himself. But in genuine autobiography I believe it is impossible for a man to tell the truth about himself or to avoid impressing the reader with the truth about himself. I made an experiment once. I got a friend of mine – a man painfully given to speak the truth on all occasions – a man who wouldn't dream a lie – and I made him write his autobiography for his own amusement and mine. He did it. The manuscript would have made an octavo volume, but – good, honest man that he was – in every detail of his life that I knew about, he turned out on paper a most formidable liar. He simply couldn't help himself!'

As Mark got up from his chair and began strolling up and down the room, he continued, 'I do not believe that it is in human nature to write the truth about itself. None the less, the reader usually gets a general impression from an autobiography whether the writer is a fraud or a good man. The reader can't give his reasons, any more than a man can explain why a woman struck him as being lovely when he doesn't remember her hair, eyes, teeth, or figure. And the impression that the reader gets is the correct one.'

Asked if he ever intended writing an autobiography, Mark drew hard on his pipe, threw up a cloud of smoke and drawled, 'If ever I write an autobiography, it will probably be as other men have done – with the most earnest desire to make myself out to be the better man in every little business that has been to my discredit; and I shall fail, like the others, to make my readers believe anything except the truth.'

After we had discussed Mark Twain, I asked Kipling if he had known any other American humourists.

'I went to Canada in 1907,' he answered, 'making the trip through to Vancouver without visiting the United States, but I spent two days with Finley Peter Dunne[4] in Montreal, and enjoyed the visit tremendously. We found in each other absolutely congenial spirits. Whenever possible I slipped away from the numerous receptions and entertainments, and retired to Dunne's sitting-room, where we spent hours in swapping one story after another. Since *Mr Dooley in Peace and War* had first appeared in 1898, I had been a warm admirer of Dunne's work. His Mr Dooley possessed wit, a bold imagination, a sharp tongue, a wide sympathy, and a rare fund of common-sense. Who can ever forget his delightful Irishisms?

' "There's no intoxicant in th' wurruld, Hinnissy, like money. It goes to th' head quicker th' whiskey th' druggist makes in his back room" ';

' "Some iv th' boldest liars I iver met wud've been truthful men if they'd dared to be" ';

' "Onaisy, as Hogan says, is th' head that wears a crown. There is other heads that're onaisy too; but ye don't hear iv them." ' '

When our talk had wandered from humorists to the game of golf, Kipling vividly described an odd golf game he had played during the winter of 1893 when he was living in the home he had built at Brattleboro, New Hampshire.

'We played the game over snow several feet deep, upon the crust, cutting holes into the soft snow, and naturally losing the balls until it occurred to my partner to ink them red. The first day we experimented with them, we dyed the plain like some football gridiron; then we had them painted. The trouble with golfing on the crust was that as the meadow was upon a side hill with gradual slope, a ball went on forever when once started unless headed off by some kindly stone wall or by one's opponent. It was not at all difficult to make a drive of one or two miles! As spring arrived, little putting greens emerged like oases in the snow, and then we arranged holes of empty vegetable cans sunk in the moist soil, round which we would manoeuvre in rubber boots. I recall my partner's intentional miss of a hole one inch away one afternoon, throwing the victory to me who was a stroke and five yards behind.'

'Did you do much writing at Brattleboro, Mr Kipling?'

'During the four years I was there, from 1892 to 1896, I turned out the two Jungle Books, some of the short stories in *The Day's Work*, many of the poems in *The Seven Seas*, and *Captains Courageous*. Joel Chandler Harris's[5] praise of *The Second Jungle Book* made me proud and happy, and I told him.

'You probably do not know how *Uncle Remus*, his sayings, and the sayings of the noble beasties ran like wild fire through Westward Ho!, my English school, when I was about fifteen. The boys used to go to battle, with boots and bolsters, and suchlike, to the tune of "Ty-yi-tungalee: I eat um pea, I pick um pea", etc., and I recall the bodily bearing into a clump of bushes solely because his nickname had been "Rabbit" before the tales invaded the school and – well, we assumed that he ought to have been born and bred in a briar-patch. A few years ago when I met an old schoolmate in India, we soon found ourselves quoting whole pages of *Uncle Remus* that had got inextricably mixed up with the memories of our school-days.'

'Some of my most vivid memories of Vermont', continued Kipling 'were of the picturesque itinerant pedlars who invaded the region each spring, hawking their merchandise from farm to farm: formidable red-and-gilt biographies of great Americans like Washington, Hamilton and Lincoln, 20-pound family Bibles, coloured steel engravings, patent electric pills, seeds, knives, needles, and flavouring extracts of infinite colour and variety. One of these wandering quacks, a florist's representative hawking seeds, who had come "to swindle every citizen from Keene to Lake Champlain" inspired my poem "Pan in Vermont", which was first published in the American *Country Life* sometime in 1902.'

Before I left, my host kindly showed me over his house and gardens, his old water-mill which was rated in the Doomsday Book at a shilling a year tax! – and his farm generally. The 'newest' wing on his house was nearly 300 years old. Not a few guns which fought the Spanish armada were cast on the farm during Elizabethan days, when there was an important armament foundry near the mill. I saw also the location scenes for *Puck of Pook's Hill*,[6] the wholly delightful fairy-stories Kipling wrote for his two children Elsie and John whose loss during the First World War was such a terrific blow to the author.

Unlike my experience with some authors, meeting Kipling personally was nothing of a disappointment, and I went away reciting to myself the closing lines of 'L'Envoi':[7]

And only the Master shall praise us, and only the Master shall blame;
And no one shall work for money, and no one shall work for fame;
But each for the joy of the working, and each, in his separate star,
Shall draw the Thing as he sees It, for the God of Things as They Are!

NOTES

Cyril Clemens, biographer of Lytton Strachey, is a distant relation of Mark Twain, author and editor of several books about him, editor of *The Mark Twain Quarterly* (from 1936 on), and founder of the Mark Twain Association.

1. *McClure's* was the first popular journal to announce Marconi's discovery of wireless telegraphy, 'and when that article appeared it was generally regarded with utter incredulity. I remember, a professor of Clark University wrote on that occasion and urged us to avoid announcing such absurdities and thereby making the magazine ridiculous' – Samuel Sidney McClure, *My Autobiography* (New York: Magazine Publishers, 1914) p. 225. ('H. H.' seems to be a mistaken remembrance of 'S. S.')

2. Guglielmo Marconi (1874–1937), Italian electrical engineer, inventor, and developer of wireless telegraphy as a practical means of long-distance communication, as well as of short-wave wireless.

3. First published in *Scribner's Magazine*, Aug 1902; collected in *Traffics and Discoveries* (1904).

4. Finley Peter Dunne (1867–1936) wrote more than 700 Irish dialect sketches, attacking hypocrisy and advocating greater toleration of diversity in American life. *Mr Dooley in Peace and War* appeared in 1898, and seven volumes followed; they were all popular. Dunne was also a political reporter and an editorial writer.

5. Harris (1848–1908) was an expert in the lore and dialects of plantation blacks, and created the American folk-character Uncle Remus, among many others.

6. A collection of ten stories and sixteen poems published in 1906 by Macmillan. The stories were first printed in the *Strand*, Jan–Apr 1906, and *McClure's Magazine*, May–Oct 1906.

7. 'L'Envoi to *The Seven Seas*'.

A Visit to Elmira, New York *

MILDRED HOWELLS

The Kiplings had invited Howells and his wife, who had spent her girlhood in Brattleboro, to visit them there, but Mrs Howells was not well enough to go and Howells would not leave her.

Rudyard Kipling to W. D. Howells

Naulakha, Waite, Windham Co., Vermont

4 June 1896

Dear Mr Howells,

We are both of us sorry and disappointed that you can't come and more sorry that Mrs Howells is below herself. (Yes, I *do* understand.) However one of these glorious summer days I despair not that we shall get you up here, for I don't think quite of quitting the land permanently. It is hard to go from where one has raised one's kids and builded a wall and digged a well and planted a tree.

As regards the other matter I do remember that once in your official capacity you said something about a book by Kipling which was salutary and chastening to that young man. But as Boswell once remarked to Dr Johnson in the stately phrase of the eighteenth century, 'It would need a hell of a lot that I took unkindly from *you*, sir' and I am cheered to think you like some of my yarns.

Affectionately always,

Rudyard Kipling

---

* *Life in Letters of William Dean Howells*, ed. Mildred Howells (New York: Doubleday, Doran, 1928) II, pp. 66–7, 100–1.

W. D. Howells to Miss Aurelia H. Howells

40 West 59th St, New York

26 February 1899

Dear Aurelia,

. . . Just now we are very anxious about Kipling, who lies at the point of death – he may be dead while I write – at a hotel, near here, with pneumonia. – I dined with him only ten days ago, and in the dressing room he saw me in a plump elderly man's difficulties with a new pair of rubbers, and the dear fellow got down on one knee and put them on for me; he said he always did it for his father. He had a coat lined with coon-skins, and he was showing it to me, and telling me about having it made. Before we left the table, he told his brother-in-law, with whom we were dining, that he must go at 10.30, for he had ordered his carriage then, and he did not like to keep the driver freezing. . . .

With love to Henry,

Your affectionate brother

Will

John Kendrick Bangs,[1] who was editor of the American edition of *Literature*, had asked Howells to write something about Kipling that could be published at once in case of his death.

W. D. Howells to John Kendrick Bangs

40 West 59th St, New York

27 February 1899

My dear Mr Bangs,

There seems now some hope for Kipling, and since I wrote you this morning I have been turning the matter over in my mind, and I find that I cannot write of him living as if he were dead. It is shocking to me; I have felt most deeply his danger; and there would be something insincere and histrionic in what I should hypotheti-cally say. I know you mean to do him honour, and I felt this so strongly that, what with my own wish to recognise his greatness in literature, I consented to do what I cannot while he lives.

I hope I have not put you out.

Yours cordially,

W. D. Howells

NOTES

William Dean Howells (1837–1920), self-educated author, consul in Venice (1861–5), editor of *Atlantic Monthly* (1871–81), and author of novels of manners up to 1881, after which he specialised in realistic fiction. He moved to New York in 1891; was a close friend of Mark Twain; and served as the first president of the American Academy of Arts and Letters. Mildred Howells (1872–1966) wrote and illustrated several books in addition to editing two volumes of the letters of her distinguished father.

1. Bangs (1862–1922) was an American humorist, editor and lecturer, and may be best known for *Three Weeks in Politics* (1894) and *A Houseboat on the Styx* (1895).

Mark Twain in Eruption*

SAMUEL LANGHORNE CLEMENS

11 Aug 1906. This morning's cables contain a verse or two from Kipling, voicing his protest against a liberalising new policy of the British Government.which he fears will deliver the balance of power in South Africa into the hands of the conquered Boers. Kipling's name, and Kipling's words always stir me now, stir me more than do any other living man's. But I remember a time, seventeen or eighteen years back, when the name did not suggest anything to me and only the words moved me. At that time Kipling's name was beginning to be known here and there, in spots, in India, but had not travelled outside of that empire. He came over and travelled about America, maintaining himself by correspondence with

* (New York: Harper, 1922); ed. Bernard De Voto (New York: Grosset and Dunlap, 1940), pp. 309–12.

Indian journals. He wrote dashing, free-handed, brilliant letters but no one outside of India knew about it.

On his way through the State of New York he stopped off at Elmira and made a tedious and blistering journey up to Quarry Farm in quest of me. He ought to have telephoned the farm first; then he would have learned that I was at the Langdon homestead, hardly a quarter of a mile from his hotel. But he was only a lad of twenty-four and properly impulsive and he set out without inquiring on that dusty and roasting journey up the hill. He found Susy Crane[1] and my little Susy[2] there, and they came as near making him comfortable as the weather and the circumstances would permit.

13 Aug 1906. The group sat on the verandah and while Kipling rested and refreshed himself he refreshed the others with his talk, talk of a quality which was well above what they were accustomed to, talk which might be likened to footprints, so strong and definite was the impression which it left behind. They often spoke wonderingly of Kipling's talk afterward, and they recognised that they had been in contact with an extraordinary man, but it is more than likely that they were the only persons who had perceived that he was extraordinary. It is not likely that they perceived his full magnitude, it is most likely that they were Eric Ericsons who had discovered a continent but did not suspect the horizonless extent of it. His was an unknown name and was to remain unknown for a year yet, but Susy kept his card and treasured it as an interesting possession. Its address was Allahabad.

No doubt India had been to her an imaginary land up to this time, a fairyland, a dreamland, a land made out of poetry and moonlight for the Arabian Nights to do their gorgeous miracles in; and doubtless Kipling's flesh and blood and modern clothes realised it to her for the first time and solidified it. I think so because she more than once remarked upon its incredible remoteness from the world that we were living in, and computed that remoteness and pronounced the result with a sort of awe, 14,000 miles, or 16,000, whichever it was. Kipling had written upon the card a compliment to me. This gave the card an additional value in Susy's eyes, since as a distinction it was the next thing to being recognised by a denizen of the moon.

Kipling came down that afternoon and spent a couple of hours with me, and at the end of that time I had surprised him as much as he had surprised me, and the honours were easy. I believed that he knew more than any person I had met before, and I knew that he knew I knew less than any person he had met before – though he did not say it and I was not expecting that he would. When he was gone, Mr Langdon[3] wanted to know about my visitor. I said, 'He is a stranger to me but he is a most remarkable man – and I am the other one. Between us, we cover all knowledge; he knows all that can be known, and I know the rest.'

He was a stranger to me and to all the world, and remained so for twelve months, then he became suddenly known and universally known. From that day to this he has held this unique distinction: that of being the only living person, not head of a nation, whose voice is heard around the world the moment it drops a remark, the only such voice in existence that does not go by slow ship and rail but always travels first-class by cable.

About a year after Kipling's visit in Elmira, George Warner[4] came into our library one morning in Hartford, with a small book in his hand, and asked me if I had ever heard of Rudyard Kipling. I said, 'No.'

He said I would hear of him very soon, and that the noise he was going to make would be loud and continuous. The little book was the *Plain Tales* and he left it for me to read, saying it was charged with a new and inspiriting fragrance and would blow a refreshing breath around the world that would revive the nations. A day or two later he brought a copy of the London *World* which had a sketch of Kipling in it, and a mention of the fact that he had travelled in the United States. According to this sketch he had passed through Elmira. This remark, added to the additional fact that he hailed from India, attracted my attention – also Susy's. She went to her room and brought his card from its place in the frame of her mirror, and the Quarry Farm visitor stood identified.

I am not acquainted with my own books but I know Kipling's – at any rate I know them better than I know anybody else's books. They never grow pale to me; they keep their colour; they are always fresh. Certain of the ballads have a peculiar and satisfying charm for me. To my mind, the incomparable Jungle Books must remain unfellowed permanently. I think it was worth the journey to India to qualify myself to read *Kim* understandingly and to realise how great a book it is. The deep and subtle and fascinating charm of India pervades no other book as it pervades *Kim*; *Kim* is pervaded by it as by an atmosphere. I read the book every year and in this way I go back to India without fatigue – the only foreign land I ever daydream about or deeply long to see again.

NOTES

Samuel Clemens, writing under the pen-name Mark Twain, wrote *The Adventures of Tom Sawyer* (1876) and *The Adventures of Huckleberry Finn* (1884). Like Charles Dickens, he achieved considerable fame as a reader and lecturer. In later years his philosophy darkened, and he became a pessimist about the human condition. He lived from 1835 to 1910.

1. Daughter of Susan Langdon Crane (1836–1924), who was the adopted daughter of Jervis Langdon. Jervis, who had bought Quarry Farm in Elmira, New York, as a weekend retreat, gave it to Susan as a present when she married Theodore Crane.

2. Olivia Susan Clemens (1872–96), talented, beautiful, and much-loved, whose premature death contributed to the sadness of her father's final years.

3. Son of Charles Jervis Langdon, the brother of Livy Clemens, who showed Samuel Clemens a miniature of her. Clemens fell in love with her picture. Mr Langdon (referred to in the text) was one of the managers of the Langdon Coal Co. Jervis Langdon (1809–70) had married Olivia, and with his adopted daughter Susan moved to Elmira in 1845.

4. Brother of Charles Dudley Warner, co-author with Mark Twain of *The Gilded Age* (1873), a novel that angrily denounced corruption in post-Civil War America.

Conversations with Some American Authors*

HAMLIN GARLAND

Somewhere in 1890 or 1891 some books of short stories by a young man named Rudyard Kipling began to find their way into American print, some of them pirated, no doubt, and one afternoon as I was buying my evening paper at a Roxbury[1] bookstand (my brother and I were then living on Moreland Street) I saw on the counter a little paper-bound volume called *Mine Own People*.[2] I

---

* *Roadside Meetings* (New York: Macmillan, 1930) pp. 168–74, 405–14.

bought it and that night I read it almost without leaving my chair. 'Here is another local-colour novelist,' I said to my brother, 'only in this book the colour is East Indian.'

There was something individual in the tang of this writing, something gay and vital, and a few days later I asked the newsdealer if he had any other books by this writer. No, he had not, but he could get me some. 'You'd better lay in a supply', I remarked. 'There is going to be a boom in his stock.'

Knowing that I was something of a literary man, the dealer followed my advice, and for several months thereafter, whenever I entered his door, reproached me by calling attention to a pile of unsold copies of *Mine Own People* and *Tales from the Hills*. I kept his courage up as best I could by repeating, 'The boom is delayed but it will come.'

My own faith in Kipling's boom was based upon reports from New York and on the opinion of two of my friends on the Boston *Transcript*. Ultimately my prediction came true and the bookseller cleared out his shelf of paper copies and bought others in regular bindings. Kipling's stories came so fast in these pirated reprints that a bit of doggerel went the rounds, 'When the Kiplings cease from Kipling and the critics are at rest.' There was reason for this sudden flare of fame. The author's note was novel, his characters vividly seen, and his region romantic. Soon every one was reading and talking Kipling.

Howells[3] told me something of his personality. 'He is a brother-in-law of my young friend, Wolcott Balestier,[4] who died recently', he said. 'He is a young Englishman who began to write on a newspaper in India. He has established a home near his wife's family in Vermont and appears to have adopted America.'

Beyond this I heard very little of Kipling, until some time in the spring of 1892, while living in New York City, I received a letter from him inviting me to dine with him. I was disposed to accept this invitation at once, but knowing that he was an Englishman and likely to insist on formal dress, I replied, 'I should be delighted to come, but the truth must be told. I have no evening suit; in fact I have never worn one. If you will excuse an ordinary frock coat, I shall be only too glad to accept your kind invitation.'

I have no copy of this reply, but it was something like this, 'My dear sir, you may come in a buckskin shirt, if you like', an expression which he knew I would understand.

The night of the dinner happened to be rainy, and as I arrived at the place appointed ten minutes ahead of time, I decided to wait in the hall of the little hotel, which was on West 46th Street (as I recall it a very obscure hotel indeed), until my watch indicated exactly seven o'clock.

While standing thus absent-mindedly facing the street door, I became aware of a moon-faced, elderly man on the sidewalk peering up at the entrance as if to reassure himself of his destination. He wore a short, light-grey overcoat and a tall silk hat perched on the back of his head, and something in the shine of his glasses and in his broad, blank face made me think of Horace Greeley.[5]

Suddenly I recognised him. 'Why, it's Riley!'[6] I exclaimed and hastened to open the door for him. 'Yes, this is the place,' I said, 'come in.'

He faced me with a perfectly blank visage, a look which he could assume at any time, and fixing me with a solemn grey eye, motioned over his shoulder with his thumb toward the interior of the hotel. 'Dining here?'

I nodded.

'With Kipling?'

I nodded again.

His eyes lightened and a slow smile widened his mouth. 'Now what do you suppose Kipling wants of two such specimens of yaller-dent poetry as we are advertised to be?'

'I give it up, Riley, so far as I am concerned, but in your case I think his interest is justified.'

Suddenly his tone changed to one of anxious pleading. Pointing a finger at me, he said, 'Now see here, Garland, you've got to insure that I get back to the St Denis Hotel. You know perfectly well that I cain't go for a walk around the block and come back to the hole I went out at.' Then placing the tip of his finger just above his ear, he added, with a grin, 'Nothing in my bump of location but mayonnaise dressing.'

Chuckling with glee over this characterisation of himself, I replied, 'I'll see that you reach your hotel in safety, but it is time to go up.' I started for the elevator.

'Wait a second', he called sharply. 'Wait till I ad-just a hame strap.'

Whilst I marvelled over his meaning, he reached under his grey overcoat and pulled out a pin. Down dropped one of the tails of his evening coat about eight inches below his reefer. Without a particle of expression, yet watching the effect on me, he pulled another pin, and as the second tail dropped he mumbled a low-voiced explanation: 'Couldn't find m' other coat. Must 'a' loaned it to a feller or left it in the street-car, or something.'

Shaking with silent laughter I finally managed to say, 'If you'll take off your topcoat and fold it and carry it on your arm the Kiplings will never know how inadequate it is.'

'Good idea!' said he but without enthusiasm, and with the makeshift garment on his arm he joined me in the elevator.

The Kiplings met us cordially if a bit apprehensively, and it soon appeared that we were the only guests and a strange pair we were. As we sat at their table in the general dining-room, Mrs Kipling occupied one end of the table and Kipling the other. Riley and Miss Balestier sat opposite me, and as I opened out my napkin I began to divine the situation. Kipling was interested in Riley and Garland as American representatives of the vernacular in verse and local colour in fiction. We were interesting as specimens and I could not decide whether we should feel flattered or resentful. 'If Riley can stand it, I can', was my conclusion.

Kipling, a short, dark-complexioned, alert young man nearing thirty, was colonial in accent, quick-spoken and humourous. He was not at all English in manner, but his outlook was British.

For a time I gave my attention to my hostess, but with those immortal talkers going on at my left, I grew distraught, and at last Mrs Kipling, sensing my predicament, gave up attempts to enlist my attention. Thereafter we all listened while Riley and his host exchanged quip for crank. It was delightful talk, but it was not till we three men retired to the small room which our host used for a study that he 'cut loose'. For half an hour his monologue was gorgeous with the colour of the East. He dealt with cobras, typhoons, tropic heat, windless oceans, tiger-haunted jungles, and elephants, especially elephants. It was all sumptuous material and his descriptions were adequately representative. He spoke of elephants 'muttering among themselves like wise old men'. He told of the quiet, calculating malignity with which one vengeful old bull chewed a stalk of cane into a swab and wound it in the robe of his cruel, drunken keeper and jerked him under his feet. He described those which went mad and those which helped capture their wild fellows. In one story he pictured a vessel with a load of these great creatures becalmed under the torrid sun of the Indian Ocean, and how they had to be loaded alternate heads and tails to keep them from rocking the boat as they swayed uneasily in their chains. One of them died, and it was necessary to cut her to pieces and throw her overboard, a gruesome task whose details I will not record. In all that he told he created marvellous pictures, filling my mind with wonder of his experiences as well as with admiration of his powers of observation and description.

Nevertheless, eager as I was to have him go on, I was jealous for the honour of American literature. I wanted Riley to show what he could do. As we were about to rejoin the ladies, I said to Kipling in an aside, 'Have you ever heard Riley recite his verse?'

'No,' he replied, 'but I wish I might.'

'He is a wonder. Ask him to read a poem.'

In response to this suggestion, Kipling said, 'Riley, read us something', and Riley, without hesitation or apology, rose to his feet and stood for a moment with his eye-glasses in his fingers. Instantly his big blond face took on something quaint and tender, something Hoosier came into it as he began to voice 'Nothin' to Say',[7] that touching and wistful monologue in which a gentle old farmer replies to his daughter's remark, 'Father, I'm going to be married, what have you to say?' with, 'Nothin' to say, my daughter, nothin' at all to say.' The poet followed this with 'That Young 'Un', which is the story of the little son of the miller who knew what the bees said, what the birds sang, but could never quite tell 'what the water is a-talkin' of'. At the close of this exquisitely truthful and deeply moving poem in the vernacular, Kipling sprang to his feet and, pacing back and forth, said with unmistakable sincerity, 'By the Lord, *that's* American literature!'

I thought so then and I think so still, although I realised at the time the marvellous skill with which Riley helped out the value of his words by voice and gesture.

In accordance with my promise, I guided Riley back to his hotel, and as we were walking along the street, he said in a musing tone, 'Will you tell me just why you and I have been so honoured by Kipling?'

'You can search me!' I replied in one of George Ade's graphic slang phrases, 'but he knew what he was getting in my case, for I wrote in warning. I told him I was not fitted to enter the dress-coat zone.'

'Well, dog the difference,' said Riley with resignation, 'we had a gorgeous evening.'

So far as I know, Kipling had no regrets. He always asked for Riley when we met, and sent his greetings when he wrote. As for his own performance that night, I had only awed admiration. That we had been specially honoured was evident, for some of the stories he told were never published, or at least I never saw them in print. All of them were new and for the most part in manuscript.

For some reason, the rights of which I never learned, Kipling found life in Vermont displeasing. Early in the nineties he removed his family to England and I saw no more of him for several years. Somehow he and Brattleboro did not rhyme and when I got a letter dated 'Bateman's, Burwash Etchingham, Sussex, England', I had a feeling that he was more at home there than he could possibly be in America or even in India. He seemed quite as far from West Salem, Wisconsin, and Greenfield, Indiana, as he had been when writing from Bombay. . . .

Bok[8] had told me that Kipling was returning to America, and the New York papers confirmed the news by front-page accounts of his landing with his wife and two children. Nearly all the reporters mentioned his fur-lined overcoat and later papers said he had taken a suite of rooms at the 'Grenoble', a small hotel near Carnegie Hall; and on my return to New York that afternoon I went up to call upon him. I had not seen him for five years, for he had been living in England, and my only news of him had been an occasional note; but he received me as if we had parted only yesterday. His reception room swarmed with visitors, mostly women, and somewhat appalled by the throng I hesitated about taking a seat. 'Let me come again when you have fewer visitors', I suggested.

With a chuckle he replied, 'I don't know when that will be! They come in endless streams. Come out into the hall; we can have a few words there.'

That he was deeply gratified by this display of interest on the part of the public was evident. There had been much adverse criticism of him at the time of his leaving the States but all that was forgotten. The whole nation was ready to honour him.

He asked after Riley, Howells, Matthews, and other of our mutual friends, and agreed to lunch with me at the club for further talk. He was older in some respects, but still carried himself with boyish alertness. When I asked, 'How are the books selling?' he replied with another chuckle, 'Hugely!'

This led me to tell him the story of the Roxbury book-seller who at my suggestion stocked up on Kipling in 1892. 'For a year or two he met me with reproachful glances, but I venture to bet he's all right now.'

This seemed to amuse him, but he broke off to say, 'I must go back to my other guests.' . . .

The city was smothered in snow, and Zangwill,[9] storm-bound, proposed that I take him to call on Kipling whom he had never met. This I was glad to do, and we spent a lively hour with this marvellous young man who is the acknowledged spokesman of the English 'jingoists'. He gave us a brilliant statement of his merciless philosophy, but qualified it by reference to 'the white man's burden'. . . . 'The races who keep the dead out of their drinking water survive and those who don't – die. Which is as it should be. The white man's duty is to rule and sanitate.'

To me he said, 'As for your Filipinos, make them work for you.'

He was vivid, brilliant, and ruthless, and did not quite follow Zangwill's subtler wit – that is, he was just an instant longer in turning the corner, perhaps because of his 'white man's burden'. He argued that England's work was to civilise and regulate.

Zangwill sat with his big head sleepily swaying, his brain lightning swift, and his voice gentle and passionless. His position was in vivid contrast to that of Kipling, who saw little to reform in the white man's country and who insisted on reforming the brown races altogether, whether or not they wanted change.

One of his side remarks stuck in my mind. 'I understand the native', he said. 'My nurse was Hindustani. I spoke no English till I was six. I knew only Hindustani.'

I remarked, 'That explains your hold upon the lore of the natives.'

He laughed as he replied, 'I don't know how much it explains, but it is a fact. I didn't speak English till I was forced to do so by my father. Ours is the job of civilising these savage and backward tribes', he summed up in effect. 'Nothing is gained by coddling weak and primitive men. The law of survival applies to races as well as to species of animals. It is pure sentimental bosh to say that Africa belongs to a lot of naked blacks. It belongs to the race that can make the best use of it. I am for the white man and the English race.'

At the end of Kipling's eloquent defence of the English as the chosen civilisers of the world, Zangwill remarked with gentle, reproachful, but humorous surprise, 'Why, Kipling, you're almost Hebraic!'

That was precisely the paradoxical situation: Zangwill, the Jew, was the disciple of Christ; while Kipling, the Christian, was a follower of Gideon and the God of Battle.

As we came away Zangwill could talk of nothing else but Kipling's resemblance to the chieftains of David's time, the men who believed in smiting 'hip and thigh', exterminating their enemies root and branch. I was opposed to Kipling's philosophy and so was Howells, with whom I discussed it; but I am not so sure that his view was not honester and more consistent than ours. Why should so much of the earth be given over to pitiless, filthy, half-formed savage races? So many billions of them have been slaughtered by their own kind. So many other billions have died like monkeys without the slightest value to the universe or their own kind. What does it matter whether such beings live or die? . . . My poor brain reels before such a problem and I long for Kipling's certitude. . . .

As I stepped out of my door on East 25th Street the morning of the 20th, I saw a small man wearing a light coat, alertly approaching, accompanied by a slender, self-contained young woman. Something in the man's compact figure was familiar – it was Kipling, and the woman was his wife. After a moment's greeting he said, 'We're on our way to McClure's office. Can you tell me where it is?'

'Certainly – I'll go with you. It's only a step!' I replied.

As we walked along he spoke of the sudden turn to warm weather. 'I have laid off my fur-coat, of which the papers made so much', he added with a smile.

At the door of the big loft in which *McClure's Magazine* was printed, I left them and turned away. They were both in happy mood, rejoicing over the acclaim which still filled the press, and which had enormously increased the sale of his books. All the dislike of America which he had hitherto expressed went for nothing. He had entered upon a new era of wealth and honour.

As I was about to leave for the West, I considered it my duty to turn over the work of Secretary of the National Institute to someone who would be on the ground; and to this end I called upon Hamilton Wright Mabie[10] in his office and gave him what records I had, telling him that I was to dine with Holbrook Curtis again and that I would ask him to surrender all his data.

The papers that morning all reported that Kipling was very ill with pneumonia, and Mabie said, 'What a tragic end of his career that would be!' Much concerned, I stopped in at the Grenoble to inquire how the case stood. I found Jacacci,[11] the art editor of *McClure's*, in the lobby. He said, 'Frank Doubleday[12] and I have just arrived. Frank has gone up to see Kipling and find out his condition.'

When Doubleday came down his face was grave. 'He's in a very critical stage of the disease. He has been unconscious part of the time today but is pluckily holding his own. The doctors have not given up. They are to employ oxygen and every other known resource, they say. It all came about from his laying aside his fur-coat on one of our deceptively warm days. It appears that his little daughter is also ill and in the care of strangers. Mrs Kipling, exhausted by the care of her husband, is unable to be with her.'

It was a bitter and tragic change in Kipling's fortunes, and the whole world was in sympathy. All that day bulletins appeared almost hourly in the newspapers stating the progress of the battle and giving details of the treatment. Recalling him as I had seen him only a few days before, so happy and so alert, I experienced a chill foreboding. 'What if he should go now?'

'Monday, 27 February. I was afraid to take up a paper this morning for fear of finding a notice of Kipling's death. Happily he is reported to be holding his own and the use of oxygen has given a hope of his coming through. The whole of America is watching the struggle and many prayers are going up for his recovery.'

For nearly two weeks his life was in danger and the whole nation shared the anxiety of the wife and others of his family. Bulletins continued to be issued as if for a great general, and when his doctors reported, 'He will live!' – every one rejoiced.

During the very worst stage of his illness, his little girl died; but by order of the physicians her condition had been kept from him. He knew nothing of her death till after her burial, and when the time came to tell him, Frank Doubleday was chosen to speak the words. 'It was the hardest task I ever undertook,' said Doubleday, who had been in almost hourly attendance upon the sick man, 'but it had to be done. I took a seat beside him and told the story in as few words as I could. He listened in silence till I had finished, then turned his face to the wall.'

NOTES

Hamlin Garland (1860–1940) was born in Wisconsin, and grew up on farms in the Midwest. He wrote short stories (*Main-travelled Roads*, 1891; *Prairie Folks*, 1893; *Wayside Courtships*, 1897), and novels that portrayed farm life as bitter and futile. A supporter of the single-tax and the populist party, he wrote two autobiographies, *A Son of the Middle Border* (1917) and *A Daughter of the Middle Border* (1921). These proved to be popular, and the latter won a Pulitzer Prize.

1. A residential district in south Boston, incorporated by the city in 1868.

2. A collection of twelve stories, six of which had been published before, in *The Courting of Dinah Shadd and Other Stories* (1890). Kipling brought out the book in 1891 to out-manoeuvre unauthorised publication in the United States.

3. See p. 247, note on Howells.

4. A reporter, novelist, campaign biographer (for James G. Blaine), dramatist, encourager of writers and artists through various publishing schemes, and, by all accounts, an attractive personality. Balestier (1861–91) was sent by John W. Lovell to England (1888) to secure original manuscripts for publication in the United States. As managing editor of Heinemann and Balestier, he met Kipling soon after he arrived in England. His sister married Kipling in 1892. Balestier contributed the American chapters to *The Naulahka* (1892), which he wrote with Kipling.

5. Greeley (1811–72) was editor of the *New Yorker* (1834); *The Jeffersonian* (1838) and *The Log Cabin* (1840); and the *New York Tribune* (from 1841 on). As a teacher and moral leader, he preached a radical egalitarianism; opposed slavery, and supported the Union. Politically ambitious, he ran unsuccessfully as Democratic candidate for President in 1872, and died insane shortly afterwards.

6. An American poet and dialect-writer (1849–1916), whose book-titles are characteristic of a turn of mind: *Afterwhiles* (1887), *Old-Fashioned Roses* (1888), *Rhymes of Childhood* (1890) and *Green Fields and Running Brooks* (1892).

7. First published in the *Century Magazine*, Aug 1887, and *Indianapolis Journal*, 31 July 1887; collected in *Afterwhiles* (1888). In this sentimental poem, a father talks to his daughter, who wants to marry on her twentieth birthday, just as he did when he married her mother. They had run away to escape parental disapproval, and now he has 'nothin' at all' to say to her, because 'Gyrls that's in love, I've noticed, giner'ly has their way!'

8. Edward William Bok (1863–1930) was born in the Netherlands, and became an editorial-writer and Editor of the *Ladies' Home Journal* from 1889 on. He supported arts and education, and helped to pass conservation laws, and the Food and Drug Acts of 1906.

9. English novelist, poet, and man of letters (1864–1926), author of *The Big Bow Mystery* (1891), *Children of the Ghetto* (1892), *Ghetto Tragedies* (1893), *The King of the Schnorrers* (1894) and *Without Prejudice* (1896), realistic portrayals of Jewish life.

10. American author, critic, editor, and lecturer (1845–1916). Closely associated with the Christian Union from 1879 on. He wrote *Under the Trees and Elsewhere* (1891), *In the Forest of Arden* (1891), *Books and Culture* (1896), and *Works and Days* (1902).

11. Augustus Floriano Jaccaci (1857–1930) used the name 'August Jaccaci' in his English publications, such as *Italian Posters and Music-book Covers* (1895), *The Modern Poster* (1895), *An Ascent of Mount Aetna* (1897) and *Noteworthy Paintings in*

American Private Collections (1909), the last title being co-authored with John La
Farge. *On the Trail of Don Quixote* (1896) was translated into several languages.
(Spelt 'Jacacci' in the Garland text.)

12. Frank Nelson Doubleday (1862–1934) was an American publisher associated with Charles Scribner's Sons from 1877 to 1895. He edited *The Book Buyer*,
and the newly-established *Scribner's Magazine*. He was President of Doubleday and
McClure Co. (1900–27), and, after the firm took the name of Doubleday, Doran
and Co. (1928), he served as Chairman of the Board.

A Children's Story for
*St Nicholas Magazine**

WILLIAM WEBSTER ELLSWORTH

[Mary Mapes Dodge's][1] ideas on the subject of children's reading
were always sane and practical, and she had the happy faculty of
suggesting, creating, obtaining the contributions she wanted from
just the people she wanted to write. She was able to persuade many
of the great writers of the world to contribute to her children's
magazine – Tennyson, Longfellow, Bryant, Holmes, Bret Harte,
John Hay, 'Ik Marvel', Charles Dudley Warner, Elizabeth Stuart
Phelps,[2] and scores of others. One day Kipling told her a story of the
Indian jungle, and Mrs Dodge asked him to write it down for *St
Nicholas*. He never had written for children, but he would try. The
result was *The Jungle Book*.

I remember Kipling the first time he came into our office and as
he sat with one leg under him, swinging the other, and peering out
at us through large gold-rimmed spectacles, he seemed like a being
out of another world – the world of 'The Phantom 'Rickshaw' and
'The Man Who Would Be King'. I can't remember ever being
really intimidated by an author except Kipling. . . .

The literary agent has his uses, and in these days of serial rights,

* *A Golden Age of Authors* (Boston, Mass., and New York: Houghton Mifflin,
1919) pp. 89–106.

dramatic rights, moving-picture rights, and second serial rights, perhaps the literary agent is inevitable. In a page of his *Autobiography* Sir Walter Besant expressed his gratitude to the dean of literary agents, A. P. Watt of London (now deceased), who with his son represented Kipling, Hichens,[3] Conan Doyle, Gilbert Parker,[4] and many other authors. 'By their watch and ward', wrote Sir Walter, 'my interests have been carefully guarded for eighteen years. During that time I have always been engaged for the three years in advance; I have been relieved from every kind of pecuniary embarrassment, my income has been multiplied by three at least; and I have had, through them, the offer of a great deal more work than I could undertake.'

NOTES

William Webster Ellsworth (1855–1936) was the great-grandson of Noah Webster; a lecturer on literary topics; Secretary (1881–1913) and President (1913–1916) of the Century Co.; and a successful publisher.

1. Mary Elizabeth Mapes Dodge (1831–1905) wrote *Hans Brinker, or, The Silver Skates* (1865), and edited the *St Nicholas Magazine* from 1873 to 1905.

2. The only English author on this list is Alfred, Lord Tennyson (1809–92). The others: Henry Wadsworth Longfellow (1807–82); William Cullen Bryant (1794–1878); Oliver Wendell Holmes (1809–94); (Francis) Bret(t) Harte (1836–1902); John Milton Hay (1838–1905); Donald Grant Mitchell (1822–1908), who wrote under the pen-name 'Ik Marvel'; and Elizabeth Stuart Phelps (1844–1911).

3. Robert Smythe Hichens (1864–1950), journalist and novelist, perhaps best-known for *The Green Carnation* (1894), a satire on aesthetes, *The Garden of Allah* (1904), and *The Paradine Case* (1933).

4. The Rt Hon. Sir Gilbert Parker (1862–1932), journalist, editor and novelist, lectured in English at the University of Toronto (1883–5); associate editor of the *Sydney Morning Herald* (1885–1889); wrote *Pierce and His People* (1892), *The Seats of the Mighty* (1896), *The Judgement House* (1913) and *Carnac's Folly* (1922).

Rudyard Kipling, Maker of Magic*

HILDEGARDE HAWTHORNE

One day my father took me into the editorial offices of *The Century* for a chat with Mr Gilder. One of the first things he said to us was, 'Kipling's round here somewhere; don't you want to meet him?' My father had met him before, but I was tremendously excited. I had read everything of his I could get hold of since Mr Stoddard's remark to me, and I was having all the fun of real hero-worship for the author.

We went into Mr Gilder's own office and met Kipling there. I looked at him hard. I wanted to be sure of him. He was broad and short and big-headed, with eyes that glowed, a brownish skin, and black hair already greying slightly. I was not disappointed in him. He gave you the feeling that here was force, power, control, and a something genial and warm that I had not looked for. I expected to be afraid of him, and, instead, I felt perfectly at home and at ease with him. He sat down by me and talked and laughed, made fun of several things, though now I cannot remember what they were, and praised the American offices. 'Nothing like this sort of thing in England', he said, waving an arm round in a short, quick gesture. 'There you have to scramble along narrow dark halls, open doors, fall down stairs, kick some one who has preceded you, and finally reach an ill-lighted, chilly, barren little room with two or three miserable clerks writing at desks.'

The contrast between this picture and the beautiful room in which we sat was so great that I have never forgotten that description, nor yet the slight horror with which I heard that he kicked the unfortunate creature who had preceded him. For I believed every word.

* *St Nicholas*, XLII (Feb 1915) 348–50.

NOTE

Hildegarde Hawthorne was a prolific writer of mystery stories, histories, and books on New England. She worked for the YMCA and the Red Cross in France during the Great War, and was well known as a *New York Times* book-reviewer during the 1920s. She died in 1952.

A Kipling Miscellany*

COLLINSON OWEN

The writer once passed a whole afternoon with Kipling in 1922, when the King visited the War Graves. Here is a digression: a group of three – the King, Haig, and Foch[1] – was breaking up; Haig and Foch were engaged in a long and hearty handshake, when the King, placing his own hand on their clasped hands said in French, 'Always good friends, is it not so?' To which Foch replied, 'Always, Sire, always – for the same cause and the same motives.' At Terlincthum Mr Kipling and the writer walked together alone, all that day; one or two of his remarks remain in memory: 'There has never been anything like this in all history – the embalming of a race.' Kipling's belief in the strength of the friendship that unites Britain and France was strong. 'It could not be otherwise with these countless British graves scattered so thickly along the battle line.'

In the United States there is the same feeling for Kipling. A certain club in New York had a Founder's Night. All present were singing choruses from Gilbert and Sullivan, when the pianist suddenly plunged into *Barrack-Room Ballads*. The whole company roared out 'Danny Deever', 'Boots', and others; the success of the evening was 'Route Marchin' '[2] to the pianist's own setting. Kipling had wiped out of those minds all feeling of America and they were so English that one could not believe it!

---

* *Kipling Journal*, no. 37 (Mar 1936) 29–30.

NOTES

Harry Collinson Owen (1882–1956) was an English journalist, and a member of the staff of various London newspapers from 1901 on. He was an official war-correspondent in the Near East (1916–19), author of a chatty and popular series, 'Monocle Monologues', and an historian of events during the second and third decades of this century in both England and the United States. He collaborated with General Sir George Milne in the writing of *Salonica and After* (1919).

1. King George V (1865–1936), King of Great Britain from 1910 to 1936; Field-Marshal Douglas Haig, 1st Earl Haig (1861–1928), commander-in-chief of British forces in France during most of World War I; and Ferdinand Foch (1851–1929), Marshal of France and commander of Allied Forces during the closing months of World War I.

2. Set to music by G. C. Stock in 1915; by J. P. McCall in 1930. A poem in *Barrack-Room Ballads, and Other Verses* (1892).

Part VI
Travels

A Snap-shot of RK*

'VICTORIAN'

A writer in the *Evening News* of 20 February 1901 recalled how some time ago he had spent six weeks in the company of Rudyard Kipling, whose aversion to the reporter amounted to a harmless mania. Kipling, he states, is not to be interviewed, and he quotes some sentiments, which Kipling expressed one day when seated alongside a trout-stream in the Canadian Rockies. 'I am always attracted to people with ink-fever,' said Kipling, 'it is irrestible while the temperature remains high, but how rarely it lasts!' Not one in fifty of those who make the trial tide over the often unbearable beginning. It wants grit – an essential quality in a journalist. Editors as a rule are very good fellows; the yarns about their desire to crush new talent is unmitigated rot. But journalists are dangerous! They may be the most kindly and honourable members of society in other relations, but the moment it is a question of copy they are without principles. A journalist myself? 'Ah,' with a chuckle, 'that is, of course, another story.' The writer goes on to say that there does not exist a person below the 'teens, who can resist Kipling. He remembered a case when a delicate, fretful baby of ten months or so, on board ship, whom even the mother could not comfort, at the sight of Kipling at the far end of the deck would cease wailing and, as Kipling drew near, the poor mite would stretch out his arms to him and sit quite satisfied resting against his knee. On another occasion he mentions that Kipling made a brief address and appealed for support for the widow and family of a deceased sailor. It was a most eloquent 'sermon', to use his own title, and the result in pounds sterling would have aroused the envy of a professional preacher. Finally the writer stated that Kipling had one parlour trick – dancing – and one superstition – palmistry. In respect of the ball-room, he tells how in Yokohama a young girl to

* *Kipling Journal*, IX (Dec 1942) 15.

whom Kipling had just been introduced showed the writer her programme and said, 'His [Kipling's] dance is the next, and I can't imagine what to say. For goodness sake, tell me something learned to talk about.'

When Rudyard Kipling Was in New Zealand*

TOM L. MILLS

Before the outbreak of the present war, distinguished visitors from the ends of the earth passed through New Zealand so frequently and rapidly that our city papers were hard put to it to keep pace with them and tell their readers about them. It was not always so. Up to thirty years ago they came unheralded, for the means of communication were not organised as they are today, nor were the news agencies so closely in touch with the movements of interesting tourists who meant 'good copy' to the papers, and interviews with whom meant great 'scoops' to the live reporter. Special reporters in New Zealand's daily papers are just as keen for 'scoops' as the world's best and, like the Canadian mounted men, they generally get their man. But Rudyard Kipling always remained the most difficult literary lion to capture. Yet he walked right into the hands of a reporter in Wellington – and walked out again some hours later without that reporter getting a line in his newspaper. The story is interesting.

The already famous Anglo-Indian, then a young man, came across without any publicity from Sydney to Wellington. That was in the early 'nineties. A shipping reporter was on board and promptly put the usual question, 'Anybody worthwhile on board – any distinguished visitors?' 'Oh, my word, yes!' was the reply of the purser. 'We have Rudyard Kipling on board.' Now that reporter could have given off-hand the pedigree of every leading horse on the

* *Kipling Journal*, VIII (Apr 1941) 13–16.

race-cards and could have named every ship of the USS Co.'s fleet; but he was not up in the writers of his day. 'Who is this Kipling?' he asked the purser, who gazed at him in astonishment, failed to find the right and fitting biography, and then shot out, 'Why he's Rudyard Kipling!' Just then the purser was asked by another visitor, 'Have you Mr Rudyard Kipling on board?' 'Yes, indeed', quickly replied the relieved officer. 'He is in his cabin getting ready for shore. I'll take you to him. Come this way.' The reporter knew this visitor, so here was something tangible to get his teeth of curiosity into. This was Herbert Baillie, of Baillie Brothers, the Cuba Street booksellers. He bought his sporting papers from that shop. So the shipping-reporter followed along the deck and asked as he walked, 'Say, Baillie, who is this chap Rudyard something or other?' In amazement – was it possible that in this year of grace there was a newspaperman who had not read *Departmental Ditties* and *Plain Tales from the Hills*? – the bookseller and ardent Kiplingite replied, 'Why, he's Rudyard Kipling, of course.'

Herbert and I had arranged to go down to the Sydney boat to give the writer a welcome to the colony. We had both read all his writings to date and had copies of his rupee editions published in Calcutta – those little books that are invaluable today. I was then on the *New Zealand Times*, employed as a proof-reader. It was a long and heavy night, and as I got home with the milkman I slept in. When I got down to the boat Kipling was away and I found no trace of Baillie. In the meantime, Herbert had taken the author in tow to act as host and show him the city. The shipping reporter tagged along. As they walked north along Lambton Quay the guide, remembering that the visitor's father was a noted curator, suggested, 'I suppose you would not care to have a look at our national museum?' 'Wouldn't I! Take me to it! That is where I can see this wonderful country's early history.' Along the quay Kipling was shooting off verbal fireworks in observations that would have made thrilling copy had the quips and acute criticisms only been reported. But the limit of the shipping reporter's capacity and curiosity was, 'Who the dickens is this Rudyard Kipling?' Entering the old museum building, Kipling exclaimed, 'Ah, here I am at home again amongst the dead bones and the ancient stones!' As for that reporter, despite the fact that he was in the company of a man of genius for over two hours and had the opportunity of the scoop of a lifetime he did not get a line into his paper, not even a personal paragraph to the effect that Mr Rudyard Kipling was in town.

But the next morning's *Times* scored a scoop of first and historic importance – historic, in that in the later days of his life when he was one of the world's foremost writers and had been awarded the Nobel Prize for Literature, Kipling declared with emphasis he had never knowingly granted an interview to any newspaper and that all the alleged interviews published in the United States were fakes. The story behind the *New Zealand Times* scoop provides another interesting bit of Kiplingiana. On the night of the only day the visitor spent in Wellington the Editor of the *Times*, the late Mr R. A. Loughnan, met him at the Club on the Terrace. Along about midnight the Editor came into my room in great glee. 'Mills!' he cried, 'I've got the scoop of a lifetime – I got a column interview with Rudyard Kipling!' 'Where did you run him to earth?' I asked. 'Up in the Club.' We both chortled. 'And did he talk for the paper?' I asked. 'I'll say rather – a whole column of it', he repeated. 'And more than that, he is up at the Club now waiting to see the proof of the article.' 'Wise man', said I. 'Why wise, Mills?' 'Why, to insist on seeing a proof,' was my reply, 'for then he is responsible for what goes into print, and not you.' In less than an hour – type was set by hand in those days, long before the linotype speeded things up on daily papers – the Editor came back, got the proof-slip and took it to the Club, where the visitor was being entertained. As an experienced reporter, Kipling read the proof rapidly. Then he threw it from him, with a gesture of disgust. 'What's the matter?' he was asked. 'Rotten!' he flung back. 'The damn thing has neither beginning nor ending. I've a good mind to dump it.' 'Oh, you can't do that, my dear fellow!' cried the Editor. 'It is in type and they are waiting to go to press. You know very well we can't dump a column at this hour of the morning.' 'Oh, very well. We shall have to let the opening go by default, but I'll round it off as a good interview should be rounded off.' And when the proof came back to me after his revision there was written on the blank paper below the type the following anecdote in Kipling's neat and small calligraphy:

He [that is, RK talking to the Editor] tells a story of having in India interviewed a dentist who had travelled in Afghanistan and there pulled the eye-tooth of His Highness the Amir of Afghanistan. The ceremony was performed in open court and the steadiness of the operator's hand was increased by the knowledge that His Highness had full power and might have the inclination to decapitate him on the spot.

I cut that bit of precious MS. off the tail of the proof-slip and have had it in my scrap-book to date. When, many years later, Kipling made the statement to Sir Robertson Nicoll,[1] Editor of *The Bookman* and the *British Weekly*, London, that he had never granted an interview to any newspaper as he abominated interviews for publication, I had the bit of MS. photographed and sent it to *The Bookman* with the story behind the scoop. When it was shown to him in due course, all Rudyard K remarked was: 'New Zealand, eh? Ah, I had forgotten that!' The great little man was not unmindful of the courtesies shown to him in Wellington, for he more or less irregularly corresponded with Mr Baillie down through the years until shortly before his death.

NOTES

Thomas Lewis Mills (1865–1955) came from Castletown, Isle of Man, and worked as a job printer before becoming a reporter for the *Evening Post*. He was one of the first to recognise the talent of Kathleen Beauchamp (Katherine Mansfield), and to encourage her to write professionally. An active member of the Australasian Provinces Press Association, he gave a series of popular radio talks, 'Famous Men I Knew', in New Zealand. He was a partner in the *Feilding Star* (1907–36). He edited *Verse by New Zealand Children* (1943).

1. A Scottish religious journalist (1851–1923). In 1885 he founded *The Expositor*, a monthly theological magazine; in 1886, the *British Weekly*; in 1891, *The Bookman*; and in 1893, the *Woman at Home*.

Rudyard Kipling*

JOHN OLDHAM and ALFRED STIRLING

In 1891 Kipling commenced a period of six years' travel, during which time he was to build for himself the reputation of being the greatest creative literary force of his generation. The sense of an expanding empire entrusted with a mission held sway throughout the British world, and in Australia Rudyard Kipling was welcomed as a first apostle of the creed.

* *Victorian: A Visitors Book* (Melbourne: Brown, Prior, 1934) pp. 120–5.

It does not detract from his later performance that his personal characteristics at this time made him appear difficult. There is a species of shyness that appears as brusqueness or even as conceit, just as there is a species of honest clear-thinking which makes it impossible for a man to suffer fools or mediocrities gladly. Perhaps some such trait left Kipling's acquaintances in Victoria and would-be friends vaguely annoyed; at any rate as a lion he was not an unqualified success. His work, however, remains quite apart from his social personality, and it would be difficult to find in the literature of any language a writer who made such a profound impression on his generation. Why he has been passed over time after time for the poet-laureateship is difficult to understand, unless the tale be true that Queen Victoria never forgave him for alluding to her in one of his earlier soldier ballads as 'the Widow at Windsor'. But such a story seems most improbable, and it is more likely that the faults of temperament he showed on his visit to Victoria have been a lifelong handicap to him.

Kipling literally blew into Melbourne in the teeth of a terrific November gale, for the *Talune*'s decks had been swept by seas almost the whole way from New Zealand. Later he recalled his introduction to Port Phillip in 'The Song of the Cities':[1]

> Greeting! Nor fear nor favour won us place,
>   Got between greed of gold and dread of drouth,
> Loud-voiced and reckless as the wild tide-race
>   That whips our harbour-mouth!

Kipling found anchorage at the Oriental Hotel and gave an interview as he lolled on a couch in his room, puffing at a cheroot. He looked exactly like his photographs, small and spectacled, studious and pensive, but his face lit up with animation and he talked breezily. His vivid conversation was obviously related to his literary style. According to one of the interviewers he had 'a lightning power of forming and phrasing his impressions, which are expressed with a lightening of the face like sparks under a blow'. He had recently been in San Francisco, and he told with gusto how he had seen two shooting affrays and the gouging-out by a European of a Chinaman's eyes.

Kipling said that he had not come to Australia to bestow his views on its inhabitants; 'he only came because the steamers happened to touch'. He was on holiday, not out to write novels, and 'besides,' he

added, 'you have a better man than me already, Rolf Boldrewood'.[2]
Still he volunteered 'a few stray imaginative ideas as to the future of
the continent'.

Speaking, perhaps, more from his experience of New Zealand, he
said, 'You don't know what work is in this part of the world. You
don't suppose that this eight-hours' work, eight-hours' rest, and
eight-hours' recreation is going to last for ever, do you?'

To a representative of the *Age* he said that Melbourne struck him
as being American, but he added, 'Remember it is second-hand
American, there is an American tone on the top of things, but it is
not real. Daresay, by and by, you will get a tone of your own. Still, I
like these American memories playing round your streets. The
trams – those bells are like music; these saloons and underground
dives are as Yank as they can be. The Americanism of this town,
with its square blocks and straight streets, strikes me much. I can't
say anything about the people, for I have not met any of them, but I
gather this much that they are very much pleased with their own
town. They don't seem to follow the Americans in their habits so
much as the city itself. I like America. When I am there I am railing
at the country, but out of it, I want to get back there.'

Kipling thought that there was too much politics in Australia for
a country 'with its character still to make'. He warned Australians
not to treat the Chinese with contempt, and described the menace of
the East in the following way: 'There is a big score to be wiped out,
and if you Australians could see them as I have in their native towns,
where you meet eyes in every crevice till you might think the very
stones in the street are made of flesh and blood, then you might get
an idea of the force you will have to reckon with, and besides their
great population, their coast and rivers give them a supply of born
sailors who would carry them just where they wanted to go. If white
men won't work other men will.'

Kipling, however, said that he realised the risk of strangers airing
their views on local questions: 'We get MPs in India, let loose there
for three weeks, who go around and tell us how to boss the country.
That is not seeing the country, and I don't intend to see it that way.'

With a final remark that Collins Street reminded him of Fifth
Avenue, he pulled on a pair of shoes which he had just bought for a
social to be accorded him that evening.

If Kipling's stay in Victoria was so fortuitous, and if it lasted less
than ten days, his stay in Sydney was even shorter. He left
Melbourne by the Sydney express on the second day of his stay, and

only remained in Sydney for twenty-four hours, returning by sea. According to the columns of 'Oriel', much of his first two days in Melbourne was spent at the Austral Salon, whither he was guided by an old school-friend. His books were already favourite topics of discussion among the literary ladies of the colony, none the less because their sensibilities were sometimes a little shocked. On his first evening at the Austral Salon the nominal star, the government geologist, was completely eclipsed, while next afternoon the ladies paid him the tribute of a special Kipling party. Perched on the arm of a chair, Kipling tried to look as though he liked it, while the ladies hovered around him in ecstasy. One enthusiastic admirer is reported to have said to him, 'When I had the influenza your books were the only things that did me good.' Meanwhile, we are told that in the background glowered 'the young men with bumpy foreheads – young lions temporarily out of employment'.

The tea-party had at last to come to an end, for Mr Kipling must catch the Sydney express. The kind hostesses flocked out to the lift to see him off. Alas for the younger ladies, 'Oriel', perhaps as a measure of protection, told next day that Kipling was reported to have recently become engaged, to a girl who, it was speculated, might very well be the original of the famous Maisie in *The Light that Failed*.

On his return from Sydney Kipling was entertained at the men's clubs. At a dinner at the Athenaeum, given by Sir Matthew Davies,[3] the Speaker of the Assembly, he astonished his fellow-guests by his compliance with a memory-test, cataloguing, with intimate detail, every object in a room just vacated. This, his hearers thought, must be one of the secrets of his realistic style. Kipling himself has given a description of an unnamed club of Melbourne in his imaginary *Book of the Overseas Clubs*:[4]

> At Melbourne, in a long verandah giving on a grass plot, where laughing-jackasses laugh very horribly, sit wool-kings, premiers and breeders of horses after their kind. The older men talk of the days of the Eureka Stockade,[5] and the younger of 'shearing wars' in north Queensland, while the traveller moves timidly among them wondering what under the world every third word means.

Kipling's movements were reported as 'pretty much mixed'; he might go home by the mail-steamer on Saturday afternoon; he might not. He particularly wanted to see Samoa and stay with Robert Louis Stevenson, but that might have to wait for another

time. It was just after the Melbourne Cup and very hot; the streets
were not then paved, and their condition was one of the details
which Kipling stored up. Later on he reproduced the impression
when he wrote, 'West away from Melbourne dust holidays begin.'
His particular holiday consisted of a quick run to Lorne,[6] then a
secluded village, but vying with Fernshaw as a show-place.
Everyone knows his memory of this trip in 'The Flowers':[7]

> Buy my English posies!
>   You that will not turn –
> Buy my hot-wood clematis,
>   Buy a frond o' fern,
> Gathered where the Erskine leaps
>   Down the road to Lorne.

After telling us that 'They that mock at Paradise woo at Cora Lynn',
he proceeds,

> Through the great South Otway[8] gums sings the great South
>   Main,
> Take the flower and turn the hour, and kiss your love again!

Saturday afternoon came and we find Kipling's name in the
passenger-list of the *Valetta* booked through to Calcutta, but he
finally decided to remain in Melbourne over the week-end, and go
overland to Adelaide by train. On Saturday night he was entertained by the literary lights of the Yorick Club at a merry farewell
supper, when his health was proposed by Mr Theodore Fink,[9] well-
known lawyer and man of letters.

Early in the following year Kipling was in the United States for
his marriage to Miss Caroline Balestier; perhaps the eulogy of
America given in Melbourne was not unconnected with the
sentiments he entertained for one of her daughters.

NOTES

John Egerton Oldham (b. 1902) and Alfred Stirling (b. 1902) wrote *Victorian: A
Visitors Book* as a history of visits to Australia by Trollope, Sarah Bernhardt,
General Booth and Kipling, among others. Stirling was the private secretary of the
Rt Hon. R. G. Menzies (who contributed a foreword to *Victorian*); Attorney
General of the Commonwealth (1934–5); High Commissioner for Australia in
Canada (1945–6); and Australian Minister in Washington (1946–8).

1. 'The Song of Seven Cities' was first published in *Nash's Magazine* and *Century Magazine*, Jan 1915, and collected in *A Diversity of Creatures* (1917).

2. The pseudonym of Thomas (Alexander) Browne, who used his experiences as farmer and gold-miner as partial background for a stream of short stories, memoirs, and twenty novels about pioneer Australia. His best-known romantic novels are *Robbery under Arms* (1888) and *Miner's Right* (1890).

3. Member of a famous family, Matthew Henry Davies (1850–1912) has been called 'the most notorious son'. He worked as a freelance journalist, and in 1886 visited London for the Indian and Colonial Exhibition. The next year, elected Speaker by a majority of one, he presided fairly, and to much acclaim. His land-speculations and bank-manipulations were more controversial. In later years he was a solicitor, and a large-scale philanthropist.

4. See ch. 4, 'Our Overseas Men', in *Letters of Travel 1892–1927*, first published in 1920 as a book. The first series of letters, 'From Tideway to Tideway', describes Kipling's trip to the Orient shortly after his marriage in 1892, and makes a number of references to such a book. It might be written (Kipling suggests) to chronicle the adventures of those who do not stay at home.

5. An armed clash in Ballarat, Victoria, between gold-diggers and military and police forces, led to thirty deaths and many casualties. The grievances of miners led to significant governmental reforms in licensing and fees for title deeds. The event, referred to ever after as the Eureka Stockade, took place on 3 December 1854.

6. A village in south Victoria, Australia, 75 miles south-west of Melbourne, and on the Bass Strait; a seaside resort.

7. First printed in the *Daily Chronicle*, 10 June 1896; collected in *The Seven Seas* (1896).

8. The Otway Range is a system of hills near the coast of south Victoria. Cape Otway is 70 miles south-west of the entrance to Port Phillip Bay, and on the north side of the western approach to Bass Strait.

9. Fink (1855–1942) was a solicitor, land-speculator, Chairman of the *Melbourne Herald*, and a powerful advocate of educational reform, particularly in vocational training.

Kipling and Edgar Wallace*

MARGARET LANE

One of the first magazines to accept and print [Edgar Wallace's] verses was *The Owl*, a weekly Cape Town review of political flavour

* *Edgar Wallace: The Biography of a Phenomenon* (London: Hamish Hamilton, 1965) pp. 77–80.

which liked to be described as the South African *Punch*. In its editor, Mrs Penstone, he found an interested and sympathetic ally, who was not only willing to buy poems he offered her but asked for more, and apparently found the poetical Tommy a sufficiently stimulating listener to hold forth to him in her office (as he noted in his journal with some pride) 'for an hour and a half on subjects ranging from the colour question to ethics'. Nevertheless it was not to the weekly *Owl* but to the daily *Cape Times* that in January 1898 he sent his 'Welcome to Kipling', the most ambitious poem he had yet attempted, written to celebrate the imminent arrival of Kipling in South Africa. The verses were topical, they were amusingly written in the Kipling vein, and – strongest recommendation of all to Edmund Garrett, the Editor – they possessed the novelty of being written by a 'common Tommy' as a tribute to the poet who had more or less made a corner in barrack-room ditties. Garrett accepted it on the spot, and wrote a long and helpful letter, pointing out several minor flaws and suggesting a useful alteration in the seventh verse. 'I changed one word in "R. Kipling",' he wrote, '"pukka"[1] for "blessed". I saw (was I wrong?) that you weren't satisfied with "blessed". It was weak, so you italicised it. "Pukka" was at least a splotch of colour, and Indian colour at that. But it's rash editing poets! I used to belong to a little club of versifiers at Cambridge who edited each other. It helps.' Delighted as much by the genuineness of Garrett's interest as by his acceptance of the 'Welcome', Edgar hurried to the parsonage to break the news to the Caldecotts,[2] and then went into Cape Town and presented himself at the office. 'Some very nice things were said about my "Welcome to Kipling",' he wrote in his diary, 'and payment was promised.' For the next few days he lived in a fever of impatience. 'Went to *CT* offices to see about getting twenty-four copies of tomorrow's *Times*. I have got an idea that my "Welcome" won't be the feature that I thought it would be. I had hoped – but hope after all is but a doubting faith.' Nevertheless, when the great day arrived and the twenty-four copies of the *Cape Times* were delivered at the hospital, he found his poem handsomely displayed, and introduced by an editorial note to the effect that 'Mr Rudyard Kipling, who is expected to arrive by the *Dunvegan Castle* today, will be interested to know that the following lines are contributed to the *Cape Times* by a private in the Medical Staff Corps stationed at Simon's Town.' The verses certainly looked very fine, and he read them over in a kind of ecstasy.

O, good mornin', Mister Kiplin'! You are welcome to our shores:
To the land of millionaires and potted meat:
To the country of the 'fonteins'[3] (we 'ave got no 'bads' or 'pores')
To the place where di'monds lay about the street
    At your feet;
To the 'unting ground of raiders indiscreet. . . .

We should like to come an' meet you, but we can't without a pass;
Even then we'd 'ardly like to make a fuss;
For out 'ere, they've got a notion that a Tommy isn't class;
'E's a sort of brainless animal, or wuss!
    Vicious cuss!
No, they don't expect intelligence from us.

You 'ave met us in the tropics, you 'ave met us in the snows;
But mostly in the Punjab an' the 'Ills.
You 'ave seen us in Mauritius, where the naughty cyclone blows,
You 'ave met us underneath a sun that kills,
    An' we grills!
An' I ask you, do we fill the bloomin' bills?

Since the time when Tommy's uniform was muskatoon an' wig,
There 'as always been a bloke wot 'ad a way
Of writin of the Glory an' forgettin' the fatig',
'Oo saw 'im in 'is tunic day by day,
    Smart an' gay,
An' forgot about the smallness of his pay!

But you're *our* partic'lar author, you're our patron an' our
    friend,
You're the poet of the cuss-word an' the swear,
You're the poet of the people, where the red-mapped lands
    extend,
You're the poet of the jungle an' the lair,
    An' compare
To the ever-speaking voice of everywhere. . . .

Oh, certainly this was very good indeed, and would show even Mr
Caldecott that he was a man to be reckoned with. 'I hear that the
"Welcome" has made me quite a celebrity,' he wrote in his
journal, . . . there was I find a notice in *CT* of Wednesday, which

referred to my poem as a "capital poem" . . . "I" returned from town today bringing very encouraging opinions concerning my thing . . . Received cheque for £11s. from *Cape Times* for poem. This day's *Owl* contains a very nice notice of my thing . . . What a happy life this is!' The greatest triumph, however, was to come six weeks later, when, as the celebrated poet who had dared to address Kipling in his own vein, he was invited by Garrett to the City Club's farewell dinner to Kipling. 'Received invitation to dine with Garrett and Kipling. Whoop!' The whoop of exultation dashed down in the diary was a heart-felt one, for the 'notion that a Tommy isn't class' had become an increasing annoyance and humiliation, and being bidden to the dinner was the first sign that Cape Town was prepared to lower the social barriers in his favour. Even with the Caldecotts, kind though they were, he had been smartly put in his place when officers came to tea; on those occasions he had not been invited to join the tennis, but had had to field balls for the others and eye the girls sulkily from a distance. He had relieved his feelings a little in a poem in the *Owl*, 'concernin'' Thomas Atkins, 'oo you all turn aht to cheer', observing with some acerbity,

> But Serciety don't call,
> An' Serciety don't send;
> Nor invite 'im 'ome to dinner, nor an afternoon to spend;
> Nor the Gov'nor to 'is Ball . . . .

And now, here he was, invited to a really slap-up dinner at the City Club to meet Kipling. He rushed to Mrs Caldecott for advice about knives and forks and some general coaching on upper-class behaviour. She gave him a practical demonstration on the parsonage dining-table.

The evening of the banquet passed in a glorious haze induced by the unaccustomed wine and marred only by a certain confusion over fish-knives. He had been presented to Kipling and had found courage to ask for his autograph, a request to which Kipling had generously responded by scribbling out a verse from the 'Song of the Banjo'[4] on club notepaper and writing 'For Edgar Wallace' at the top. He seems to have been genuinely touched by the admiration of the young soldier, who, spruce and rigid in his private's uniform in a crowd of boiled shirts and condescending faces, concealed his nervousness under a show of poker-faced assurance which Kipling probably understood well enough. The meeting with Kipling was at

all events magnificent news to send home to the Freemans and Mrs
Anstee.[5] 'Kipling was exceedingly nice to me,' he wrote
exuberantly, 'and not only gave me his autograph attached to a
verse of the "Song of the Banjo" but wrote me a fine letter the
following day, complimenting me on my "London Calls" [a poem
which had appeared in the *Cape Times* the day before]. . . . He gave
me his London address and said that he would be very glad to give
me any advice that lay in his power. Wasn't that nice? My writings
have given me a certain amount of "tone" and I am received in the
best houses, in fact I have asserted myself, and overcome the social
barrier that debars "Tommy" from getting a good many priv-
eledges [*sic*] that he would obtain, were it not for his "cloth".'
Actually Kipling's advice, though kindly meant, had not been too
encouraging. 'His last words', Edgar confided to his diary, 'were,
"For God's sake, don't take to literature as a profession. Literature is
a splendid mistress, but a bad wife!"'

NOTES

Margaret Lane (b. 1907) is a novelist, biographer, and journalist, married at one
time to the eldest son of Edgar Wallace, and later to the Earl of Huntingdon. She
worked as a reporter for the *Daily Express* (1928–31). In addition to her well-
received biography of Wallace (from which this excerpt comes), she has written
about the Brontës and Beatrix Potter.

   1. A variation of 'pucka' or 'pakka'. From the Hindi word *pakka*, which means
cooked, ripe, mature; hence thorough, substantial, permanent, genuine, etc.
(*OED*).

   2. Marion Caldecott, regarded by Edgar Wallace as his intellectual godmother,
was wife of the Revd William Shaw Caldecott in Simonstown, South Africa. They
met in 1897. Wallace married their daughter Ivy.

   3. A Dutch word, used throughout South Africa to denote a fountain or spring.

   4. First printed in the *New Review*, June 1895, and collected in *The Seven Seas*
(1896).

   5. George Freeman and his wife loved children, and adopted Edgar Wallace as
'Dick Freeman'. Mrs Fred Anstee ran a small tea-and-coffee shop, and discussed
literature with 'Dick', while her husband, a part-time scene-shifter at a theatre,
interested the boy in dramatic productions of all sorts.

Kipling's Days at the Cape*

BASIL FULLER

Some people living in Cape Town till remember the slightly built figure, short-sighted gaze and fierce, semi-military moustache of Rudyard Kipling, who once lived here, at intervals, for several years.

Recently I met one of these people. He said, 'Kipling was a man of curious temperament. His brusque manners caused many strangers to misjudge him. And, indeed, he could be very rude to anyone whom he thought presumptuous. An incident which occurred on board ship in Cape Town harbour will illustrate this point. The vessel – I think it was the *Norham Castle* – was about to leave. Most passengers stood at the rail waving to friends ashore. But Kipling sat apart.

'Presently, a young man approached and made a casual remark. Probably he had recognised the author and hoped for his company during the voyage. But Kipling merely stared through the unfortunate youth.'

Another acquaintance, a man who served aboard a vessel in which Kipling travelled several times, agreed that the author's manner frequently was misleading.

'Many thought that he did not wish to know people. But if, sometimes, this was so there was an excellent reason for it. I was a young man at the time, and he put up with me without quibble, but I noticed that some older people tried to impose on him quite shamelessly. For instance, there was the woman who had a nephew who was a really brilliant writer, "if only he had just that little bit of assistance and advice, Mr Kipling; now if only you could spare the time to read one or two of his poems . . . "! And then, of course, there were those others who delighted in being seen talking to a

* Originally published in *Cape Times Magazine*, 6 Jan 1951, p. 4; reprinted by permission in *Kipling Journal*, xx (Apr 1953) 12–14.

"lion". It is my belief that years of this treatment had caused Kipling to react in an unfortunate manner. You see, he was very easily recognisable.'

On the other hand, Mr C. J. Sibbett recently told me about an amusing incident which occurred during the South African War and which shows that Kipling sometimes took a far milder view than the average man on judging inconvenience caused by strangers. I called upon Mr Sibbett because I knew that his memory is usually good and that he was a wealth of stories concerning the days when Kipling lived in Cape Town.

It happened one day that Mr Sibbett travelled north on a train which also carried the author and the general manager of a well-known bank. The train was held up by troops commanded by a one armed major, who flatly refused to allow it to proceed. In the upshot, the travellers were detained on the veld for twenty-four hours at Norvalspont.

I gather that, quite naturally, the general manager of the bank was indignant because he considered that the delay was unnecessary, and that most of the passengers expressed very forcible opinions. But Kipling seems to have been amused rather than annoyed. Indeed, later he described the incident for a British journal in a contribution which he called 'An Episode at Folly Bridge'.[1] He told the story humorously and without a trace of rancour.

In his autobiography, Kipling records another amusing story of this difficult railway journey. Apparently, his carriage was unlit. So he obtained a pair of three-wicked signal-lamp candles from a member of a party of 'tommies' to whom, earlier that day, he had distributed tobacco. He wrote, 'I naturally wanted to know how he had come by these desirable things. He replied, "Look 'ere, Guvnor. I didn't ask you 'ow you come by the baccy you dished out just now. Can't you b—— well leave me alone?"'

Kipling's first memories of Cape Town concerned 'a sleepy, unkempt little place'. These memories dated from 1891 when he landed from a liner named *The Moor*. At once, he began to make happy contacts which he recalled with pleasure to the end of his life. On the voyage from Britain he had made friends with a certain naval captain who was on his way to a new command at Simonstown.[2] So, in due course, he was introduced to the Admiral of the Cape Station who, he says, 'lived in splendour, with at least a brace of live turtles harnessed to the end of a little wooden jetty, swimming about till due to be taken up for turtle soup'.

He came to Cape Town again in 1897 and went to live in a boarding-house at Wynberg.[3] This house was kept by an Irish-woman who, said the author unkindly, 'spread miseries and discomforts round her in return for good monies'. But, despite such inevitable complaints, already he loved the Cape, for he adds, 'the colour, light, and half-oriental manners of the land bound chains round our hearts for years to come'.

Indeed, 'for years to come' it was to be, for at this time Kipling made a friend of Cecil Rhodes. Immediately Rhodes saw in the author a means of obtaining for South Africa increased favourable publicity overseas. So he tried to persuade Kipling to make his home permanently at the Cape and, to lend force to persuasion, even built for him a house on the slopes of Devil's Peak. This house, the Woolsack, stands hard by Groote Schuur and, in Kipling's day, was even more closely surrounded by trees than it is now.

Rhodes offered Kipling the use of this beautiful home for life. And so, 'to this Paradise we moved each year-end from 1900 to 1907'.

Delighted in his beautiful Cape Town home, Kipling makes many references to the Woolsack in his book *Something of Myself*. He tells how many of the tame animals from the zoo on Rhodes's estate made friends with the children and even found their way to the house. For a time, even a lion cub became a household pet.

'Close to the house lived a spitting llama, whose peculiarity the children learned early. But their little visitors did not, and if they were told to stand close to the fence and make noises, they did – once. You can see the rest.'

Sometimes Rhodes would walk across for a chat. Indeed it was with the Kiplings in the Woolsack that he first discussed his great scholarships scheme, and it was on Mrs Kipling's suggestion that he increased the £250, originally proposed, to £300.

Kipling seems to have been fond of telling stories of the Woolsack. For instance: 'We were showing off our newly built little Woolsack to a great lady on her way up-country, where a residence was being built for her. At the larder the wife pointed out that it faced south – that quarter being the coldest when one is south of the Equator. The great lady considered the heresy for a moment. Then, with the British sniff which abolishes the absurd, "Hmm! I shan't allow that to make any difference to me."'

During the South African War, when the Absent-minded Beggar Fund, sponsored by Kipling, was making £250,000 for comforts for the troops, the author would sometimes take parcels to certain Wynberg hospitals where, at the time, he was well known. Once he offered a bale of pyjamas to the wrong nurse. He said afterwards that he was confused by the red capes.

'Sister,' he cried, 'I've got your pyjamas!' But it seems that she lacked humour, for Kipling remarked sadly, 'That one was neither grateful nor very polite.'

Early in 1898, Kipling met Edgar Wallace in Cape Town and helped to start the crime writer on his meteoric career. The author arrived in the *Dunvegan Castle* and, on the morning the vessel docked there appeared in the *Cape Times* a poem called 'Welcome to Kipling'. It imitated the famous Kipling metre. . . .

Contributed by Edgar Wallace, then a 'Tommy' in the military hospital at Simonstown, the poem appealed to Kipling, who asked that the soldier poet should be invited to a dinner to be given in the City Club. At the dinner, it seems that Kipling was kind and gave Wallace his London address, an invitation to call, and strong advice not to attempt writing as a career.

Kipling certainly loved Cape Town. One gathers that during the greater part of the first decade of the country the thrill of each year became the outward journey from Britain. On the slopes of Table Mountain[4] one might escape from life's realities – always a little frightening to Kipling, whose fierce manners were, perhaps, a mere protective mechanism. The author was full of feeling for the Cape, and this feeling often escaped quite beautifully in his writings.

'Into these shifts and changes we would descend yearly for five or six months from the peace of England to the deeper peace of the Woolsack, and life under the oak-trees overhanging the patio, where mother-squirrels taught their babies to climb, and in the stillness of hot afternoons the fall of an acorn was almost like a shot.'

He also had cause to bless the Cape for the health it restored to him. And he himself summed up his days in Cape Town in four simple words – 'Life went well then.'

NOTES

Basil Fuller (b. 1901) has written *Bid Time Return* (1954), on Rhodes; *Canada Today and Tomorrow* (1935); books on politicians and 'pirate harbours and their secrets'; and *Springbok round the Corner* (1951).

1. 'Folly Bridge' appeared in the *People's Press* on 15 and 16 June 1900, but was not collected until the Sussex Edition.

2. In earlier days written Simon's Town. Small seaport in South Africa, in Cape Province, about 18 miles south of Cape Town.

3. A town south of Cape Town.

4. Immediately south of Cape Town, about 3500 feet high, with a remarkable flattened summit.

RK and his Rolls-Royce Car*

G. R. N. MINCHIN

During the period referred to in this chapter, Claude Johnson[1] was still the organising genius of Rolls-Royce Ltd. A letter from Rudyard Kipling to Claude Johnson written in those days has recently come into my hands. One would expect something well written from the famous poet, but as an example of how a letter can be worded and composed to such perfection, I reproduce it as follows:

Costebelle Hotels, Hyères[2]

25 March 1921
Began: 11 a.m. Finished: 4 p.m.

Dear Claude Johnson,

Here is a story to the credit of your firm showing how business should be done.

I had been in Algiers for a month which is no place for a Christian's car: so I left the Duchess at home with orders to join me at Marseilles, on my return from Africa, for a farewell honeymoon tour ere I forsook her for another – my fourth, or fifth is it? – from the same harem.

I reached Marseilles on the evening of the 23 March, the Duchess met me at the Docks, loyal and devoted as ever, but not

* *Under My Bonnet* (London: G. T. Foulis, 1950) pp. 116–17.

quite well. On these cursed Avignon roads she had snapped a leaf of her offside forespring and lost, or scraped off, her exhaust apparatus pipe behind the exhaust-box. You can see the situation!

I gathered that with care and the cut-out in use, she could hobble from Marseilles to Hyères without collapsing in front or lighting up behind. It was too late that evening to attempt to legislate for the situation. So, next morn, into Hyères she took us – 2 hours 45 minutes for 50 miles of hell's own pot-holes variegated with road trimmings and surface railways. (I had never been east of Marseilles before: nor had she, and we groaned in unison.)

Arrived at these hotels, I recalled that you had an agency in Nice. At this point the concierge, armed with a pre-war directory, assured me that you hadn't. I could get no definite address so in despair (after having killed the concierge who will appear in the bill) I sent off a wire to 'Rolls-Royce Agency, Nice', and outlined my appalling situation. Simultaneously I wired RR at Paris for the Nice address, and resigned myself to the worst.

Remember that was Thursday evening (5 p.m.) before Good Friday; the Easter holidays were ahead of us; I had Mrs Kipling, my daughter and a niece with me, all the Riviera to play with for the next ten days; every conceivable *wagon-lit* berth filled up for a month ahead; all day trains occupied, as far as I could make out, the night before, and my sole link with life and the decencies was a semi-paralytic, only too inflammable Duchess! The utmost I dared hope for was that I could send her alone to Nice (180 kilometres). I might by Divine Providence, call her my own again after the Easter holidays. I was not angry. I was calm with the chill melancholy of despair.

This morning at 9.30 a.m. (25 March) I got a reply from the Rue Malakoff giving me the Nice agency address. To make sure, then, I repeated my overnight telegram plus proper address, to Nice and sent it into the hotel office to be despatched. It was brought back to me with the announcement that the concierge assumed Monsieur would not now wish to despatch it as 'they' had already arrived.

At first I took this for a bad jest of the sort that destroys ententes – but when I went to the garage – *it was true*. Parsons who used to be in your Paris repair shop, and an assistant had arrived in an horizon-blue lorrylette,[3] with spare spring and exhaust pipe. The Duchess's front was already jacked up and work was in full swing (10.15 a.m.) (morning of 25 March). They had got my wire, had pulled out of Nice at five of the morning when French telegraphists are abed, and to my hungry eyes they looked like fairies in goatskin coats.

They had her all finished, tried and done with by 3 p.m. this afternoon. Then they folded their horizon-blue wings and vanished in the direction of Nice. A field ambulance could not have been quicker than that travelling circus. When did you start 'em?

(Incidentally at our garage lay an open body 1907 RR which in old age, had developed a habit of heavy drinking and could not do more than 8 miles per gallon. I presume this would be equivalent to inflammation of the prostate gland among the aged. Anyhow, when the Duchess's wants had all been attended to, I believe the travelling circus prescribed for the poor old dear.)

And it is to make you all my compliments that I send you this with gratitude and admiration, still warm and panting after my rescue. Literally I was not delayed one minute; for, after the Havre-Hyères run she would have had a day off anyhow.

With every good wish,

Most sincerely,

Rudyard Kipling

NOTES

George Robert Neville Minchin wrote one novel (1930) and *Under My Bonnet* (1950), about motoring adventures.

1. Claude Goodman Johnson (d. 1926) organised Rolls-Royce and served as its managing director. He was educated at the Art School, South Kensington; was the first secretary of the Royal Automobile Club; and set up both the first purely automobile exhibition in England (1899) and the 1,000-mile reliability trial (1900).

2. Commune, Var department, in south-east France, 32 miles south of Draguignan; founded in the tenth century, Hyères, near the Mediterranean, has gained considerable popularity as a winter resort.

3. An anglicising of *camionnette*, i.e. a light lorry or motor-truck.

Kipling and Winter Sports*

ALFRED FRÖHLICH

On the day of the great earthquake at Messina[1] I met Kipling at Engelberg on the Lake of Lucerne and helped him to take his very first steps on the ice. In the following winter I had nice warm wash-leather gloves made for him and he acknowledged receipt in the following words: 'All the rink is prostrated with envy at my beautiful lemon-coloured hands; they are certainly good gloves and impart a fine tone to my edges.' He mistrusted bob-sleighing and tobogganing, made only one or two feeble attempts at ski-ing, but was interested in curling and spent hours assiduously handling the broom with verve. It was my ambition to steer a bob-team, but I never attained much skill at bobbing and generally upset my team. After one of these feats of mine Kipling sent me the following verse:

> There was a Professor who led
> The deuce of a life in a sled.
>   Miss Knapp and Miss Hall
>   Now represent all
> His live ballast which isn't quite dead.

In the evenings there were entertainments of all kinds: music, gaming, dancing. At one of the fancy-dress balls I appeared as – Rudyard Kipling. I donned his well-known skating-costume and a theatrical wig-maker converted me into a second Rudyard Kipling while the original posed as the model. He owned to having experienced an uncanny feeling when he saw his 'double' gradually evolving under the hands of the skilful hairdresser. I entered the ballroom with Mrs Kipling on my arm. Kipling followed soon after in a dinner-jacket. The ball guests, on seeing two RK's, thought they were the victims of an illusion caused by the heady Christmas

---

* *Kipling Journal*, no. 38 (June 1936) 42–4.

punch. Both Mr and Mrs Kipling caught a slight chill at this ball, and I, their friend, was naturally appointed their family doctor. From the very start of the treatment a difference of opinion arose between us. The Kiplings desired to have some pills to 'relieve the liver', but I doubted the efficacy of pills in the case of a simple cold. Kipling then sent me the following quatrain:

> Heaven help the Nations of the Continent,
> Send, send our missionaries out to teach 'em!
> They never knew what Salts and Senna meant,
> They never heard of Cockles or of Beecham!

On the wall of my working-room there hangs a water-colour by Kipling representing an enormous bacillus with the designation 'Bacillus Tussis Engelbergensis, var. Frölich. Enlargement 1:1,200,000. Pictor Ignotus. The name of the artist is unknown.' In this picture Kipling has given free rein to his genial humour and his great pictorial talent. The long antennae of the monster are clinical thermometers showing a temperature of more than 50 degrees of fever heat, the joints are covered with pins and barbed hooks, the menacing tail resembles a fir cone. The swollen clumsy body is full of suppurating sores typifying the irritating effect of a catarrh on the mucus membranes of the air passages. The protruding eyes glower horridly out of their cavities.

I met Kipling winter after winter in Switzerland and his invitations to visit him in his own home in Sussex became more and more pressing. In the spring of 1914 his last invitation closed with the following words: 'Remember, you are pledged to tell us when you come to England. Keep your promise or I'll make an international affair of it. I'll send the British fleet up the Danube and destroy the Austrian Empire.'

Here are some lines in another letter from Kipling – 'I also have bought skis – a pair for John and a pair for me. We will wallow in the snows together.' 'That maniac Stockar yesterday broke all records for the new bob-run in $1.22\frac{3}{4}$ seconds. The previous best was 1.25. How good is God to the insane?' 'We have had the Zurich match – in which John played. One man (a Belg) got his rib broken and the captain of the Zurich team was knocked silly. Also his front teeth were loosened. As the Zurich team came up with the loudly expressed intention of killing as many of our team as they could, I feel that, for me, Providence looked after its own. Engleberg had no casualties, but we lost the game by 2 goals to 3.'

The tragic war put an end to a further exchange of letters. But on the 30 December 1935, his seventieth birthday, I sent him a small album containing only two photos. One, taken at Christmas, 1905, showed me arm in arm with the then world champion of figure-skating, the Viennese Gustav Hügel, who had also been staying at Engelberg, and the second at Christmas 1935, again of Hügel and myself. We wrote on the photos: Professor Fröhlich and Hügel, the skaters, in the heyday of life and in old age. I also added a few words of congratulations on his seventieth birthday. A week later Kipling sent me a card thanking me heartily for the kind attention. Another week and we heard of his serious illness, and yet another week and the greatest poet of the British Empire had passed away.

NOTES

Dr Fröhlich (1871–1953) was associated with the Neurological Institute at the University of Vienna, and was an expert on intraspinal routing of fibres of some of the posterior nerve-roots of the spinal cord. In 1923 he published a handbook of economic and efficiency factors bearing on the preparation and dispensing of medicines, 'with special consideration for German and Austrian conditions'.

1. A port, archbishopric and university town; the capital of Messina province in the island of Sicily. The great earthquake of 28 December 1908 killed approximately 80,000 people.

Part VII
The Final Years

Something of Kipling*

B. S. TOWNROE

In his *Something of Myself*, Mr Kipling told in 1937 many facts about his earlier life. Here are some new stories about him which have never been published before.

I first met Kipling in Liverpool in 1915 when, of course, his reputation was world-famous. At that time as Assistant Secretary of the West Lancashire Territorial Association,[1] it was my privilege to assist Lord Derby,[2] when the President of the Association, in his recruiting campaign, which led to him becoming Director-General of Recruiting at the War Office, and laid the foundation of the 'Derby scheme' of voluntary registration. But that, as Mr Kipling so often wrote, is another story.

Recruiting in the spring of 1915 was very sluggish in the Lancashire seaside town of Southport.[3] Normal methods of arousing local interest had failed. Accordingly Lord Derby gave me permission to telegraph to Mr Kipling at his home at Burwash, to ask him to speak at an open air meeting to be addressed from the balcony of the Town Hall, Southport. It was a forlorn hope, but to our surprise a few hours later arrived a telegram accepting.

I met Mr and Mrs Kipling as they stepped out of their train at Liverpool, and over tea he asked many questions about our recruiting methods, the response of public opinion, and the attitude of the Labour Party and the local trade-union leaders. These were, in fact, giving very great assistance in Lancashire to Lord Derby. We then set off by car to drive to Southport across the Fylde, that little known, rather remote, and very rich agricultural district of West Lancashire. Mr Kipling took the keenest possible interest in everything he passed, but particularly in rural methods of farming, the state of the fields, the shape of the stacks, and pointed out special features of interest with the zest of a boy with a new toy.

* *Kipling Journal*, XIII (Dec 1946) 12–13.

On arrival at Southport he was so intrigued by the distant view of the sea miles away that he asked to be allowed to make a personal exploration of the town and to drive out to the beach and the distant view of the Lake District. Eventually he met the local 'big-wigs' in the town hall, and then spoke through loud-speakers to thousands of people gathered together in Lord Street and the gardens below. He indicted the Germans for all their cruelties and infamous treatment of the civilian population in Belgium. His words were profoundly condemnatory of German militarism. The theme was the way France and England were being attacked by barbarians. It was the most powerful attack on German methods that had been made, and it was cabled to all parts of the world. It had an immense press at the time.

After the war I was lucky enough to serve on a committee which Mr Kipling attended regularly, but at which he rarely spoke. He used to sit there looking at times profoundly bored, especially when certain people talked at too great length. During such orations he amused himself by 'doodling' on scrap-paper in front of him, or making little impromptu sketches. He was, however, careful to tear up all this artistic work before he left the table, knowing, I suppose, how quickly it would be seized upon by souvenir-collectors. After one of these lengthy meetings he remarked with a twinkle in his eye, to Miss Cook, the lady who was taking down notes – 'How men do talk!'

I met him at that time in both London and Paris. One of my most vivid memories is the sight of him and Mrs Kipling standing alone, and looking tired and rather forlorn, at an Embassy garden-party in Paris given by the late Lord Crewe.[4] It was surprising that they had not been recognised by the French and lionised, for he was of course, extremely popular in French literary circles.

I searched for two vacant chairs and offered these to them both. They were very glad indeed to sit down and so I had the good luck to have a quiet talk with him all alone. He referred to his Southport speech and expressed grave anxiety about the future relations of France and Great Britain, remarking that we were still wandering in the confusion of the no-man's-land which lay between the old world and the new.

During the remainder of his life he helped our Franco-British work in many directions, but we tried in vain to persuade him to be the guest of honour at one of our banquets as he disliked the possibility of being broadcast. He expressed, however, again and again his hope that the two countries would re-establish together the foundations of the peace of the world, not on pious dreams or amiable hopes, but on those ancient virtues of logic, sanity and laboriousness with which her history and her own indomitable genius have dowered France.

NOTES

Bernard Stephen Townroe (1885–1962) earned his reputation as an authority on architecture, beginning with *A Handbook of Housing: How to Meet the Problem* (1924), and continuing with a series of studies on rebuilding to eliminate slums, bombed structures, and the like. Like Kipling, he loved France, and he wrote *A Wayfarer in Alsace* (1926) and *A Pilgrim in Picardy* (1927).

1. After the Territorial and Reserve Forces Act had received the royal assent, King Edward VII summoned the Lord-Lieutenants of the Counties of England, Wales, and Scotland to a meeting at Buckingham Palace (20 October 1907). He urged them to cooperate with the Secretary of State in launching the new County Associations. The Duke of Norfolk replied on behalf of his colleagues. The West Lancashire Territorial Association administered twenty-nine units, of cavalry, artillery, engineers, infantry, service, and medical corps.

2. Stanley, Edward George Villiers, 17th Earl of Derby (after 1908) (1865–1948), served as Director General of Recruiting at the War Office during World War I. (He had also been secretary to Lord Roberts in Cape Town.) Although his efforts to enlist volunteers on a scale large enough to avoid the need for conscription failed, the conscription bill which was passed avoided acrimonious debate because the Derby scheme had been tried.

3. On the Irish Sea, 17 miles north of Liverpool.

4. Crewe-Milnes, Robert Offlet Ashburton, 2nd Baron Houghton and Marquess of Crewe (1858–1945), son of Richard Monckton-Milnes. He served as Secretary of State for the Colonies; then for India. Between 1922 and 1928, he was the British Ambassador in Paris. A Liberal, he wrote a notable biography of Lord Rosebery, his father-in-law.

A Kipling Memory: the Oneness of All Life*

COULSON KERNAHAN

Was it in the late summer of 1913 because a slender moon lay, like a finger, upon the lip of night, as if to command silence, that Kipling

* *The Times*, 3 Oct 1939, p. 11.

turned suddenly to me to say, 'That was a true word of yours to the Chief [meaning Lord Roberts][1] about peace and silence – that even to mention silence is to break it, and that the same often holds good about peace, for peace-palavers are generally followed by war, as history shows.

'In April 1898, the Tsar addressed a rescript to the nations, inviting international discussion on the means of ensuring universal peace for the world.'

'In the same year we had the Spanish-American War.'

'The first Hague Meeting peace agreement was signed, on behalf of the assembled powers, in July 1899.'

'Two months later, October, England was involved in the Boer War; and we had the Manchurian War in 1902 and the Russo-Japanese War in 1904.'

'The second Hague Meeting was in 1907, since when we have seen the Italian–Turkish War in 1911, and mark you, less than one year before that, Mr Carnegie had placed $10 million at the service of the Carnegie Fund for the ending of war and the consummation of universal peace.'

'In 1911, too, England and America negotiated a treaty, by which matters of dispute were to be submitted for arbitration for the prevention of war. When France also joined, this treaty was hailed as the coming of the Millennium, and thanksgiving services were held and sermons announcing the arrival of universal peace were preached in countless churches and chapels.'

'And that very year, which was to see the end of war, plunged Europe into the bloody Balkan war, and, after it was over, some of the very allies who had fought together against Turkey wanted to go to war among themselves for the division of the spoils. And that Balkan business isn't over yet, and God only knows into what wars it may not lead Europe and the world, one of these days.'

Then Kipling swerved aside to exclaim, 'A glow-worm, by Jove! The first I've seen this year. Look here, you fellows!'

He squatted, Hindu-wise, on his haunches by the hedgeside; and as an officer signals silently to his men, instead of using a spoken word of command, so Kipling, by an inward movement of his extended hand, palm open, signalled to us to do the same, and the three of us crouched there together.

Then he seemed to forget us, and to be talking to – not about – the glow-worm, communing with his tiny fellow-sharer in the inexplicable miracle and boon of life. As for reproducing from memory, and long years after, what was said by a man of genius, all I can do is to attempt to convey the gist of what was said and to convey the impression left upon us who listened.

Kipling was musing, aloud, on the 'oneness' of life, as if he held that there is one and the same life-element in all which is animate; and as if, so holding, he saw, in the minute creature over which he was musing, that which strangely related the minute creature to our own scarcely less minute existence; and as if he held, too, that, just as a mere dewdrop on a blade of grass may mirror the great sun in the sky, so the flickering and uncertain spark which – be it in man or be it in glow-worm – we call 'life' is but the infinitesimal reflection of the one great Source of all light and all life.

Then, not as he who turns aside from, but as he who continues the same thought, Kipling passed on, in his musings, to find in the infinitely little, as in the infinitely great, the same 'oneness' of which he had been speaking, thus relating the vast and multitudinous universe, and the vaster and more multitudinous system of universes which are revealed by the telescope, with the multitudinous and teeming life revealed by the microscope.

Dull, commonplace, and colourless this summary – in my words – of Kipling's musings may be. But each of his words was weighed and chosen (as David weighed and chose the stones he slung at Goliath), and all that he said was so illuminated by Kipling's own flashing phrase and metaphor, that his musings seemed to afford his two listeners a glimpse, at least, of 'those cycles of God's providence', as Robertson of Brighton called them, which are on so unimaginably vast a scale that no mortal and finite eye can follow them in their orbing. Yet, none the less, those musings seemed to bring the slender moon in the heavens, the luminous glow-worm on the grass, and our little insignificant selves into some close and mystic relationship, each with the other – and with God.

NOTES

Coulson Kernahan (1858–1943) worked in support of Lord Roberts for eight years preceding the First World War, and was Hon. Recruiting Officer. A prolific writer, he gave book-length treatment to the Territorials, Swinburne, spiritualism, various poets (including Kipling), and recruiting experiences. He was literary adviser to Ward, Lock and Co.

1. Frederick Sleigh Roberts, 1st Earl Roberts (1832–1914), fought in the Indian Mutiny (1857–8), the second Afghan War (1878–80) and the South African War (1899–1902). He was commander-in-chief in India from 1885 to 1893. He served as the last commander-in-chief of the British Army (1901–4), after which the post was

abolished. His final rank was that of field-marshal. His reminiscences, *Forty-one Years in India*, appeared in 1897. Kipling was much impressed by his abilities.

Kipling's Precaution[*]

CHRISTOPHER MORLEY

There's an odd little story about Kipling that has never been in print. It was told me by his publisher and intimate friend the late Frank Doubleday. Those who have marked some excesses of modern biography and editing will understand it. As a gloss upon the episode one can look up two savage little poems by Tennyson: 'To——, After Reading a Life and Letters', and 'Poets and Their Bibliographies'.[1]

Mr Doubleday went down to visit Kipling in Sussex. It was a beautiful summer day, and the publisher, arriving by an unannounced train, was not met at the station. He decided to walk and enjoy the countryside. As he approached the house he was surprised to see, on a blazing day, a dark plume of smoke rising from one of the chimneys of 'Bateman's'. So much so, indeed, that he even wondered if the flue were on fire.

Doubleday quickened his pace. The front-door stood open to the summer heat; no one had noticed the visitor's approach; as an old friend of the house he walked in and went straight to the author's study. He tapped at the door and entered. Kipling was crouched in front of a roaring fireplace, feeding the flames with bundles of papers. Even as the publisher stood in the doorway he saw a mass of manuscript in that well-known small handwriting go into the hearth. Every instinct of a publisher was appalled.

'For Heaven's sake, Rud,' he said, 'what are you doing?'

Kipling, perspiring by the blaze, gave the mass of burning papers a rummaging thrust with a poker. He looked at his friend keenly from under those heavy brows.

'Well, Effendi,[2] I was looking over old papers and I got thinking. – No one's going to make a monkey out of me after I die.'

---

[*] *Saturday Review of Literature*, XIII (1 Feb 1936) 11.

NOTES

Christopher Darlington Morley (1890–1957) was a Rhodes Scholar who moved easily into heavy editing responsibilities at Doubleday, Page and Co. (1913–17), *Ladies' Home Journal* (1917–18), and the *Saturday Review of Literature* (1924–40). Of his many novels and books, perhaps the most famous are *Thunder on the Left* (1925) and *Kitty Foyle* (1939). He was editor-in-chief of the revised editions of *Bartlett's Familiar Quotations* (1937, 1948).

1. Tennyson may have written this first poem after reading Richard Monckton-Milnes' *Life, Letters and Literary Remains of John Keats* (1848). Biographers believe that the poem was addressed to Charles Tennyson Turner, the poet's brother, who had largely abandoned the writing of poems. At any rate, the poem praises one who might 'have won the Poet's name', but made the wiser choice of 'a life that moves to gracious ends/Thro' troops of unrecording friends'. The second poem calls on Virgil, Horace, and Catullus as 'old poets foster'd under friendlier skies' who wrote

> Before the Love of Letters, overdone,
> Had swampt the sacred poets with themselves.

2. Title of respect ('sir'), particularly in Turkey.

The Unfading Genius of Rudyard Kipling (1)*

ARTHUR WINDHAM BALDWIN

One of my sources of the early married days of Kipling's parents was a close friend of my grandmother and all her sisters, by the name of Miss Edith Plowden. Circumstances being as they were, I came to know her well; and I think, if I read you an extract from one of Rudyard Kipling's letters to her, it will show clearly what he thought about private writings falling into hands other than those they were intended for.

People are sometimes vexed by this attitude, but Kipling held the not unreasonable view that an author should have sole control over which of his writings should be published and which should not, on

* *Kipling Journal*, xxxv (Mar 1968) 8–14.

both this and the other side of the grave. I am well aware of the cogent argument that ALL the private papers of famous men and women should become the common heritage of a nation, or a world, only too eager to do them honour; but *I* don't happen to be persuaded by it; nor did my father. In this, as in most matters of principle, Baldwin and Kipling saw eye to eye.

Let Kipling, then, state *his* case in a letter written to Miss Plowden in January 1915:

> I gladly accept your offer of my copybook of early verses with the Father's drawing and I shall be more grateful than I can say if you would extend your kindness so far as to give me the copies of the schoolboy poems on notepaper. After all, they were sent from me to you, and if they are going to be given or willed away why should they not come back to me for myself and my children? They are of more interest to me than anyone else and though I am quite certain that Stan would deal honestly *by* them, I know by bitter experience how difficult it is to prevent other people from gaining access to such things and giving them a baleful publicity. Whence got you the idea that I am reckless about my letters and poems? For more than twenty years I have done my best to try and get all such letters and papers into my possession. That I have not always been successful is proved by the fact that I have seen the most *sacred* and *intimate* matters concerning myself and my people printed in newspapers and periodicals; and it has been the same with a good deal of my early work. It is for this reason that I hope you will, of your kindness, give me all the old work that you may have of mine and above all that you won't have Father's drawing photographed. *Nothing* is safe from the Press these days . . . .

So those things were sent back to him and he did with them what he thought best, in that cruel year when his only son was killed at the Battle of Loos.

All that I have to tell you is innocent, and, it may be thought, superficial; but it's the best I can do, in selecting from such papers as I possess.

I wish I had ever been able to get to know Kipling as closely as my elder brother Oliver did. But I have at least a record of an early kindness on my behalf, in the form of a letter Kipling wrote to my father telling of a visit he had just paid to me during my first week at a boarding-school at Rottingdean.

The year was 1912. I was eight. This is some of the letter describing our encounter . . .

He charged forth with a pal – no sign of any pensive steps and slow about A. Baldwin. Elsie and I hailed him and he came to anchor, legs very wide apart, the new, very new schoolboy overlying the child now four days in the background . . . Conversation short and naturally weighted with the knowledge that he was on his way to cricket . . . then he dashes off like a trout across the field in the sunshine, picks up a scarlet-headed yaffingale[1] of a kid called Buzzard and the two prance off with their arms on each other's shoulders . . . Then the master appeared and they all ran to him like young hounds – almost you could see their sterns waggling . . . The last I see of him is a flourish of a bat and a man-of-the-world wave of the hand. Quite full of beans and evidently realising his new world with pleasure. Bless him.

Another record of his exceeding kindness I have in the form of written emendations on an essay I had done at Eton. I was about seventeen – a poorish specimen of an unattractive age – and was *appalled* when my mother asked Kipling, who was staying with us, to look at it. The consequence was that he went to the trouble not only of going through the miserable scrawl *with* me, but, when he got back to London, of ordering a dozen or more books from the classics, which he thought might be of benefit to my literary development, with an explanatory letter. I will read some of it, written in 1922:

There is now on the way to you a packet of books – some of which may serve your turn by opening up your young (alleged) mind in various directions. I admit some of 'em look tosh, but you browse among 'em and see what strikes you. *Hazlitt* isn't as out of date as he looks. He makes one take notice. *Crashaw* is for words and emotions, *Swift* is purely for style. *Coleridge* is an out-of-the-way bird with a habit of approaching the ordinary at extraordinary angles. *M. Aurelius* is the heavy lead and awful stodge in most places but about $\frac{1}{10}$ percent of him goes. *Donne* may or may not catch hold of you. Anyhow, keep him for a bit and see if he doesn't

affect you later. Anyway, he will teach you words and tropes and
such things . . . .

I *must* just give you one more example of the trouble he would
take in this embarrassing matter of giving his literary services when
asked, to his admiring relations. It must have bored him
unspeakably, yet he gave no indication of it.

Faulty and uninspiring as were *my* school essays, they were
scarcely worse, and far less formidable to deal with, than some of the
verses of his Aunt Louise, my father's mother. Yet I possess four
sonnets of hers in typescript on the subjects of Love and Christianity,
written in 1909, upon which her patient and world-famous godson
has crossed out, changed, inserted and added final comments on
each with a gentle firmness beyond all praise. For instance, he
wrote, after his improvements, 'I think it will do now. Type out
complete and send in to me and we'll look over it.' On another: 'I
don't like this. There is no specific word to lay hold of: but I don't see
how it can be altered. You must recast from end to end.' And so on.
Quite amazing, I think. No wonder we all loved him. Everyone
knows, from his books, of the way he had with children and with
animals, but not much else, except in his less read latter works, of his
infinite humanity. Many know of the strength, but too few know of
the sweetness, of his character.

Now I will try to give you a few disconnected glimpses of the
affectionate understanding that existed between himself and my
father. Naturally, Kipling could not approve of *all* the actions and
reactions with which Baldwin was associated during his twenty
years of high political life; but at the roots, as I have said, they were
of similar moral outlook and they understood and trusted one
another with an easy comradeship that had established itself in
boyhood.

I can remember an evening at Astley between the wars when they
fell to reminiscing about the holiday they had both spent as boys on
a farm in Essex under the indulgent control of Kipling's mother,
lately returned for a spell from India. As they recounted incidents
they laughed and they laughed till they could hardly speak.

Another time, so one of my sisters tells me, these two middle-aged
men were discovered sitting on the stairs, their arms round one
another's shoulders, rocking and weeping with ungovernable mirth.
What the cause of it was neither would ever say. I can promise you it
wasn't liquor, anyway.

But my main glimpses come from one angle: principally in letters written to friends or relations by my father. Without doubt Kipling will have destroyed any letters from *my* father to *him*. These references of mine are nothing much, but they do give out a faint echo of the days when they were written, most of them round about fifty years ago.

The first is from Bateman's summer 1911: 'I am writing in the drawing-room, and Rud is upstairs, with his Muse in first-class working order, for I hear him tramping up and down and singing. Bless him!'

'Bless him' or 'her' was very much a *family* term of affection among the older generation of Macdonald descent.

Next: from London, November 1916. 'I had breakfast with Kipling at Brown's Hotel and two hours' talk. . . . I was highly pleased to find that he had come to the same conclusion about the Government that I had, *and* by the same road, after almost as long and anxious a cogitation. We have common puritan blood in us and he said a thing I have so often said and acted on: "When you have two courses open to you and you thoroughly dislike one of them, *that is* the one you must choose, for it is sure to be the right one." How much happier not to be made like that!' added Baldwin.

I wonder if you know why the Kiplings always stayed at Brown's Hotel? To the best of my recollection this is what my father told me. After their wedding at All Souls', Langham Place, in January 1892, they repaired to Brown's in Dover Street for a few days before leaving for the United States. The manager, at the end of their stay, presented them with a receipted bill.

Next: from London, June 1919, after a visit: 'Bateman's was a peculiarly happy and peaceful time. For two days I never stirred outside the garden and the weather of course was perfect. For more than one reason it is the completest haven to me that the world affords, and I shall be there again before long . . . . '

Baldwin was a great walker, swift and far; and that letter was possibly written at some period after a visit when he had found the following notice pinned up in his room at Bateman's for his especial attention.

It read,

RULES FOR GUESTS.

1. No guest to walk more than 5 miles an hour. 2. No guest to walk more than two hours at a time. 3. Guests are strictly

forbidden to coerce or cajole the natives to accompany them in said walks, as the proprietors cannot be responsible for the consequences.

Signed, Rudyard Kipling, Caroline Kipling, Elsie Kipling
(natives)

Next: from Astley three days before Christmas 1921 (when the Coalition Government, of which Baldwin was an uncomfortable member, was in some disrepute). 'I met Carson in Downing Street from whom I got a very chilly nod, and the sort of greeting a corpse would give to an undertaker. There was some restraint about cousin Kipling too, whom I saw at the Carlton in earnest conversation with Rupert Gwynne. I hope it'll wear off by tomorrow when he is due here.' (Of course it did. No temporary political snag could trip up that intimate and ancient friendship.)

I think it must have been *that* Christmas at Astley which stays clearest in my memory, when the Kiplings and the Baldwins of both generations spent the evenings in various light amusements, such as billiards and paper games, before the advent of radio and television discouraged such goings on. We sometimes used to converse in a kind of literal dog-French. If one could slip in a murderous pun, so much the merrier.

Once, when *my* brother Ollie, as we called him then, put his hands to the piano and lifted up his voice in song – he was no good – I remember composing a few rhyming couplets in facetious dispraise of the singer, which Kipling eagerly took up, improved and extended. This is the result of our joint work, almost all of it his:

> When Ollie sings, the amorous Cat
> Says; 'Praised be Pasht, *I* don't do that.'
> The Cartwheel in the frozen lane
> Grunts: 'Here's my rival loose again.'
> The envious Owl replies, and then
> Drops dead beside the chicken-pen;
> And well the Kine of Astley know
> The note that sours their lacteal flow;
> While in the sty the gravid Sow
> Loses her litter at the row.
> The Handsaw and the screeching File
> Together mutter: 'Oh, how vile':
> And strive in chorus, up and down,

> The melancholy noise to drown.
> Far off a Train, with grinding brakes,
> A counter-demonstration makes:
> Feeble and futile, None compete
> With Ollie on the music-seat.
> A Factory-whistle, fierce and shrill,
> Bellows despairing and is still;
> And anguished Earth and Heaven attend
> The intolerable solo's end,
> Where four mixed voices from one throat
> Keep neither key nor time nor note,
> But treble, tenor, alto, bass,
> Riot in one ungodly chase
> After a tune which flatly strays
> 'Twixt 'Auld Lang Syne' and 'Marseillaise'.

It must have been in the early 'thirties (when the two cousins have allowed themselves to be pulled asunder by the Government of India Bill), that Kipling wrote four noble lines of verse which he presented to Baldwin as a tribute of admiration and understanding. They used to hang, framed, on a wall of the library at Astley. Like a fool I never wrote them down nor got them by heart; for after my father's death, I have learnt, they were disposed of.

Disposed of, too, are the bulk of his letters to my father: sold, like the many that he wrote to my brother; and I don't know where they are. Enough of that.

'But that's all shove be'ind me, long ago and fur away . . . ' and I don't propose to end my speech in rancour or dismay; so let me make a final return to something jolly.

Some of you may remember reading in the Press of Baldwin's alleged liking for pigs. So far from being assumed, this liking was real and lifelong. I came on *this* in a letter of his the other day, written in 1919 from Astley: 'In the meantime I stay on, reading Monte Cristo, talking with my eldest son, paying bills, going to bed early, and living as nearly like a pig as I can, except that so many people look over the top of the sty and poke me up whenever I try to settle down in the straw . . . . '

For Christmas in that same year Kipling made a poem for his cousin and inscribed it on the flank of a toy wooden pig, as a token of their common affection for pigs alive and, alas, pigs dead.

In Baldwin's words, Kipling 'went into Harrods and said, "I

want a pig." And they: "We have one at four guineas." "That",
said the poet, "is no good to me. My limit is half a crown." So he
bought one made by a wounded warrior.'

Perhaps I should apologise to this non-political audience for the
slighting reference to the old Liberal leader in the last line but one of
the poem. It was written, as I said, nearly fifty years ago, and all
concerned are gone, including, I need hardly add, the little wooden
pig.

This is it:

> Some to Women, some to Wine –
> Some to Wealth or Power incline –
> Proper people cherish Swine.
> Cattle from the Argentine –
> Poultry tough as office twine –
> Give no pleasure when we dine.
> But, from nose-tip unto chine,
> Via every *intestine*,
> *Nothing* is amiss in Swine.
> Roast or smoked or soaked in brine –
> (We have proved it, Cousin mine)
> *Every* part of him is fine.
> So, till Income Tax decline,
> Or Truth exist across the Rhine,
> Or George can speak it, praise we Swine,
> Common, honest, decent Swine.

Mr Chairman, Ladies and Gentlemen, on that prandial note I ask
you to rise and drink with me the toast: 'To the Unfading Genius of
Rudyard Kipling.' Bless him.

NOTES

Arthur Baldwin (1904–76), the second son of Stanley Baldwin, defended his
father's reputation in *My Father: The True Story* (1956). After serving in the Royal
Air Force (1941–5), he succeeded his brother (1958) to become the 3rd Earl
Baldwin of Bewdley. He was a director of the Great Western Railway, and of
various insurance companies. In addition to *The Macdonald Sisters*, he wrote an
autobiography, *A Flying Start* (1967). The essay reprinted here is the text of a speech
given at the Kipling Society Luncheon, 25 October 1967.

1. Dialect word, appearing first in 1609, used in the south and south-west;
echoic of the ending of *nightingale* and the laughing cry ('yaffle') of the green
woodpecker.

Life at The Elms, Rottingdean*

ANGELA THIRKELL

My grandmother had a great deal of natural self-possession and dignity and a power of accepting every one – no matter what their social position – entirely for what they were in themselves. She could talk to working-people in their cottages with as much ease as she received royal princesses who came to look at pictures. I must say that I think the first of these tasks by far the most difficult and I was always paralysed with shyness if my grandmother took me with her on one of her cottage visits. There was no condescension in her visits and no familiarity, though the child who accompanied her was ready to cry with confusion as she sat with her large blue eyes fixed on some gnarled unlettered old woman, telling her tidings of comfort from *Fors Clavigera*.[1] Only her entire absence of self-consciousness made these visits possible and there were other and – to us – even more shameful occasions when she would have a worthy carpenter of wheelwrights to the house once a week to discuss the socialism in which she so thoroughly and theoretically believed. All the snobbishness latent in children came to the fore in us as we watched the honoured but unhappy workman sitting stiffly on the edge of his chair in his horrible best clothes while my grandmother's lovely earnest voice preached William Morris[2] to him. Then there were times when she believed that a hideous but favoured maid was worth educating. In the evening there would be an embarassing ritual and the maid would sit in the drawing-room, though at a respectful distance, and read aloud to my grandmother from such books as she thought suitable to the domestic intellect on *The Distribution of Wealth*[3] and the *Early Italian Painters*.[4] How we

* *Three Houses* (London: Oxford University Press, 1931) pp. 78–80, 82–91, 107–8, 110–11.

hated it all and how uncomfortable it was for every one concerned except the kind giver of these mental feasts. There can rarely have been a woman who was so absolutely unconscious of self, though it was carried to such a pitch that even her sense of humour fell into abeyance. Now and then her humour did get the better of her, as when she described a visit she had paid to some poor family who had an invalid child 'surrounded with medals for abstaining from vices of which he was uncapable'.

In spite of her wide affections and deep understanding she was curiously removed from real life and I think she honestly believed that *The Seven Lamps of Architecture*[5] on every working-man's table would go far to ameliorate the world. She was absolutely fearless, morally and physically. During the South African War her sympathies were with the Boers, and though she was at that time a widow, living alone, she never hesitated to bear witness, without a single sympathiser. When peace was declared she hung out of her window a large blue cloth on which she had been stitching the words 'We have killed and also taken possession.' For some time there was considerable personal danger to her from a populace in Mafeking[6] mood, till her nephew, Rudyard Kipling, coming over from the Elms, pacified the people and sent them away. Single-minded people can be a little alarming to live with and we children had a nervous feeling that we never knew where our grandmother might break out next. . . .

Inside the sweetbriar close a tent was sometimes pitched for us in summer. I do not know why it had been bought and it was the most wretchedly uncomfortable and stuffy form of shelter that could be devised, but naturally we felt its romance deeply. It was a round tent with a rickety wooden table on two legs encircling the centre pole and it was our supreme joy to have tea in it and equally Nanny's supreme detestation. To her it must have meant stuffiness, table-manners running riot, the carrying out of heavy trays, mess of milk and crumbs, overpowering breathless heat and deep discomfort, and now I think I would agree with Nanny. But to us then it was glorious adventure. One might easily be a Knight of the Round Table in his pavilion, or Saladin receiving Richard, or the Greeks before Troy, and the highly uncomfortable meal eaten reclining on a rug in the atmosphere of the Black Hole of Calcutta among swarms of flies became Alexander's feast. Or if we happened to be Cavaliers at the moment and the Roundheads were known to be approaching in force, what was easier than to slip out, on one's stomach under the flaps of the tent and, re-forming rapidly in upright position, take them in the rear. We threw ourselves into the fray with all the more ardour when the Roundhead of the day happened to be our cousin, Rudyard Kipling, who lived at the Elms across the village-green.

The three Kipling children, Josephine, Elsie, and John, were about the same ages as our nursery three. Josephine, very fair-haired and blue-eyed, was my bosom friend, and though we both adored her father, the stronger bond of patriotism drew us yet more firmly together as Cavaliers against Cousin Ruddy's whole-hearted impersonation of an Arch-Roundhead. For the purposes of Civil War I had assumed the name of Sir Alexander of the Lake and under this title I had sent a cartel of defiance to the Roundhead, but Alexander is a long word for seven years old and the Roundhead's answer to my challenge ended with the searing words, 'And further, know that thou hast misspelled thine own miserable name, oh, Alixander.' For months I went hot and pink with the memory of this rebuff. The war between Cavaliers and Roundheads raged furiously every year as long as the Kiplings were at Rottingdean, Josephine and I leading forlorn hopes against the regicide and being perpetu-ally discomfited by his superior guile, or by the odious way in which the nannies would overlook the fact that we were really 6 feet high with flowing locks, a hat with feathers, and huge jack-boots, and order us indoors to wash our hands or have an ignominious midday rest. How would *they* have liked it if they were plotting to deliver King Charles from Carisbrooke[7] and *their* nannies had suddenly pounced upon them with a 'Get up off the grass now Miss Angela and come and lie down before lunch, and there's Lucy waiting for you Miss Josephine, so put those sticks down like a good girl and run along.' Fools! Couldn't they see that these were no pea-sticks, but sword, dagger, and pistol, ready to flash out or be discharged in the service of the King? But nannies are by nature unromantic, so we had to submit and pretend to be little girls till we could meet again later.

Our nanny had come to us when my sister was a few weeks old and though she did her duty by my younger brother and myself, she naturally put 'her' baby first and our plans and make-believes were only tolerated as they did not interfere with nursery routine. Romance in her was expressed in song. She had an enormous repertory of what had been popular songs ten years earlier and could bring tears to our eyes by 'Just a Song at Twilight'[8] and curdle our blood with 'The Gipsy's Warning',[9] or cause a wave of revivalism to sweep over the nursery by 'Beulah Land, Oh, Beulah Land'.[10] She had a real passion for the lower forms of creation. The higher mammals she feared and loathed and never alluded to cows except as 'them vicious cows', but to anyone with more than four legs her heart was open. It became an embarrassing trait, for insects recognised her as a kindred spirit from afar; daddy-long-legses in particular would come for miles to get between her stiff collar and her neck, where they spent the day in calm repose and were taken out at night with the utmost gentleness when she undressed and put out of the window on to a leaf, usually leaving a leg or two behind in the disconcerting way they have. How very interesting were the dressings and undressings of nannies when one was small enough to share a room with them. Their undressing of course we rarely saw as we were asleep before they went to bed, but I have fascinating visions of their getting up by candlelight on winter mornings and clicking themselves into black stays which appeared to stretch from neck to knee. It was one of my highest ambitions to be old enough to have black stays that clicked down the front and to imitate Nanny's masterful handling of the mechanism; the way she fastened them first in the middle and then with two skilful movements brought the upper parts together and then the lower parts.

The Kiplings' nurse Lucy was also given to song and her (and our) special favourite was a melancholy affair called 'The Blue Alsatian Mountains',[11] which seemed to us the most romantic thing we had ever heard. I can only remember a few hauntingly beautiful lines, or so they seemed to me then:

> Ade, Ade, Ade [this line was, of course, in German],
> Such thoughts will pass away.
> But the Blue Alsatian Mountains
> Their watch will keep alway.

It gives me lumps in my throat even now.

That summer must have been a year of song, for besides Lucy who really looked after the younger children, there was a governess for Josephine and that particular year there were two. I imagine now that one must have stayed on for a fortnight to get the other into the ways of the house, for two governesses at once seems unusual, but the result was delightful, for they sang Mendelssohn duets together all over the downs, much to Josephine's delight and mine.

It is many years now since Josephine died one cruel winter in New York while her father too was desperately ill and her mother had to show all a woman's deepest courage in bearing what must be borne and keeping the death of the adored child from the adoring father till he was well enough to stand the blow. Much of the beloved Cousin Ruddy of our childhood died with Josephine and I feel that I have never seen him as a real person since that year. There has been the same charm, the same gift of fascinating speech, the same way of making every one with whom he talks show their most interesting side, but one was only allowed to see these things from the other side of a barrier and it was sad for the child who used to be free of the inner courts of his affection. I still have a letter from Josephine, written in sprawly childish capitals. 'I will help you', it ran, 'in the war against the Roundhead. He has a large army but we can beat him. He is a horrible man let us do all the mischief we can to him.' It must have been a very real game that made her call the father she loved a 'horrible man'. The world has known Josephine and her father as Taffimai and Tegumai in the *Just So Stories* and into one short poem he put his heart's cry for the daughter that was all to him. This letter, a nursery-book which had been hers and a silver button from a coat are all I have of Josephine, but her fair-haired, blue-eyed looks and her impish charm and loving ways are not forgotten.

Although she and I were usually a devoted couple, there were plenty of quarrels. There was the terrible day when I offered to do Josephine's hair according to the White Knight's recipe for keeping hair from falling off, by training it upwards on a pea-stick, and the result was an awful tangle of yellow hair, shrieks and tears from the victim, and the descent of a governess on the culprit. Manners at meals were another subject for quarrels. Our nursery had somehow acquired the right to eat cutlet bones in its fingers unchecked, a proceeding which shocked our cousins inexpressibly and led them to call us pigs. They, on the other hand, being half American, had an odious habit of breaking their boiled breakfast eggs into a glass and stirring them up with a spoon. It was a pink glass which somehow made matters worse, and with the complete candour of the nursery we stigmatised the whole proceeding as disgusting.

During those long warm summers Cousin Ruddy used to try out the *Just So Stories* on a nursery audience. Sometimes Josephine and I would be invited into the study, a pleasant bow-windowed room, where Cousin Ruddy sat at his work-table looking exactly like the profile portrait of him that Uncle Phil[12] painted; pipe always at hand, high forehead, baldish even then, black moustache, and the dark complexion which made gossip-mongers attribute a touch of Indian blood to him. As a matter of fact I believe the dark complexion came from a Highland strain in his mother's family, for it occurred in other cousins sharing a grandfather whose forebears came from the Isle of Skye, and two at least of them could have passed as natives anywhere in Southern Europe. Or sometimes we all adjourned on a wet day to the Drill Hall where the horse and parallel bars made splendid forts and camping grounds, and when the battle was over and the Roundhead had been unmercifully rolled upon and pommelled by small fists he would be allowed by way of ransom to tell us about the mariner of infinite resource and sagacity and the suspenders – you must not forget the suspenders, Best Beloved. The *Just So Stories* are a poor thing in print compared with the fun of hearing them told in Cousin Ruddy's deep unhesitating voice. There was a ritual about them, each phrase having its special intonation which had to be exactly the same each time and without which the stories are dried husks. There was an inimitable cadence, an emphasis of certain words, an exaggeration of certain phrases, a kind of intoning here and there which made his telling unforgettable.

Or, if it was a blazing August afternoon, we might all three lie panting on the shady side of a haystack up on the downs, a field of ripe corn rippled by the warm wind before us, with scarlet poppies and blue cornflowers gleaming among the wheat, and hear his enchaining voice going on and on till it was all mixed up in a child's mind with the droning of a threshing-machine up at Height Barn and sleep descended on us; sleep from which one was probably roused by having the soles of one's bare feet tickled with straw by way of vengeance from a slighted story-teller. Our highest heroics were apt to be pricked by Cousin Ruddy and collapse ignominiously. There was a period during which I happened to be Queen Zenobia, a role in which Josephine, who always played second fiddle in our entertainments, loyally supported me as waiting woman or some useful super. Cousin Ruddy was cast for the part of Aurelian, but he became mortifyingly matter-of-fact and wouldn't respond. The harrowing climax came when he met the nursery procession coming up from the beach one day, myself carrying for some unknown reason a quantity of wet sand in the upgathered skirts of my blue serge frock. Queens in adversity deserve some consideration, but Cousin Ruddy only said,

> There was a Queen Zenobia, and
> She filled her pinafore with sand

upon which the queen dissolved in tears and became a very furious little girl.

One winter I devoted hours of hard work to making a book of poems for Josephine whom I dearly loved. They were all written out by hand, but looking back I cannot say that they had any merit at all, being poor in thought and construction and largely borrowed from other sources. The only poem I can remember will illustrate the graver defects of my immortal works:

> The antlered monarch of the waste,
> Sprang from his heathery couch in haste,
> And worked his woe and my renown,
> And burnt a village and sacked a town.

Not good, you will say, and indeed you will be perfectly right, but Cousin Ruddy, who as a poet himself should have been kinder, so criticised my unhappy attempts that I sank into a state of dejection which lasted several days and was only really cured by being allowed to come into the study and see him write his name, very, very small, with a very, very large pen – a much coveted treat. It was his kind custom at the end of the holidays to give me a sheet of paper covered with autographs which I was able to swap at school at the current rate of exchange for stamps and other valuables.

If I had been over from North End House to spend the afternoon with Josephine Kipling at the Elms, it was quite likely that I would find a little knot of sightseers gathered outside the high white gate which screened the house from the road. All through the summer months charabancs, drawn by four skinny miserable horses (how mysterious the word *sharrabangs*[13] was to us), would disgorge loads of trippers at the Royal Oak, and as there was little for them to see in the village besides my grandfather's house and the church, they spent a good deal of time round Cousin Ruddy's gate. The Kiplings had been obliged to have the gate boarded over in self-defence, leaving a little hole with a sliding shutter through which you put your hand to open it. Through this hole tourists would stare with a perseverance worthy of those individuals who looked through the grating in Mr Nupkin's gate[14] at Ipswich. Not once nor twice did Aunt Carrie (she had been a Balestier from Vermont and Cousin Ruddy wrote *The Naulahka* in collaboration with her brother Wolcott Balestier) have to ask a kneeling crowd of sightseers to move aside and let her go into her own house. The tourists were marvellously misinformed as a rule and I am afraid we took a perverse pleasure in lingering near the gate and deliberately misleading any one who asked us questions, though in the case of the gentleman who wanted to know 'where Rupert Gilpin lived', but little misleading was necessary. Nor did we find it needful to undeceive the inquirer in the churchyard who asked in a hushed and reverent voice 'where Rudyard Kipling lay'. . . .

The personality of Mrs Ridsdale was the life of the Dene. Who in Rottingdean does not remember her sailing down the village street, commanding of figure, a large silver-topped leather bag always hanging at her side, a word for every one, an eye to every one's business, and always the first to do a kindness? A person too of immense character. Was it not she who invented and carried out the questionnaire for Kipling-hunters? 'Can you tell me where Rudyard Kipling lives?' a tourist would ask. Mrs Ridsdale would stop and fix him, or her, with her shrewd eye, saying, 'Have you read anything of his?' Very often the answer was 'No', when Mrs Ridsdale would remark, 'Then I won't tell you', and pass majestically on. . . .

The Dene possessed the first telephone that reached Rottingdean and the first we had ever seen. It was the kind that you had to wind up with a handle for a long time before it would start and you had to hold the combined receiver and mouthpiece in a tight nervous grip to keep it connected, so that you were nearly paralysed if your talk lasted any length of time. It was one of our treats to be allowed to hear Mrs Ridsdale telephoning to Brighton.

Rottingdean must have been well abreast of the times, for not only did it introduce us to telephones, but to our first motor. From our eyrie in the drawing-room window we could see on the other side of the green the Kiplings' motor pawing the ground before the door. It was one of those incredible machines raised high from the ground with a door in the middle of the back and it didn't like starting and when it had started it didn't want to stop, except half-way up a hill, and it perpetually ran dry on the tops of lovely downs miles away from even a dew-pond and when the grown-ups went in it the ladies wore tweed motor caps of gigantic size with veils swathed tightly round them and stuck through with enormous hatpins. When we saw the Kipling children dancing round it, we were consumed with longing to go and dance too, so slipping from the room we ran across the green and kicked up the dust with bare feet to express our joy. Finally the majestic machine got under weigh and drove off with a trail of smoke and smell behind it and we were left lamenting. To the best of my remembrance I never went for a drive in the monster, because whenever a ride had been promised it refused to go and we sat and sat in it while the chauffeur tinkered at its inside and then had to get out with a promise for a real ride some day. But 'some day', as my brother very truly remarked, 'is in the days that never come'. Just at this moment the young Kiplings were descended upon and carried off by a horde of nurses and governesses and we betook ourselves to the churchyard for further entertainment.

NOTES

Angela Thirkell (1890–1961) was the granddaughter of Edward Burne-Jones, daughter of J. W. Mackail, and a cousin of Rudyard Kipling. She wrote more than thirty novels about the middle-class and upper-class descendants of Trollope's Barsetshire characters.

1. The ninety-six letters of Ruskin's work (1871–84), written to an educated artisan, expressed a distrust of liberal democracy. Kipling read it while at Westward Ho!

2. English poet, novelist, designer, craftsman, and socialist (1834–96). Associate of Burne-Jones, friend of the Rossettis. Helped to change aesthetic standards in the decorative arts.

3. Thomas Nixon Carver (1865–1961) published this work in 1904.

4. Written by Anna Brownell (Murphy) Jameson (1794–1860), *Early Italian Painters* (1859) went through at least ten editions in England, and was also very popular in the United States.

5. Ruskin's famous study of the 'poetry of architecture', attempting to show how architecture relied on moral and spiritual values, was printed first in 1849.

6. Mafeking, a town in the north-east Cape Province, South Africa, near the Transvaal, was under attack during the Boer War. The lifting of the siege led to great rejoicing in England.

7. A town and parish on the Isle of Wight, Hampshire, just south of Newport. Charles I and his children were imprisoned here in the ruins of an eleventh-century castle.

8. Also known as 'Love's Old, Sweet Song', by J. L. Molloy, with words by G. C. Bingham.

9. Written by H. A. Coard, and published in Ditson's *Old-Time Song Hits* (c. 1909).

10. By J. R. Sweney, with words by E. Page or E. P. Stites.

11. By S. Adams, with words by Claribel.

12. Sir Philip Burne-Jones, 2nd Baronet (1861–1926), brother of Margaret Mackail.

13. From *char à banc*, literally a car with a bench; an open sightseeing bus, with transverse seats facing forward.

14. See Charles Dickens's *The Posthumous Papers of the Pickwick Club* (1836–7) ch. 25.

Memories of Rudyard Kipling (1)*

JULIA TAUFFLIEB

It is with hesitation and real emotion that I respond to your request and send a few reminiscences of the great man who honoured me with his wonderful and rare friendship, from the day when we met to the day when he passed to another world, mourned by all people.

We first made acquaintance in my mother's house in Morristown, New Jersey. My mother had met Rudyard Kipling on a trip going to Bermuda. Mr Kipling appreciated my mother's great intellectual qualities, and it was one of the joys of her later life to come in contact with such a true genius as Rud was. My mother invited Mr and Mrs Kipling to visit her at her house, and needless to say what a joy it was for us all to meet and know them.

---

* *Kipling Journal*, x (Oct 1943) 6–7. (Article signed 'Madame J. H. C. Taufflieb'.)

For some years I only saw the Kiplings at intervals, but kept in close touch with them and after 1907 when I went to live in Europe, we saw each other constantly. The Kiplings would come to stop with me in my chateau in France and we would go across the Channel to stop with them in Burwash. They had three children: Josephine, their first and she was a fairy child. When she was taken from them at a very early age, Rud never seemed to become reconciled to her loss. The second child, Elsie, 'Ladybird', as Rud called her, was so full of life, so intelligent and attractive. She is now Mrs George Bambridge. John was a bit younger and such a dear. He bade fair to be very brilliant.

Rudyard Kipling was always 'Uncle Rud' to my beloved daughter, Frances, and I was 'Aunt Julia' to his children. One Christmas the four Kiplings came to visit me over the holidays, and Mr and Mrs Henry Van Dyke,[1] Minister to the Hague, and two of their children were of the party. You can imagine what a Christmas that was. One not easily forgotten by old or young. Each year the Kiplings' and ourselves would be somewhere together. They would come to me, or I would go to them in their quaint Elizabethan house snuggled away on the Sussex Downs. We were in Marienbad, Vernet-les-Bains and several other trips, and the last winters of Rud's life we were all in Cannes.

When the war came in 1914, John insisted on enlisting, and in a letter Rud wrote me, dated 28 August 1914, he says, 'John is trying very hard to get his commission but as he is only seventeen and his eyes are not what they should be, it is somewhat difficult.' Lord Roberts was an intimate friend of Rud's and John insisted so much that I believe Lord Roberts rather overlooked the calendar. Suffice it to say that John joined the Irish Guards on 2 September 1915, and immediately left for France, and on 27 September 1915, after the Battle of Loos, he was reported missing. He was never heard of again. Some years later I met Colonel Vesey,[2] John's colonel, and heard from him all there was to know. John and another young lad started on a hazardous mission without real orders, and they were last seen leaning against a barn. A shell came, destroyed the barn, and nothing was ever heard of those two gallant young soldiers again.

For months the Kipling family heard nothing, and neither the father nor the mother believed John killed. I was in London in December 1915, and went to see them at Brown's Hotel. One could never imagine that a tragedy had occurred in their lives. They seemed absolutely cheery and evidently had not allowed themselves to believe that they would not see John again. However Rud, seeing me to my car that evening, at the foot of the stairs, took hold of my arm, and pressing it so that it almost hurt, said, 'Down on your knees Julia, and thank God that you have not a son.' I knew then that he knew. Rud was never the same in any shape or manner after John's death.

After the war, in 1919, General Taufflieb, the three Kiplings and myself, took a motor trip along the battle-front to Verdun. In a letter written after this automobile journey, and after having passed two days at Verdun, where the General took such pleasure in showing Rud all over the scarred battle-fields, Rud writes, 'I got more information from the General on certain matters than I would have gathered from a whole war-staff. He gave me an explanation on the top of his fort with the landscape laid out before us that cleared the situation up like a photograph.' The evening of the last day at Verdun Rud came in, took off his cap, passed his hand over his head and said, 'For the first time in my life, I have come to the place where I feel that if anyone gave me another idea my head would not stand it – it would burst.'

Some years later he was to be received at the Sorbonne and the Kiplings were stopping at the Hotel Meurice in Paris. We went to call on them in the afternoon previous to the presentation and such an array of caps and gowns came to my eyes. Naturally Rud had none of his own, and the professors of the Sorbonne, not knowing his stature, had sent him all sizes. Rud was like a boy trying them on, and I wish I could recollect the amusing comments he made. At last he found one to fit him.

The reception at the Sorbonne was tremendous. Rud had always loved France since his father took him as a small boy to the Exposition of 1879. He spoke French fairly well; fluently, but not always correctly. He was more beloved by the French people than any English writer (I was going to say than any Englishman). I know of one French general who carried some of Rud's books with him all through the four years of war. One day Rud showed me a paper-covered copy of *The Light that Failed* translated into French. It had a bullet hole right through it. A young French soldier had sent it to Rud with the words, 'You have saved my life, so I think this book belongs to you.'

Again we were together when Rud was received at the University of Strasbourg. The President and Mme Poincaré[3] were present, and the Alsatians were as enthusiastic in their welcome of Kipling as their brothers of the Sorbonne had been before them.

One evening in Paris I gave a reception for the Kiplings in my home at Neuilly. I procured the services of one of the great actors of the Comedie Française to recite Rud's great 'Ode to France' which alone would have endeared Rud to the French people. The poem had been translated by a great many authors, and I was literally persecuted as to whose translation I should select to be recited.

NOTES

Julia Catlin married General Taufflieb, who, after Alsace returned to French rule, became Commissioner there. She enjoyed entertaining in her home, near Strasbourg, after World War I. The Kiplings stayed at Cannes with them during the winter season. Indeed, Kipling died (January 1936) while *en route*, with Carrie, to join the Tauffliebs in Cannes.

1. Van Dyke (1852–1933) was a clergyman in Newport, Rhode Island, and in New York City; a professor of English literature at Princeton; a lecturer at the Sorbonne (1908–9); Minister to Holland and Luxembourg (1913–16); chaplain in the US Navy (1917–19), and author of numerous popular books of stories and religious sermons.

2. Lieutenant-colonel the Hon. T. E. Vesey, twice wounded, and awarded the Croix de Guerre on 17 August 1918.

3. Raymond Nicolas Landry Poincaré (1860–1934) was President of the French Republic (1913–20), Prime Minister (1922), and the public official most responsible for occupation of the Ruhr and halting the collapse of the franc (1926).

Memories of Rudyard Kipling (2)*

JULIA TAUFFLIEB

We often went to stay at Bateman's, where life was delightful. Every morning after breakfast Rud's study door would be shut, and no one

* *Kipling Journal*, x (Dec 1943) 4–5. (Article signed 'Madame J. H. C. Taufflieb'.)

was allowed even to knock. No! – one person was allowed to sit in one corner of the room and paint, and that was General Taufflieb. Rud said, 'The General is the only person in my life that I have ever allowed in the room when I am writing. I seem to work better when I feel his presence there.'

Luncheon at one o'clock was always a cheery meal, and in the afternoon we generally took a walk to see Carrie's cows and pigs. After tea Rud would say, 'Well, Julia, how about a story?' and we would go up to his study and he would light the fire. I stretched out on the settle and in truth it could never have been any other piece of furniture, so hard was it. But what did I care! Rud would take up one of his manuscripts, and read aloud one of his latest stories. He read delightfully, and lost himself completely in his reading. When he came to some pathetic passage he would 'choke up' and when there was a funny part, how he would laugh! These hours were precious, and I appreciated them; few people had the rare privilege that I enjoyed.

After an eight o'clock dinner, we would adjourn to the drawing-room. Rud's special playfellows, his dogs, were ready for their game. The childlike side of Rud was very strong, and it enabled one to understand his wonderful impersonations of children. 'Mike', I think, was his pet Scotty, and down on the floor in front of the fire Rud would throw himself, and the dogs always knew it was their hour. The rugs were turned up and a game of ball with Rud and his dogs was on the programme. What a room when the fun was ended! Then there would always be interesting discussion.

In the last few years of Rud's life he had serious stomach-trouble which eventually caused his death, but which was kept in check, he thought, by the French doctors. In those years the Kiplings spent most of their winters in Cannes. There Dr Brea,[1] the celebrated physician, looked after Rud with a never-tiring devotion. We saw the Kiplings daily, and Rud's patience and courage under the attacks of pain which assailed him from time to time, were almost superhuman. He would even joke when suffering agonies. Rud had always liked good food, but when he was obliged to forego certain dishes he would always pass them off with a joke.

In 1920 when we first went to Strasbourg to live, we sent him a *pâté-de-fois gras* for Christmas, and in a letter dated 25 January 1920 he writes to me 'a man's heart, as you know, is in his stomach, but in this particular case although my stomach rejoiced in the freshness of that *pâté*, and although Carrie and Elsie ate far too much of that *pâté*, as I told them, my heart rejoices much more in addressing for the first time a letter to Alsace, France. I was hoping and praying for the chance, and I am glad it is to you that my first letter goes.'

When in November 1935 we went to Bateman's we found Rud better than he had been for a long time. I rarely saw him when he acknowledged that he was ill. Our visit was a singularly happy one, and we expected them both out at Cannes for January. The morning we were to leave, Rud said to my husband, '*Mon Général*, I have called you General for so many years, may I call you Émil?' Alas, that was the last time that we ever saw our dear friend.

Rud never seemed to change, or really grow old. He had eternal youth, which bars all changes. When I last saw him he walked with the spring that he had when I first knew him. He never was really young-looking; he had such a look of wisdom. He naturally had some faults, but in all the years that I knew him it would be difficult for me to name one. Perhaps he was not always diplomatic in his veiled allusions to some highly placed people, but truth, loyalty and patriotism surrounded the flame of genius burning in him. What can one say more? He never wished nor sought honours; in fact he declined them.

He was taken ill in London on a Sunday. Captain Bambridge telephoned to me the terrible news Monday morning: that an emergency operation had been performed, and that Kipling's condition was grave. Then followed three days of suspense, and on Thursday morning I received a wire saying 'He is making a splendid fight, if his heart holds out he may pull through.' But alas, he passed away on Saturday, 18 January 1936.

One day I asked Rud why he had refused the honours offered him. He said, 'I prefer to live and die just Rudyard Kipling.' Some months later, when I stood in Westminster Abbey, and saw the simple slab with 'Rudyard Kipling' on it, I felt that Rud had been right. The American writer who after Rud's death said that the works of Kipling would live as long as those of the Bible and Shakespeare, and that he would be known for generations to come as 'The Immortal', understood also.

NOTE

1. A misprint in the original text. Dr Bres was one of the doctors who treated Kipling during his long, painful, and complicated medical history. See Lord Birkenhead's *Rudyard Kipling* (London: Weidenfeld and Nicolson, 1978) p. 320.

Kipling Interviewed at Last*

Sherlock Holmes came back, and so also did the Brigadier Gerard,[1] and doubtless many other living and dead heroes of fiction. But Mulvaney,[2] whether or no he be dead already and Dinah Shadd's tears[3] dried, will never come back. So Mr Kipling recently declared to Mr Irvin Cobb, who has achieved the nearest known approach to an interview with the man supposed to be non-interviewable. Mr Cobb has been making his first journey to Europe, touching 'all the high spots in just two months' with the idea of writing a 'Cobb's Baedeker'. But 'Mr Kipling won't be in it at all.' Still, he visited Mr Kipling and heard many interesting things from him which Theodore D. Rousseau[4] has put into three columns for the New York *Evening Post*. He asked somewhat cautiously about Mulvaney, insinuating that that personage was not in the class with Huckleberry Finn and Henry Esmond – 'so rounded out and complete that no one thinks of meeting them again'. Mr Kipling replied,

Yes, to be the best of my knowledge – the best of my memory, I might say, Mulvaney is dead. The last mental picture I had of him was on the edge of a cut in India, where he was directing a gang of coolies building a railroad extension. There is no doubt that he was a bit seedy and down-at-heel. So I am sure that if he has not already passed away, he soon will, and *Dinah Shadd* will bury him.

No, he cannot come back. It won't do, you know. A character is born in your thought, and grows and is developed, and takes on virtues and vices, and becomes old, and then – well, just fades away, I take it.

And that is the way with Mulvaney. I couldn't revive him – I could only galvanise him. He would be a stuffed figure with straw for bowels and glass balls for eyes, and the people could see the strings I pulled him with. No, he is gone. . . .

* Unsigned article in *Literary Digest*, XLVII (27 Dec 1913) 1277.

On the point of Kipling's literary likes and dislikes we are told 'he doesn't care for the ultra-moderns of his craft in England', and his 'disfavour falls most heavily' upon one of them – 'perhaps the most widely known', says Mr Cobb, without mentioning Bernard Shaw. The new generation in this country have escaped him, but the mention of *Mr Dooley* brought a quick exclamation of praise:

'Ah, Dunne!' he said. 'There you have a great man – one of the greatest of the writers of English of this century! It is an extraordinary combination. There is an Irishman writing as an Irishman, yet if I were asked to pick four samples of literary achievement that most fitly typified the impulse and the humour of your American life, three of my selections would be from *Mr Dooley*.'

This from Kipling – with a reputation for being so chary with his praise – it was one of the surprises of the day to his visitor.

Kipling's description of modern war is a 'mathematical problem, with some of the aspects of a surgical operation by the highest paid specialists'. He sees 'no more romance or glamour'. On this theme he is interesting:

I have seen very, very little fighting in India. I wrote mostly of what I had been told. But I did see war in South Africa. I said to myself before I went out, 'I'll see the dash and get the rattling inspiration of it. I'll see charges, and thin red lines, and hear hoarse commands and stand silent and thrilled in that dread hush before the battle.'

But what a disillusion! The hush before the battle was like the quietness of surgeons and nurses before they go into the operating-room. Nobody galloped up on a lathered horse and fell unconscious after handing the general the long-waited dispatch. The general himself bestrode no charger, but sat in a comfortable camp-chair beside a neatly spread tea-table. You heard a few tick-ticks and somebody handed him a slip – the substitute for the dispatch – and he read it and drank his tea and said, 'Um-m-m, good. Workin' out just as I thought. Wire Binks to bring up that battery', etc., etc.

And all this method and precision and application of modern efficiency ideas makes the carnage that follows all the more ghastly. You don't know in advance just what is going to happen, you don't know how it happened; you just look at the dreadful dead men and the shrieking wounded men, and they seem to you like innocent bystanders who have got in the way of some great civil-engineering scheme and been torn and blown up.

The American Civil War Kipling calls 'the great epic of the Anglo-Saxon breed – more, it was the greatest epic in the history of mankind': 'And it hasn't been written – no, nobody has written it yet. It is not yet far enough in the past; you can't get the perspective. But it will be written, and when it is written as it should be, a master-work will be born.'

The talk from here fell away to pastoral affairs:

On a walk after lunch Mr Cobb remarked the number and the tameness of the pheasants and the little English robins.

'Ah, you know birds', said Kipling. 'I don't know birds so well, though I'm fond of them; but I do know trees. There are some good yews here. That one is said to be more than 800 years old. You'll know those – the sumach and the American dogwood and the goldenrod – I had them brought over. I love the sumach; it seems to me like the red Indian of the American forests. But I can't make it blaze here – it turns pale.

'I wish you would stay until after dinner', he went on. 'I'd like you to hear a nightingale that comes every evening to our garden. I'd like you to compare him with your mockingbird. Tell me about the mockingbird – what's he like?'

Mr Cobb said the Southern mockingbird was the troubadour of the woods, a licentious scoundrel, who left Mrs Mockingbird at home with the little ones and went serenading other bird-beauties – but withal, a fellow with romance in his soul, a true poet.

'Well,' said Kipling, 'I wish I could say as much for the nightingale. I know all the popular illusions about him, but the truth is, he's blackguard with a gift of music in his throat that he can't control – a noisy, swashbuckling blackguard of the garden. He comes here at night and he proceeds to abuse all his enemies for all he's worth. It's feathered profanity in a disguise of harmony, and he gets so worked up over it that he finally ends in an inarticulate gurgle.

'But I would like you to see a thrush crack a snail on a stone', said Kipling. 'I dare say you've never seen that. Well, it's most interesting. You see, when a thrush finds a stone that he likes, he brings all his snails to that particular stone, and he becomes so proficient that it takes just one crack to demolish the shell and lay the unfortunate snail bare for consumption. There's one thrush here that does it particularly well, and I know where his stone is, but I'm afraid we're too late for him.

NOTES

1. Étienne Gerard, a lieutenant and later a general, is a character in A. Conan Doyle's *The Exploits of Brigadier Gerard* (1899).

2. Terence Mulvaney, an Irish soldier, is the constant drinking and fighting companion of Stanley Ortheris and Jack Learoyd. He was first introduced in *Plain Tales from the Hills*.

3. Dinah Shadd is Mrs Mulvaney, appearing in four stories: 'The Big Drunk Draf' and 'Black Jack', in *Soldiers Three* (1888); 'The Courting of Dinah Shadd', in *Life's Handicap* (1892) (in which she cries 'like a sorrowful angil' at the sight of Mulvaney's bloody cheek), and 'His Private Honour', in *Many Inventions* (1893).

4. Newspaperman in Nashville and New York (to 1914); secretary to Mayor John P. Mitchell of New York during World War I, handling receptions for important visitors; later a banker for Guaranty Trust, and a leading figure in the American colony in Paris.

At Thomas Hardy's Funeral*

BLANCHE PATCH

It was rare in those days for a week to pass without Shaw's name bobbing up here and there. I should say that he grew indifferent to recurring references to what he was about: emphatically he resented those who were impelled to pry, and I can recall only two instances of people who did not want to meet him. One of them was a young lawyer, from the United States. 'You can tell Shaw', he said to me, 'that I am not one of those who want to see him', a reluctance which was probably mutual. Rudyard Kipling was the other who scorned GBS. When Shaw and he were pall-bearers at Thomas Hardy's

* *Thirty Years with GBS* (New York: Dodd, Mead, 1951) p. 132.

funeral in Westminster Abbey on 14 January 1928, Kipling, it is recorded, 'shook hands hurriedly and at once turned away as if from the Evil One'. They would not have shaken hands at all but for the ubiquitous Edmund Gosse who pushed forward and introduced them, which is just what anyone would have expected Gosse to do. GBS wanted to pair with John Galsworthy, but Kipling was alongside him, and Shaw said to me afterwards that he thought the arrangement was very bad stage-management as he was so much taller than Kipling. The difference in height may have added to Kipling's exasperation with ideas which he imperfectly understood. One thing which pleased Shaw at this service was the organist's fine rendering of the Funeral March from *Saul*[1]. . . .

NOTES

Blanche Patch (1879–1966) wrote *Thirty Years with GBS* as a record of her work as Shaw's secretary.

1. The Dead March in Handel's *Saul*, first performed in London in 1739.

A Conversation with Kipling on Conrad*

EDMUND A. BOJARSKI

One of the few areas of Joseph Conrad's life and work which remain almost completely unexplored by the literary historian is his relationship with Rudyard Kipling. Although both writers lived in the same vicinity for years, shared a pioneer passion for the automobile, and competed with each other for the favour of the reading public, there seemed to be few, if any, direct personal contacts between them.[1] In December 1885 when Kipling's first work, 'Quartette', appeared in the *Civil and Military Gazette* of Lahore, Conrad was the second mate aboard the *Tilkhurst*, a coal-

* *Kipling Journal*, XXXIV (June 1967) 12–15.

freighter docked in Calcutta. The Polish-born British merchant-seaman had evidently not as yet felt the urge to fictionalise his adventures – his first short story, 'The Black Mate', was still almost a year in the future – and it is unlikely that at that time the young second mate of the *Tilkhurst* came across this first work of the man who, ten years later, was to be his rival.[2] In a letter dated Christmas 1898, however, Conrad advised Mrs Karol Zagorski, a relative in Poland collecting material for an article on English literature, that 'Among the people in literature who deserve attention the first is Rudyard Kipling. . . . '[3] By this time Conrad, who was working on *Heart of Darkness*, had moved to Pent Farm at Stanford, near Hythe in Kent, not far from Kipling's home at Rottingdean. Conrad, hardly an avid reader of poetry, who 'seems to have had little interest in his British contemporaries and only to have read their books when the author was a personal friend',[4] evidently made an exception in the case of his famous neighbour. Earlier that same year he had written a defence of Kipling (and indirectly of himself) against Arthur Symons who criticised *Captains Courageous*[5] and *The Nigger of the Narcissus*.[6] The article, called 'Concerning a Certain Criticism', was submitted to *Outlook* early in 1898, but was never published.

Four years later the Kiplings moved to Bateman's (later renamed Welcoming House), their dream home on Pook's Hill in Burwash, but they were still practically within hailing distance of the Conrads at Pent Farm. It was from Welcoming House that Kipling wrote on 9 October 1906:

> Dear Conrad,
> What a book – *The Mirror of the Sea*![7] I took it up as soon as I arrived and sailed along with it until I went to bed. Certainly I recognised the description of the winds, which I consider almost as splendid as the description of the darkness in 'Typhoon', but I have read and reread it all and I thank you sincerely and gratefully. This ought to make an even more vivid impression on someone who has sailed in sailing ships than on me, and that's saying a lot.[8]

Conrad's reaction in a letter to Galsworthy gives an indication of the relationship between the two men: 'Kipling sends me an enthusiastic little note. The Age of Miracles is setting in! . . . The End of the World is at hand . . . '[9]

A much less well known Kipling assessment of Conrad and his work which has escaped the attention of Western Conradists was made in a conversation more than two decades later with one of Conrad's countrymen, a Polish linguist, diplomat, and literary essayist named Jan Perlowski.[10] Perlowski (1872–1941), like Conrad, was a ward of Conrad's uncle and guardian, Tadeusz Bobrowski,[11] and met Conrad in 1890 during the novelist's visit to Poland.[12]

In 1928 Perlowski served his government as a diplomatic representative in Madrid. One morning he was summoned to the telephone to be told by a familiar female voice, 'My father arrived yesterday. Please come over tonight. You will find only my father, my husband, and me.' The invitation was extended by the charming Mrs Bambridge, wife of a member of the British Embassy in Madrid and daughter of Rudyard Kipling.

That evening Mrs Bambridge introduced Perlowski to her father as one of Kipling's sincerest admirers, and Perlowski added that he did indeed ascribe great meaning, not only in the literary sense, to Kipling's work. The conversation soon turned to Conrad, and Perlowski was impressed by the generosity with which Kipling brought up and discussed the unusual talent which in recent years had been overshadowing his own work.

Speaking with quiet animation, Kipling began with the familiar observations on Conrad's language and style. 'When he spoke English,' he observed, 'it was sometimes difficult to understand him, but with a pen in his hand he was first amongst us.' When reading Conrad's novels, Kipling often wondered about the origin of some particular turn of phrase used by this foreigner, not encountered anywhere previously and not only reflecting a remarkably fresh thought, but in a thoroughly English way. Kipling thought that this was simply some 'substitution of his former personality', the replacement of Conrad's original personality by another. But this was true only in the sphere of language since in spirit, according to Kipling's conviction, Conrad had within himself nothing English. 'Reading him,' he said, 'I always have the feeling that I am reading a good translation of a foreign writer.'

Kipling then went on to clarify this idea, which was strangely synonymous with the impressions of many of Conrad's readers in Poland. Kipling believed that in addition to his enormous talent and unequalled technique, the exoticism of Conrad's soul was probably what attracted English readers. There is in the average

Englishman a complex of emotions suppressed by a puritan culture, and Conrad set free those suppressed emotions. His characters, masterfully drawn and understandable to the English reader, have an emotional temperature higher by a few degrees than is normal for the English. In their intensity, Conrad's characters usually move 'to the pitch of emotion', but since the gradual progression takes place virtually before the reader's eyes, even he succumbs to what is, for him, an unusual increase in emotion and 'getting red in the face', experiences sensations unknown until now.

'Have you noticed', continued Kipling, 'the countless types of people in Conrad obsessed by one idea or emotion? Have you observed to what intensity the specific feeling of fear and terror is brought in Conrad? That man must have suffered horrible nightmares himself. And love, too, is in his work of the most romantic kind imaginable. The English reader, outwardly unemotional, enjoys that sincere exaltation, just as every English-man enjoys Chopin's romantic music.' Perlowski listened, struck by this analogy from Kipling, who did not know a line of Polish poetry, but did know the greatest of Polish poets in melody.

Beyond that, in Kipling's judgement, Conrad's moral world was also non-English. 'In English writing', he said, 'one can obviously find anything, especially in these times when every author pursues originality. But Conrad was sincere. In the novel which he prized most highly of all his work and which is really his masterpiece, *The Nigger of the Narcissus*, we find attitudes foreign to our society. In this novel he is more akin to the Russians than to the English. His "purely humane" attitude toward that Negro does not suit the English spirit, which is Christian but not "humanitarian". This book might have been written by Maxim Gorky. Conrad's foreign spirit stands out even more clearly in another of his novels, equally excellent from the artistic point of view, *Lord Jim*. In its very fundamentals the novel has something distinctly non-English. First, it should be noted that in its foundations it is by no means, as some maintain, the internal drama of a man guilty of transgression and suffering the pangs of conscience. The real theme of the book poses the question of whether or not a man is responsible for his actions. Conrad expresses the view that under certain circumstances, that responsibility may be reduced to such a degree as to be almost non-existent. Undoubtedly Conrad has a point, and in specific instances that is how it really is. In general, however,' said Kipling, 'I would not advise Conrad to put forward such a thesis before any of our

English juries, which retain to the present our old Anglo-Saxon conviction that every man bears responsibility for his own actions.'

At this point the conversation turned to the autobiographical character of *Lord Jim*. Perlowski described Conrad's past in detail and Kipling laid down some restrictions. 'If', he said, 'the sinking ship which Lord Jim, one of the officers, left in a moment of some kind of obscuration of the spirit, is supposed to be Poland, then why, having discovered his error, does Conrad not return to the deck of the *Patna*? In the novel this was impossible. The ship luckily reached port and Lord Jim's return would have been of no use. But the Polish *Patna* remained in danger for many long years after the publication of the novel. Conrad could have corrected his mistake at any time, and yet he did not do it. It becomes obvious that there is a misunderstanding here, and that Conrad's novel is not autobiographical.'

NOTES

Edmund Bojarski, a dedicated Conradian (b. 1924), has been the manager of rare books in the Conradiana Bookshop, McMurry College, Abilene, Texas, and is an authority on several Polish authors. (In what follows, Bojarski's own notes are signalled 'EAB'.)

1. Not one of the major Conrad biographers describes a meeting with Kipling. [EAB.]

2. Gérard Jean-Aubry, *The Sea Dreamer: A Definitive Biography of Joseph Conrad*, trs. Helen Sebba (London: Allen and Unwin, 1957) p. 108. [EAB.]

3. Jocelyn Baines, *Joseph Conrad: A Critical Biography* (London: Weidenfeld and Nicolson, 1960) p. 144. [EAB.]

4. Ibid. [EAB.]

5. Serialised in *McClure's Magazine*, Nov 1896–May 1897, and in *Pearson's Magazine*, Dec 1896–Apr 1897; printed as a copyright edition in 1896, and in a trade edition in 1897.

6. Published in 1897.

7. Published in 1906.

8. Jean-Aubry, *The Sea Dreamer*, p. 249. [EAB.]

9. Ibid. [EAB.]

10. Perlowski (1872–1941) was educated in philosophy and classical studies before taking up an active career as diplomat in Warsaw, Paris, Berne, the League of Nations, Rome, the Holy See, Lisbon and Madrid. He contributed articles on Polish history to the *Petite encyclopédie polonaise*, edited by Esame Piltz (1916).

11. Member of the Polish land-owning nobility, whose *Memoirs* (1900) described Conrad's father as a 'brooding melancholiac, consumed by despair and religious mania'. He was Conrad's maternal uncle, and took over his guardianship in 1869, when Conrad became an orphan. He finally gave Conrad a reluctant

permission to go abroad, for reasons of health. See *Conrad's Polish Background: Letters to and from Polish Friends*, ed. Zdzislaw Najder and trs. Halina Carroll (1964).

12. Jan Perlowski, 'O Conradzie i Kiplingu', *Przeglad Wspolczesny* (Warsaw, 1937) *passim*. [EAB.]

Kipling at Home (1)*

DOROTHY PONTON

In the hot dry summer of 1911, I paid my first visit to Kipling's home.

Outside the little station of Etchingham, on the borders of Kent and Sussex, stood a one-horse vehicle which conveyed its passengers through the picturesque country-side to Burwash, about 4 miles west of the station. For three parts of the journey, the ground rose gently, then a sudden dip brought you to the outskirts of the village, where stood the Rector's house. A steep hill, skirted by primitive cottages on the one side and an old-fashioned inn (called 'Admiral Vernon') on the other, led to the village proper. At the top of the hill the road bore a little to the left; past another hill topped by the old church, and straight on through the village to the Bear Inn where the passengers descended. For a small sum the driver offered to convey me to Bateman's. A five minutes' drive brought us to the top of Bateman's lane, made conspicuous by a modern house, known as the 'Red House', and a less red letter-box let into the wall. Here the bus turned due south down a very steep and rough lane. On the right hand extended fields, with an orchard and an old house off the lane (called 'Little Bateman's') a spinney darkened the other side of the land. In the valley, but not quite at its foot, rose Bateman's, the Jacobean house of Rudyard Kipling. Beyond the lane it was a mere track, but a wider lane met it at right-angles and ran almost due east to Dudwell Mill Farm.

A dense yew-hedge screened the grounds from inquisitive eyes; an oak gate gave entrance to the flagged, beautifully kept lawns, which led to the massive porch, bearing the date 1634. Creepers adorned

* *Kipling Journal* ix (Apr 1942) 7–9.

the porch on either side and climbed to the windows of Mr Kipling's study.

A tug at the bell brought a grey-haired parlour-maid to the door. She led me across a large hall, paved with black and white squares, and ceilinged with oak and beam rafters; the walls had oak wainscoting and a vast arched chimney-piece occupied the west wall opposite the leaded-light windows. A massive draw-table, with carved legs and oak benches on either side, stood near the windows, and an oak cupboard against the south wall.

Passing under a stone doorway, opposite the staircase, the maid opened a door on the left and ushered me into the parlour, simply furnished in keeping with the character of the house. Opposite the parlour was a smaller room, used at that time as a school-room.

Just before passing under the stone doorway in the hall, a few steps on the right-hand side led up to a small room, used by Mrs Kipling for transacting business. It made an ideal little study, lined on three sides with book-cases, below which were roomy cupboards. At the other end of the hall, opposite the stone doorway, lay the dining-room, the walls of which were covered with Spanish leather. A little hatchway, hidden behind an oak panel, revealed the kitchen.

On ascending the stairs, the chief bedroom lay on the left of the landing. This room contained a fine old carved French bedstead and furniture to match. The room opposite the stairs served as Mr and Mrs Kipling's bedroom, and that on the right of the staircase led to Mr Kipling's study. This was a large room over the porch and hall. The main windows faced east, overlooking the front lawn and down the lane leading to Dudwell Mill Farm. The west and north walls were lined with bookcases, reaching almost to the ceiling, and here the author kept his collection of cherished books. A long table, facing the window, contained his writing-materials and favourite pipe-rack. A couch stood near the wide fireplace. A narrow passage, opposite the stairs, had a bedroom off the left and, at the end of the passage was another. Another flight of stairs led to a spare-room, and the rest were attics used for the domestic staff or for storage purposes.

Near the school-room door was a massive oak door leading into the grounds which faced south. The first thing that caught the eye, on looking straight ahead, was the beautiful lawn with its avenue of limes and at the end of the lawn, the flower-beds, quiet in colouring except for a sudden streak of vivid hue standing out from the rest. A

road flagged terrace, the cracks of which were filled in with tiny
erbs that wafted an odour of peppermint as you passed them, bore
o the right and faced undulating pastures beyond the garden. At
he end of this terrace a path ran to the right and left. That on the
ight went round the main house to two hop-kilns, converted into a
ottage where the gardener at this time lived. Later on a new
ottage was built for the gardener outside the garden, and the hop-
ilns were used as servants' quarters, with one room reserved as the
ecretary's office. Beyond the kilns the path broadened into a motor-
rive eastward, but continued in a northerly direction past the
arden sheds and into the vegetable garden.

The flagged path to the left of the terrace ran south along the edge
f the lawn, beyond which was the square lake and a glorious rose-
arden set about a circular pool. Continuing south, the path skirted
grass tennis-court, and was edged with borders of snowy
arnations. The flagged path ended abruptly at the river-bank, but
gravel path to the right continued along the bank, edged with
weetbriar, hazel, alder and spindle-trees. A few yards farther on
as a wooden bridge beside an old forked pear-tree, which crossed
he main stream; a few steps downwards brought you to another
ttle bridge, overhung with elder bushes; this crossed an arm of the
tream which fed the old water-mill, and was helped by the quiet
chug-chug' of a dynamo, to supply electric power to Bateman's. A
ow wooden gate separated the grounds proper from Park Mill and
ark Mill Cottage.

The old Mill House was a white wooden building of very ancient
ate; the part adjoining the stream was used as a store-place for
imber and other things necessary for repairing old buildings
ithout descending to the use of modern contrivances; the residen-
al portion was at that time occupied by the chauffeur and his wife.
ark Mill Cottage consisted of a converted hop-kiln used at this time
s the residence of the secretary and the governess, with a maid in
ttendance. A rough field occupied the frontage of these houses, and
it was the well – the sole supply of water. A wooden gate gave
ntrance to the rough cart-track which was, in fact, a continuance of
he main Bateman's lane.

The Dudwell, in the summer of 1911, was hardly more than a
rickle of water, and the stream looked innocent enough, but stormy
eather soon converted it into a rushing torrent, and the dusty lane
ecame a bog of Sussex clay. Even Bateman's itself was not immune
om invasion when the stream was in spate and Mr Kipling, on one

occasion at least, dashed from his bed in the dead of night to rescue
some valuable rugs from being submerged by the muddy water that
welled over the great hall like a lake of pea-soup. Part of the tennis
court disappeared into the stream after a storm, and its place was
later taken by a modern 'en-tout-cas' court which rather spoilt the
old-world look of that part of the garden.

When the river was in spate it made strange sobbing noises, and
the wind, rushing through the valley, often sounded like a woman's
scream. Legend attributes these sounds to a tragedy that occurred in
the neighbourhood during the reign of Queen Elizabeth. At that
time the place belonged to an iron-founder, Richard Moyes, a
widower with an only daughter. Among his workmen was a
Frenchman, Jean Crapaud, who fell in love with the daughter.
Moyes dismissed the man, but he would not leave the
neighbourhood. One night, when the river was in flood, Moyes
heard someone creeping downstairs. Finding his daughter's room
empty, he seized his sword and rushed towards the mill. There, on
the bridge, he found the lovers and, as he sprang at the Frenchman
with drawn sword, his daughter threw herself between them,
received the thrust and fell screaming into the river. Her body was
never recovered.

NOTE

In her years as governess to the children of Rudyard and Carrie Kipling, Dorothy
Ponton taught John mathematics, and Elsie Latin and German. After the Great
War, she returned to Bateman's as a secretary. Her small book *Rudyard Kipling at
Home and at Work* was privately printed.

Kipling at Home (2)*

DOROTHY PONTON

Between 1911 and 1913 the verses and chapter-headings of Mr
Kipling's prose works were collected in *Songs from Books*[1] and many

* *Kipling Journal*, IX (July 1942) 9–11.

of the short stories and verses written, which were later published in *A Diversity of Creatures*.[2] While the suffragettes were very active, Mr Kipling drafted his verses 'The Female of the Species'.[3] The suffragettes, as a body, objected to Mr Kipling's view on votes for women, and threats to burn down Bateman's reached him, but he quietly ignored them and pursued his own policy.

On the declaration of war against Germany in August 1914, Mr Kipling sounded a rousing call to arms in his verses, 'For All We Have and Are',[4] followed by the prophecy of the German moral collapse in 'Zion',[5] and a moving eulogy on the death of Earl Roberts when visiting the Indian troops at the Front. At the beginning of 1915 he visualised the mental sufferings of a sick German woman in 'Swept and Garnished',[6] followed by 'Mary Postgate',[7] which showed how an unimaginative English woman reacted against a German airman, who had fallen from his machine after dropping bombs on the village and killing a little girl.

After the loss of his only son (Second Lieutenant John Kipling of the 2nd Battalion, Irish Guards), who was reported 'wounded and missing' after the Battle of Loos in September 1915, Mr Kipling revealed, in some measure, his unspoken grief, in the verses, 'A Nativity',[8] and 'My Boy Jack'.[9] 'En-Dor'[10] uttered a stern warning to all who hoped to trace their lost ones by resorting to spiritualism and 'A Song at Cock-crow'[11] ruthlessly criticised the attitude of the Vatican towards atrocities committed by the enemy, as did also some of the 'Epitaphs'.[12] But through the gloom of those years, Mr Kipling always welcomed anything that lifted the pall for a moment and in 'A Recantation'[13] he praised the music-hall artists for their invaluable services in lightening the burden of the troops at the front by their entertainments. And when rumour attributed the manufacture of margarine from corpses, he electrified some friends by reciting the following lines:

> Charlotte, when she saw what Hermann
> Yielded up when he was dead,
> Like a well-conducted German
> Spread him thickly on her bread.

In 'Mesopotamia'[14] he severely blamed the Government for its lack of proper medical provision for the wounded in that part of the world, and in 'The Hyaenas'[15] he denounced the Press for its unfair criticism of Lord Kitchener[16] after his death in the *Hampshire*. His verses 'The Choice'[17] were written as a sequel to 'The Questions',[18] after America joined the Allies. In 'The Song of the Lathes',[19] he describes the feelings of a widowed munition-worker, and 'Gethsemane'[20] provides the poignant monologue of a soldier before he is gassed. In 'Justice'[21] he sternly warns the Allies against the folly of offering too-easy terms to the enemy. His verses, 'The Irish Guards',[22] outlined the history of the regiment his son joined, and he was already collecting material for his history of *The Irish Guards in the Great War*.[23]

In 1921 Mr Kipling was made a Master of the Sorbonne and in November the family went to France for a brief period. At the Sorbonne Mr Kipling gave an address entitled 'The Virtue of France',[24] and read a thesis before the assembly. At Strasbourg he delivered three speeches, 'A Return to Civilisation'[25] at the University, 'The Trees and the Wall'[26] at the University Banquet and 'Waking from Dreams'.[27]

During my secretaryship from 1919 to 1924, Mr Kipling's chief work was *The Irish Guards in the Great War*, a work of two volumes written as a memorial to his son. It was a work of poignant memories; for he knew many of the men who had been killed in action. Some of the material for the book was collected from the diaries of officers – mere scraps of paper stained with the mud of the trenches – or even flecked with blood.

The Irish Guards, 1st Battalion, returned to England in March 1919, and the 2nd Battalion were disbanded later. Some of the officers spent weekends at Bateman's, when they doubtless gave the author first-hand information of certain engagements at the front, which he skilfully wove into the fabric of the whole story. Often Mr Kipling would take his visitors along the banks of the Dudwell to fish. 'It's a strange thing,' he said, 'these war-worn youngsters, who didn't mind killing Huns, will blanch and squirm when the moment arrives to attach a worm to the end of a hook. "Please, would you mind doing it?" they will plead and look the other way.'

As the regiments were disbanded, many of the young officers – whose education had been interrupted by the call to arms – returned to college. Mr Kipling's verses, 'The Scholars'[28] and 'The Clerks and the Bells'[29] describe their attempt to return to the studies of youth. But with an occasional sidestep to create some vivid word-picture on some important current event, or to find relaxation in some lighter vein, Mr Kipling bent his whole genius to completing this masterpiece of the Great War. 'This will be my great work', he once said, and at another time. 'It is being done with agony and bloody sweat.'

He worked at it methodically and with the utmost care to get all details correct. His usual method of procedure was to study the subject closely and then set down, in his own inimitable style, the result of this study. This formed the original manuscript. When the typewritten copy was presented to him, he pruned or expanded it, and the next copy would be subjected to the same process till – perhaps not until four or five copies had been carefully revised – the finished article would be laid aside till a final revision of the whole was made just before publication.

His handwriting was sometimes difficult to decipher and he once accused me of making 'pot shots' at an undecipherable phrase. But, when I admitted my guilt and asked what I was to do about it, he smiled and said, 'Continue the pot shots. They sometimes give me an idea; anyway I like 'em better than blanks.' At another time he threatened to get a typewriter of his own – and did. But the work composed on it was, at first, much more undecipherable than the other. 'The beastly thing simply won't spell', he complained. One day he came stealthily to the office window and stood for a moment listening while I was typewriting. 'How did you know I was there?' he exclaimed, as I turned to see what he wanted. I pointed to a glazed calendar standing on the roll-top desk. 'Oh, I see!' he observed solemnly. 'A perfect reflector of all that goes on behind your back. I shall have to be more circumspect in the future. This visit was prompted by professional jealousy to discover your speed on that infernal machine.'

On one occasion a whole chapter of the Irish Guards history, which had been sent for a fourth revision, disappeared. Mr Kipling asked me to return it, and when I said it had already been returned there was some consternation. Nobody could find it and it was not until the library was being checked some weeks later that it turned up inside another book in Mr Kipling's study.

Every scrap of manuscript was supposed to be returned as soon as it had been copied, and Mrs Kipling jealously guarded these till the end of the year, when they were sent to London to be mounted and then placed in safe custody. One day – not long after the typescript had gone astray – Mr Kipling asked for the copy of a page of manuscript, which he supposed had been given to me. I denied having received it, and Mrs Kipling looked very suspiciously at me. 'Are you sure it is not in the office? I'm almost certain it was given

out', remarked Mr Kipling seriously. I asked what it was about and
then added, 'I have no recollection of receiving that piece'
whereupon Mr Kipling went off humming, as was his wont when
bothered. But, before I had been in the office half-an-hour, he
appeared at the window with a broad smile and placed the missing
sheet on the table. 'Here it is. I'd only forgotten to tear it off my
block. Sorry!' he said. 'Thank you. I'm glad it has been found',
replied I. 'And I'm glad I didn't say "Quite certain it was given
out"', added he.

In the early summer of 1922 Mr Kipling, as a member of the
Imperial War Graves Commission, went to visit the graves when
King George V made his pilgrimage there. Mr Kipling's verses,
'The King's Pilgrimage',[30] were published on this occasion.

By the end of the summer, the Irish Guards history was ready for
publication – at least almost ready. But when Mr Kipling handed it
over to be forwarded to the printers, Mrs Kipling chanced to turn
over a few pages and her keen eyes lighted upon certain alterations
in Mr Kipling's handwriting. 'But this is not the final copy, Rud',
she remarked. Mr Kipling raised his eyes to Heaven in despair, and
then glanced quickly at me. 'It's all right, Carrie,' he said after a
blank pause, 'I've made only a few alterations; they're quite
clear.'But Mrs Kipling was adamant. No typescript, bearing any
alterations in Mr Kipling's handwriting, must leave the house. He
bowed wearily to her wishes and the work was handed to me to be
retyped at high pressure. 'I appreciate your industry,' said Mr
Kipling when the last fifty pages were handed to him, 'and still more
the fact that you never turned a hair when the whole thing was
decanted upon you and you settled to the load.'

In August Mr Kipling, whose health had been troubling him for
some time, suddenly became desperately ill and was rushed to
London for an X-ray examination. On his return he kept to a special
diet, but though this restored him partially to health, he always
looked ill. 'Shall I always have this pain?' he once asked wearily, but
the doctors assured him all was well. During the autumn the proofs
of the Irish Guards history were corrected by dint of sheer will-
power. In November Mr Kipling became ill again, and as he was
then strong enough to bear an operation, this was decided upon in
the hope of effecting a cure. The operation was performed at the
Middlesex Hospital and he returned to Bateman's within three
weeks. Gradually he recovered some of his former vitality and,
while convalescing, wrote portions of 'Propagation of Knowl-

edge'[31] – a new chapter on the immortal *Stalky and Co.*, and 'The Janeites'[32] which was published later with other tales.

In February 1923, Mr Kipling attended the annual dinner of the Royal College of Surgeons and eulogised the skill of the surgeon in his speech 'Surgeons of the Soul'.[33]

When he was strong enough to travel, Mr Kipling went abroad with his family, and on their return in May 1923, turned his attention to writing short stories, many of which appeared later in the collection of prose and verse entitled *Debits and Credits*.[34]

NOTES

1. First published in England, Canada and the United States in 1912.

2. Published in 1917.

3. Kipling's 'The Female of the Species: A Study in Natural History' was published as a broadside in 1911, and in the *Ladies' Home Journal*, Nov 1911. It was collected in *The Years Between* (1919).

4. First published in *The Times*, and other British and American papers on 2 September 1914; separately in 1914; collected in *Twenty Poems from Rudyard Kipling* (1918).

5. 'The Doorkeepers of Zion' was first printed as one of the four octavo pamphlets *Destroyers at Jutland* (1916), and collected in *Sea Warfare* (1917).

6. First published in *Nash's Magazine* and *Century Magazine*, Jan 1915; collected in *A Diversity of Creatures* (1917).

7. First printed in *Nash's Magazine* and *Century Magazine*, Sep 1915; collected in *A Diversity of Creatures*.

8. First printed in *The Years Between*.

9. Published in *The Destroyers at Jutland* (1916); collected in *Sea Warfare*.

10. 'En-Dor' was first printed in the *Morning Post*, 20 Oct 1911; the *Ladies' Home Journal*, Nov 1911; collected in *The Years Between*.

11. Published in *Sea Warfare*.

12. Published in the *Morning Post*, 20 Oct 1911, and *Ladies' Home Journal*, Nov 1911.

13. Published in *The Years Between*.

14. Printed in the *Morning Post* and the *New York Times*, 11 July 1917; collected in *The Years Between*.

15. Published in *The Times*, 24 Oct 1918; collected in *The Years Between*.

16. Herbert Horatio Kitchener, 1st Earl Kitchener of Khartoum and of Broome (1850–1916), embarked on the cruiser *Hampshire* for Russia in June 1916. The ship struck a mine off the Orkneys and sank, drowning Lord Kitchener and many other people.

17. Printed in the *Daily Telegraph* and the *New York Times*, 13 Apr 1917; collected in *The Years Between*.

18. 'The Neutral' was printed in a pamphlet written for the Minister of Information (1916). Retitled 'The Question', it was republished in the same format, and then collected in *Sea Warfare*.

19. Published in the *Sunday Herald*, 24 Feb 1918, and the *Philadelphia Ledger*, 17 Mar 1918; collected in *The Years Between*.

20. Published in *The Years Between*.

21. Printed in *The Times*, 24 Oct 1918, and collected in *The Years Between*.

22. Printed in *The Times*, 11 March 1918, and collected in *The Years Between*.

23. The two-volume work, published in 1923, carried the full title *The Irish Guards in the Great War, Edited and Compiled from their Diaries and Papers by Rudyard Kipling*.

24. An address given at the Sorbonne, 18 Nov 1921; collected in *A Book of Words: Selections from Speeches and Addresses Delivered between 1906 and 1927* (1928).

25. An address given at Strasbourg University, 17 Nov 1921; collected in *A Book of Words*.

26. An address given at a banquet, Strasbourg University, 27 Nov 1921; collected in *A Book of Words*.

27. A speech at the High Commissioner's Luncheon, Nov 1921; collected in *A Book of Words*.

28. First published in the *Daily Telegraph*, 29 Jan 1919; collected in *Songs of the Sea* (1927).

29. Published in *Hearst's International Magazine, Nash's Magazine*, and *Metropolitan Magazine*, Feb 1920; collected in *Rudyard Kipling's Verse: Inclusive Edition 1885–1926* (1927).

30. Printed in the *New York Times, New York World* and *Boston Globe*, 15 May 1922; collected in *Rudyard Kipling's Verse: Inclusive Edition, 1885–1926*.

31. Printed in *Strand* and *McCall's Magazine*, Jan 1926; collected in *Debits and Credits* (1926).

32. Published in *Hearst's International* (May 1924); collected in *Twenty-one Tales* (1946).

33. 'Surgeons of the Soul', an address given on 14 Feb 1923, and collected in *A Book of Words* (1928).

34. The first English edition appeared in 1926.

Kipling at Home (3)*

DOROTHY PONTON

During the 1914–18 War, Mr Rudyard Kipling bought some Guernsey cows which supplied Bateman's with milk and butter. As the leases for land and farms on the estate expired, they were not relet (with the exception of an orchard farm on the north-west boundary of the estate), and Mr Kipling began to farm his own land and to employ a staff of farm-labourers.

Each time a Guernsey calf arrived, it was duly named by its mas-

---

* *Kipling Journal*, IX (Oct 1942) 5–7.

ter, its markings and all details about its pedigree were set down and forwarded to the Guernsey Herd Book for registration. Bateman's Baby, Bateman's Blizzard and Bateman's Bunting were successfully reared, besides others, and joy came to the heart of the author when they gained prizes at the Tunbridge Wells Cattle Show. The Guernseys were kept for dairy-produce only, and the farm accounts soon showed that these ladies cost far more to keep than their produce warranted.

A Sussex herd of red Shorthorns roamed the pastures and were fattened for market, and two handsome dray-horses worked on the farm to supplement the use of the mechanical appliances for farming. A poultry-farm was run, and I was much impressed by the fact that the farm accounts revealed that geese cost next to nothing to feed, and sold at a high price at Michaelmas-tide. The orchards, too, provided good crops, and the piggeries yielded very profitable litters.

A new cottage, which had been erected behind Park Mill Cottage, now housed the gardener, whose wife acted as dairymaid. An elderly cowman occupied the residential portion of the old Mill House. He was one of the Sussex breed – almost stone deaf, but alert, and accustomed to be astir long before his neighbours. He possessed a speech peculiar to his kind, and, in addition to this being almost unintelligible to ordinary mortals, I soon discovered that he found what others said equally unintelligible. Often Mrs Kipling gave him orders, which he assured her he understood perfectly, and as often he would tap at my office window two minutes later. 'They do tawk so funny up theer', he would explain apologetically. 'What do she want?' and he would sidle up and present a very large ear close to my mouth for information.

When a calf was born he always reported the matter thus: 'Tell the master and the missus, will 'ee, she be a beauty?' quite regardless of the sex. When the birth had been announced, Mr Kipling would tramp half a mile, or more, across fields to the farm where the baby lay. There it would be duly named 'Bateman's Butterpat', or whatever name seemed appropriate to the author, and its markings sketched on the form to be forwarded to the society which kept the Guernsey Herd Book. Rudd, the cowman, would get the calf to pose in suitable positions while Mr Kipling intimated, by nods and smiles, that the old fellow could take all the credit for the fact that the calf's star and saddle markings were perfect and that its switch was the finest he had seen.

In the summer of 1919 the Kiplings decided to enlarge their

Sussex herd, so a pedigree bull was introduced. He seemed a gentle creature, and was therefore allowed to roam at will in the pastures set aside for the Sussex herd. But one morning he fell from grace, for as Mrs Sands, the foreman's wife, tripped across the fields to feed the poultry, the bull tossed his head and began to follow her. As he approached, she thought he did not look so gentle after all, so she bolted inside one of the poultry-houses, much to the consternation of the feathered inmates. After the bull had playfully trundled the poultry-house along some distance, bellowing at intervals to accompany the shrieks of the woman and the cackling of terrified hens imprisoned therein, he began to get annoyed, and started charging in earnest. Some farm-labourers, attracted by this unaccustomed sight, approached, and then heard the din issuing from the poultry-house. After a struggle the bull was secured and condemned to solitary confinement.

Once, when the Kiplings were away for the weekend, a Guernsey and a Sussex cow, which had recently calved, met. The calf belonging to the Sussex Shorthorn had been taken away from her, and she cast envious eyes upon the little Guernsey calf. A fight ensued in which the Guernsey mother was nearly killed. The vet, summoned in haste, gave no hope of her recovery, and the foreman was in a panic over what the owners would say. His wife, however, pressed a flask of brandy into his hands, which I had given her permission to use in emergencies. Together they approached the exhausted cow and offered her the stimulant. She drank it all! 'And in half an hour she stood up on her own legs and ate some hay', announced the foreman gratefully as he returned the empty flask. 'And my man's better than any old vet', added the wife. I felt a little apprehensive that a relapse might occur, but the cow progressed favourably and made a perfect recovery. When the matter was reported to the Kiplings' return the foreman and his wife were complimented on their prompt action in saving the life of a valuable beast, and my flask was refilled with the finest cognac. 'Only to be used in emergencies, remember!' advised Mr Kipling.

The bullocks were reared for beef and sold at market. In the autumn all the fat stock was disposed of and a herd of sheep roamed the pastures from Michaelmas till Lady Day. Mr Kipling alluded to these as 'our paying guests', for the owners paid a fixed price per head for feeding, and they cost little to feed.

Such fields as were not under pasture grew crops. Bateman's Farm became a hive of industry when the crops were being gathered. Most of the harvesting was done by mechanically propelled machines, but the actual carting was always performed by the dray-horses, Captain and Blackbird, which took a keen interest in watching their winter stock accumulated and stored. Captain had a sense of humour, and a dislike for work, which sometimes led him astray. One hot autumn day, as I was returning to my office, I encountered Captain trampling idly about in the vegetable-garden, his loose harness jingling as he moved. Before I could shut the gate he politely pushed me aside with his nose and stalked ponderously into the lane. A shout from one of the farm-hands, from whom he had escaped during the dinner-hour, reminded him of labour, so he jogged cheerfully home to Dudwell, and tried to dispose of his harness by rolling in the very muddy pond much to the consternation of the geese and ducks. Soon the enraged farm-hand arrived. At the crack of the whip Captain stood up; but, finding that he was just beyond reach of the lash, and that his master had no intention of wetting his feet, he remained standing in the cool water till working-hours were over.

Blackbird was more sedate. She never shirked work, and she usually treated Captain's frivolities with complete indifference. When work was over, and they were loosed together, Captain always showed his delight by galloping off and then rolling on the grass. If Blackbird refused to join in this pastime, he would pretend to kick her. Once Blackbird retaliated with a real kick, and Captain was disabled from active service for a while. But he revelled in his ease, and, even when his leg was apparently restored, he managed somehow to run up a temperature when the vet paid his periodic visit. However, Mrs Kipling discovered a quick, and permanent, cure by ordering his diet to be severely restricted. When Captain saw only a wisp of hay in his manger, while Blackbird was munching oats, his temperature dropped to normal, and he was pronounced 'fit for work'.

At a time when, after Mr Kipling had not been very well, the family spent several weeks on the Mediterranean coast, he said to me before going away, 'You'll get on all right with the farm-hands if you treat the men as boys of fourteen and the women as younger in intellect', and I found the advice invaluable when petty feuds sprang up among the workers.

Meeting Kipling*

ROGER BURLINGAME

I was eight. All day I had been scrubbed in honour of the great man who was coming to dinner. A terrifically spotless sailor-suit had been ironed out for me. All day I was allowed to touch nothing that might contaminate me. The great man would be coming at eight o'clock.

It was not customary for eight-year-old boys to meet distinguished authors from England, and my father and mother had only decided on me as a bait at the last moment. The fact was that a few nights before Rudyard Kipling had been given a dinner in New York which had greatly distressed him. The house at which the dinner was given had been decorated at vast expense so that it looked like a jungle, even to the point, I believe, of monkeys jumping from limb to limb of the exotic trees. As he arrived on orchestra played 'Gunga Din'. I think it was also sung by a hired baritone. The report was that Kipling had left before the dinner was over with the briefest of words to his host and hostess.

My father, hearing of this, was determined that Kipling should not be embarrassed at our house. My father was his great friend and well knew of the author's shyness and his general dislike of social occasions. The inspiration my mother had was to put me in my sailor-suit at a point which Kipling could not pass without seeing me. Everyone knew his fondness for children and it was thought that when he entered in trepidation if he saw nothing but a child he would immediately be put at his ease.

So there I sat trembling on the tiny love-seat in the little room which in New York houses for some inexplicable reason was called the foyer. Suddenly the bell rang, the door opened, and the maid ushered Mr Kipling directly into the room where I sat. As soon as he

* *Kipling Journal*, XXVII (Dec 1960) 4–5.

saw me he shouted, 'Oh, there's the young 'un!' and sat beside me on the little couch.

I can't remember anything but his eyes. Those are as vivid before me now as if I were still looking at them there in the foyer. They were hypnotic. They seemed to see right into my innermost thoughts – whatever those might have been. I had rehearsed things that I was to say about the Jungle Books and the *Just So Stories*, both of which I knew almost by heart. But when he began to talk I said nothing. I think he talked about the British Navy. I think he talked about how boys of fourteen in England went into training to be naval officers. Suddenly he asked me what I wanted to grow up to be. I wanted to say 'a writer', but I could not bring myself to say it. I think I must already have been smart enough to look at myself, a little prig of a boy in a sailor-suit pretending that he wanted to be like the great man. I probably said something about a policeman or a locomotive-engineer or a sailor – some conventional answer. It did not really matter to me then. I was hypnotised as I have never been since. All I knew was that I was in the presence of a kind of superman, and I do not think that I have ever been deeply moved by his stories or his poems that some memory of this scene did not bring back to me.

I think it was only a day or so later that Kipling came down with the siege of pneumonia that almost killed him. I remember my concern during that time as I read the daily bulletins given out by his doctor.

There is only one more thing that happened between Kipling and me. As a child I had the usual fancy of an imaginary country of which I was the president or king or something of the sort. This country had an unusual economic system. The money grew on trees – but it wasn't as simple as that. The seeds of the money trees had to be processed by a factory which got a percentage and then turned the finished money over to the tree-owner. The factory was called 'The National and Four Buildings Money Seeds Association'. Evidently my father told Mr Kipling about this because a year after I had met him he wrote my father a criticism of the US Government's handling of the Philippine situation in these words: 'Seems to *me* your national money-seeds and Four building corporation is rather puzzled in its mind. If it doesn't annex the Philippines, it ought to be hung. I hate to see a job left half-finished.'

The letter hangs framed with Kipling's portrait in my study.

NOTE

William (Roger) Burlingame (1889–1967) was educated at Harvard and the Sorbonne; taught at Barnard College and Massachusetts Institute of Technology; and worked, at various times, for the *Independent* (New York), for the Office of War Information, and as a war-correspondent. His interests were primarily focused on biography (his book *Benjamin Franklin: The First Mr American*, 1955, was highly acclaimed), and the impacts of invention on American society. He wrote the history of the publishing-house of Scribner's.

Kipling Memories*

J. A. DE COURCY HAMILTON

I was brought up by my mother on Kipling's stories. Some of my earliest memories are of being read to from the *Just So Stories* and the Jungle Books, and as I grew older I was introduced to *Puck of Pook's Hill* and *Rewards and Fairies*. The Boer War was just coming to an end and I can remember the words and music of the Absent-minded Beggar. Kipling was at his most popular at that time, but he himself seems to have had his doubts about the flag-wagging, and expressed them in 'Recessional'. That poem was prophetic, though I do not think we ever became 'drunk with sight of power', and anyhow we have been forced by circumstance to surrender much of what we had.

By the time I was eighteen I had read nearly all that Kipling had published up to that date, and so, when I was sent to India in 1914, I felt almost at home both in Anglo-India and amongst the peoples of the continent. India was also in the blood, as many members of my family had served there before me.

My battalion was stationed at Quetta,[1] which immediately recalled to mind Jack Barrett.[2] But by then Quetta was a healthy station and typhoid no longer took a heavy toll on the troops. One of the local figures was Beatty of the India Police,[3] and it was often, and wrongly, alleged that he had been the original Strickland.[4] The

---

* *Kipling Journal*, xxx (June 1963) 11–12.

true prototype, I have always understood, was another famous policeman, Warburton of the North-west Frontier Province. There was also at that time in the station a lady who was rumoured to be the original Mrs Hauksbee's daughter; but again I believe this was entirely untrue. Later I was to go north and see something of the country described in the, to my mind, greatest (after *Kim*) of all Kipling stories, 'The Man Who Would Be King'. I never went through Mach on the Bolan Pass[5] where Billy Fish[6] of the story used to drive the tank-engine without thinking of that wonderful tale. On a visit to Lahore I saw the Zam-Zama gun on which the little Kim used to sit and play.

A few years later I found myself with my battalion in Kurdistan, building a road up through the Pai Tak Pass into Persia. We had heard rumours of a hush-hush expedition under the name of Dunsterforce being formed in Mesopotamia to go through to the Caucasus and parties of officers and NCOs passed in due course through us on their way to the Caspian. One day General Dunsterville and his staff arrived and spent the night in our camp. I knew enough of my Kipling to know that the General had already achieved immortality as the original of Stalky.

Some seven months later, after fighting in the Jangli country[7] around Resht, I was about to embark with a company of my regiment for Krasnovodsk[8] in Central Asia, when I received a summons to replace General Dunsterville's ADC, who had gone sick, and to go with him to Baku, where a small British force with Russian and Armenian allies was holding the town against a mixed force of Turks and Germans. The story of those operations has been told elsewhere. After our evacuation back to Enzelli (Pahlevi)[9] the General was recalled and, although he pretended to take it all in good part, he was visibly moved. 'I do not know', he muttered rather sadly, 'whether it is the port or senile decay.' Funnily enough, I found this phrase of his embodied in a later Stalky story. Before departing he gave me a large tin of tobacco, a most welcome gift in those parts. I did see him once again at some lecture in London, after the war.

After a spell at Cambridge I joined the Sudan Political Service and there again I found myself among scenes made familiar by Kipling. 'Little Foxes',[10] the story of the Gihon hunt, is well known and there were still people serving the Sudan Government who had known Hickman,[11] the Governor of Dongola, the original of the Mudir who imported the hounds from England. Fate also made me for four years District Commissioner of the Fuzzy Wuzzies,[12] who had caused so much trouble on the Red Sea coast in the early' eighties and who feature in *The Light that Failed*. They also, according to the poem, 'broke a British square'.

Kipling himself later visited Egypt and the Sudan and painted some brilliant prose pictures of the two countries in *Letters of Travel*.[13] He incidentally paid my service a somewhat ambiguous compliment by saying that its death-rate was only a little higher than its own reputation.

But my big moment came years later when I was on leave cub-hunting in Sussex. I had been invited over to lunch by a local land-owner who told me to come just as I was in my rat-catcher clothes. I drove up to the stately home in my disreputable car and was ushered in by a dignified butler. I greeted my host, who was a bachelor, and he immediately presented me to two of the other guests, who, to my astonishment and delight were Mr and Mrs Kipling. I sat next to Kipling at lunch and, as I had just come from the Sudan, I was, or so he made it appear, just his 'cup of tea'. He talked of nothing else and pumped me all through luncheon about my life out there. He said he was contemplating writing a story about a young district official who, being all alone, had trained his two servants and some of the police to play polo, and so made up enough players to make some sort of a game. He had also been invited to suggest names for the desert railway-stations between Wadi Halfa and Abu Hamed, which up to then had only been known by numbers. He thought they might be called after some of Kitchener's generals.

After lunch we were taken out to see the stables, but Kipling gradually drew me off into a walk about the gardens. He could not have been more agreeable, and talking to him one saw how he had managed to pick up other people's 'shop', which he had later himself distilled into his stories. The secret was, I am sure, that he himself was so sincerely interested, and therefore was able to draw out the best from the people he was talking to.

In Kipling's stories the expert will find some mistakes of fact – there is a bad one in 'Little Foxes', though I did not dare to tell him so. But this does not detract in any way from his genius. He was a great story-teller; and I fancy that in the latter part of his life when the drum-beating phase was over, and he himself had realised that some of his early idols had had feet of clay, he developed a depth of compassion and an understanding of all sides of human nature which have rarely been surpassed. He himself had experienced personal sorrows and knew how greatly common humanity is in need of pity and forgiveness.

NOTES

John Almeric de Courcy Hamilton (b. 1896) was educated at King's College, Cambridge, and served with the 4th Battalion Royal Hampshire Regiment (1914–19). He carried out several assignments in the Sudan, Iraq and Egypt, before retiring in 1957.

1. See p. 61, n. 10.

2. See 'The Story of Uriah', published in the *Civil and Military Gazette*, 3 Mar 1886, and reprinted in *Departmental Ditties* (1886). Jack Barrett is posted to Quetta from cool Simla. His wife mourns his early death – 'five lively months at least'.

3. Probably Major-general Sir Guy Archibald Hastings Beatty (1870–1954); served in India, France, Egypt and China.

4. Called by Angus Wilson 'Kipling's unconvincing Sherlock Holmes of all disguises', Strickland, connected with the Indian police, appears in several stories, and twice in *Kim*.

5. Mountain pass in Pakistan, between Sibi and Quetta in northern Baluchistan; about 60 miles long, and some 5900 feet above sea level.

6. Dravot and Carnehan, in 'The Man Who Would Be King', call one of the chiefs 'Billy Fish' because he looks like an old comrade who drove his big tank-engine at Mach on the Bolan in the old days.

7. 'Resht' is also spelled 'Rasht'. Pesht Resht is an industrial city, capital of Gilan province in north-west Iran near the Caspian Sea.

8. A city in south-central Asian USSR, in the Turkmen Republic, across the Caspian Sea from Baku. A fort was built here in 1717, but the city was founded later, in 1869.

9. Caspian port in Gilan, northern Iran, 15 miles north-west of Resht, noted for its naval base and royal palace. Built in the nineteenth century and called Enzeli; renamed Pahlevi, Pahlavi, or Bandar Pahlavi.

10. First printed in *Collier's Weekly*, 27 Mar 1909, and *Nash's Magazine*, Apr 1909. Collected in *Actions and Reactions* (1909).

11. Colonel T. E. Hickman, the first governor of Dongola province, the Sudan, imported foxes for hunting purposes in 1899.

12. The *OED*, which cites Kipling as one of its authorities, defines the term as 'a soldier's nickname for the typical Sudanese warrior, from his method of dressing his hair'.

13. Published in England and the United States in 1920.

The Unfading Genius of Rudyard Kipling (2)*

ARTHUR WINDHAM BALDWIN

It is only four years since I addressed the Kipling Society in this building, and I must say I was under the impression that that would last you and me for the duration. Unlucky circumstances, however, have dictated that I should be put up to speak again this year to propose the undying toast. None the less, I do feel honoured at being given a second chance, and my wife and I are most grateful to the Committee for having invited us to be your luncheon guests today.

Those of you who were kind enough to listen to me before may have wondered how much I really knew of Kipling's works. I must tell you at once: far too little. Don't be deceived by my occasional quotations. There are wide gaps in my knowledge, which can very soon be spotted; and that is why I walk – or talk – pretty warily in company such as yours, and keep as much as possible to what I do know a little about: that is, the family. Please forgive me if my address is rather discursive: it seems to compose itself in that way.

You will perhaps understand why it did, when I tell you that (for some reason unknown to me) last December a gentleman (also unknown to me) asked me if I would write three or four thousand words on Kipling's father, for a book by many contributors to be called, I think, *The World of Kipling*. Having agreed to do this, I found that I knew very little indeed about John Lockwood Kipling – according to his son, who didn't use words vaguely, 'a marvellous man' – and, if I were to make any sort of showing, I should have to read and travel and note and think a great deal more than I'd bargained for. I won't bore you with fine details of my searches and excursions, but, as you may suppose, I picked up quite

* *Kipling Journal*, XXXVIII (Dec 1971) 4–9.

a hotch-potch of material, and was provoked to quite a few traffics and discoveries, guesses and conclusions.

After a most helpful visit to Miss Punch at our Society's office in Northumberland Avenue, I went to Yorkshire, root-land of the Kiplings; there I found the Methodist school where John had been educated – and, incidentally, another of my great-uncles, the Revd Frederic Macdonald, too. At that pious academy they still preserve what had always been thought to be one of John's exemplary reports. *Was* thought; until I discovered that, from the date on it, it was in fact that of his younger brother, Joseph. The subjects taught in those days were formidable: Greek, Latin, French, English, Arithmetic, Algebra, Trigonometry, Mensuration, Euclid, Drawing, Scripture, Conference Catechism, Evidences of Christianity, Scriptural Antiquities. And I thought of the influence of the Bible language on Rudyard Kipling's writing, and, although he had been schooled at Westward Ho!, how early he had absorbed the Scriptures at the hands, among others, of his loving grandmother, Hannah Macdonald of Bewdley. Have you observed, for instance, that the modern-sounding phrase recurring in the poem 'Boots' – 'There's no discharge in the war' – comes practically straight from the book of Ecclesiastes, chapter 8, verse 8? Perhaps it's perfectly well known; but not to me, until I noticed it a year or two ago.

I went to Burslem, where John had worked, as a young man, at pottery; and I failed to find where he had lodged. But I learned that his sketches were all signed 'JK' – not the familiar 'JLK' of his book illustrations. I went to Somerset House for his birth-certificate; and there I learned that he had not been named Lockwood at all, but plain John. I went to the South Kensington Museum, now called the Victoria and Albert, where he had done much important work as a designer and architectural sculptor. I found absolutely no written record of him at all, either there or at any other office in London where I was told such information might be stored. I went to St Mary Abbott's Church, Kensington, to inspect the marriage-register of 18 March 1865 (when an older church had occupied the site), and I read his careful signature, 'John Lockwood Kipling', and realised that his self-bestowed second name had now been established. And I thought it strange that John, the father, had chosen to *add* a name to his baptismal one, and that Rudyard, the son, had chosen to *subtract* one of his: Joseph, as I am sure you know. And, looking at that wedding signature, as I have at many of his autographs before and since, I noticed that the initial 'J' was given an especially ornamental twirl that day; and I remembered how Rudyard's many signatures also would vary according to his fancy. Has anyone, I wonder, ever drawn attention to the differing styles of the 'D's of Rudyard and of the 'P' and even the 'G' of Kipling? I don't think my own signature varies. Does yours? Trifling. I know; but rather odd, isn't it? Indicative of the artist, perhaps.

I went to admire the Indian rooms at Bagshot Park and at Osborne House; and after that I was given permission to look at the relevant royal letters and journals in the Windsor Castle archives, where, among references to John's work, I was pleased to read that when he was in India the Duke of Connaught had first supposed Mr J. L. Kipling's name to have been Mr Tippling. I tell you I've lived this year in quite a Kipling dream; and I've enjoyed it. There's nothing like research for generating shocks, even what is known as serendipity, which is finding useful things you were not looking for. Only, of course, you *must* do all the work yourself, because to delegate it is to risk missing too much.

One Sunday, this spring, after Matins in the village church, where I live, our lay reader took me aback with the information that Lorne Lodge No. 4, Campbell Road, Southsea – Kipling's House of Desolation – was at present owned and occupied by a cousin of his, and that she would be very pleased to show me the place any time I liked. It didn't take me long to accept *that* invitation. And there I saw the bedroom that must have been shared with Harry Holloway, the bully boy; and the street along which had walked a very small child, with his smaller sister trying to tear off the cruel letters LIAR which had been stitched on to the back of his coat. And I reflected that it was the very centenary of the year when my great-aunt Alice – Mrs Bambridge's grandmother – that's why we are second cousins – had taken train from Bewdley – the precise date was 13 October 1871 – with Ruddy and Trixie and had left them with Mr and Mrs Holloway.

All of us who care about the heart of Rudyard Kipling must have worried over this period of his life. I know from my readings that he wasn't easy to manage. How, with his Indian upbringing and his phenomenal spirit, could he have been? I am fortunate in possessing letters and diaries written by my grandmother, Mrs Alfred Baldwin (Louisa, a younger sister of Mrs John Kipling's), and by their mother, my great-grandmother, Mrs Macdonald. I find there that, when he was staying with them for months in 1868 – before he was three years old – he was indeed a handful. His tantrums, or would a mad purist say 'tantra'? – were awful. Here is Mrs Macdonald's verdict: 'Ruddy, after being sweet and pleasant for a little while, screamed horribly just before leaving. . . . I cannot think how his poor mother will bear the voyage to Bombay with an infant' – that's Trixie – 'and that self-willed rebel. I hope his father will train him better.' He must have done, for on returning to England in 1871 at the age of five and a half the boy appeared to be much improved, except perhaps for this (and I quote): 'Ruddy, having no little companion, talked me almost to death. He was very disorderly while his parents were here, but he behaved much better when they were gone.'

Grandmother and grandson wrote to one another from Bewdley and Southsea – letters both ways must have been previewed by pseudo Auntie Rosa Holloway – and there is no hint of trouble in the diaries. After the child had been a year at Lorne Lodge, and had spent some of his holidays in Worcestershire, I find: 'Ruddy was fetched back to Wilden'[1] – that's where his younger cousin Stanley lived – 'today. We were sorry to part with him.' Improved, do you think, or broken, by Mrs Holloway? That boy wasn't going to let on. There are those, I know, who feel sure that the suffering described in 'Baa Baa Black Sheep' and in *Something of Myself* has been exaggerated. I believe that we all subconsciously desire to think so too. But what I say to those who insist on that assumption is: 'Have you ever yourself been bullied, systematically and for a long time?' Those who have not been so treated can have no real understanding of it. Children's feelings can be extraordinarily intense. I am tempted now to say 'Hands up, those who contemplated murder or suicide before the age of ten.' But I won't.

I proceed now on a happier note, with two or three memories of the Kipling–Baldwin relationship. I have been asked to comment on the suggestion that one of my father's most pungent phrases from a political speech originated with his cousin; and it may be that some have even searched Kipling's works for evidence. The phrase I'm referring to is 'power without responsibility', etc. This, unlike many an attribution of authorship, happens to be true, and I merely amplify it, if only (as they say) for the record, as told me by my father. This is the way of it. 'In the days when everybody started fair, Best Beloved. . . . ' (Isn't that a perfect beginning to a political tale? Who knows which of the Just So Stories[2] opens with it?) Or one might use another Just So beginning: 'In the High and Far-Off

Times. . . . '³ Kipling was attracted by the charm and enthusiasm of a rich young Canadian imperialist whose name was Max Aitken,⁴ later to become Lord Beaverbrook. They became friends. When Aitken acquired the *Daily Express* his political views seemed to Kipling to become more and more inconsistent, and one day Kipling asked him what he was really up to. Aitken is supposed to have replied, 'What I want is power. Kiss 'em one day and kick 'em the next'; and so on. 'I see', said Kipling. 'Power without responsibility: the prerogative of the harlot throughout the ages.' So, many years later, when Baldwin deemed it necessary to deal sharply with such lords of the Press, he obtained leave of his cousin to borrow that telling phrase, which he used to some effect on 18 March 1931, at – I am pretty sure, for I believe I was there – the old Queen's Hall in Langham Place.⁵

Whilst on the subject of integrity, I should like to digress by recalling a bizarre test of character to which Kipling was subjected very early in his career as a journalist. Professor Carrington – and may I say how sorry I am that he could not come to our luncheon this year? – refers to it in the biography. The tale was first told by Kipling in a letter to his aunt, Edith Macdonald, the day after the event. He had not then been sixteen months in Lahore, and was only just eighteen years old. He recounts how he was invited by an old Afghan chief to call upon him. This khan, or *sirdar*,⁶ as he was styled, was under not very strict detention by the authorities in a house somewhere in the city, and was most anxious to be released to go back to his wives and women at Kabul, supposing that a favourable mention of him in the pages of the *Civil and Military Gazette* would have more effect even than an appeal to the Lieutenant-governor himself. The conversation was carried on in flowery Urdu, and the whole letter is enthralling to read. It is enough to mention that Kipling was shown successively three objects of a man's desire that were to be his for the taking, so only that he might print the few words required. The first temptation was a bundle of currency notes to the tune of about £1300; the second was a beautiful Kashmiri girl; and the third, which he says he did find hard to resist, was the pick of three among seven of the most beautiful horses he had even seen. I will quote the conclusion in his own words, fresh as the day that they were written, on 2 February 1884:

> I am so thoroughly indignant with the old beast that I resolved to inflict myself upon him for a time till I sobered down. When I had

smoked out one pipe, drunk my coffee and talked oriental platonics with the Kashmiri I rose up to go and my host didn't attempt to hinder me. He had lost about three cups of coffee, one smoke and about a couple of hours of time (but that didn't count) and had heard some plain truths about his ancestry. Of course, I couldn't do anything for him – though his case is a hard one, I admit, but I can mention the subject to Wheeler, and he can, if he likes, take notice of it, so that I shan't be concerned in the affair. When I mounted my old Waler[7] (he *did* look such a scarecrow) I found that beneath the gullet-plate of the saddle had been pushed a little bag of uncut sapphires and big greasy emeralds. This was his last try, I presume, and it might have seriously injured my brute's back if I hadn't removed it. I took it out and sent it through one of the windows of the upper storey where it will be a good find for somebody. Then I rode out of the city and came to our peaceful civil station just as the people were pouring out of church – it seems so queer an adventure that I went and set it down and am sending you the story thereof. I haven't told anyone here of the bribery business because, if I did, some unscrupulous beggar might tell the Khan that *he* would help him and so lay hold of the money, the lady or, worse still the horses. Besides I may be able to help the old boy respectably and without any considerations. Wasn't it a rummy adventure for a Sunday morning?

And, we might add, a not ignoble epitome of British rule in India?

After that interlude I return to my old home and generation in England between the two world wars. I think I spoke last time about Rudyard Kipling's gentleness and patience and sense of fun. He never demurred when I, as a schoolboy, used to ask him to sign one of his books which I might have been awarded as an examination-prize. Once, I remember hearing my tutor at Eton, a very learned man, speculate on the meaning of the title *Rewards and Fairies*.[8] He wondered whether the word 'reward' meant what it seemed to mean, or whether it was perhaps pronounced 'ree-ward' and was some archaic sprite or gnome. I silently resolved to enquire of the author next holidays. The answer I got wasn't entirely satisfactory to my ignorant mind. Didn't I remember Corbet's[9] 'Farewell, rewards and fairies?' I suppose I gracelessly mumbled something and crept away abashed; and it wasn't until years afterwards that I discovered Corbet and the very simple clue in the last two lines of the verse:

Yet who of late, for cleanliness,
Finds sixpence in her shoe?

Rollicking games we used to play in the evenings on the billiard-table: games like 'Slosh' and 'Pots and Cannons', exchanging the while quips in an affectedly laborious dog-French, at which Kipling was, of course, particularly ingenious. Once, and I think only once, we persuaded the elders to join us in a paper game. Even my father, who had long lost most of his appetite for such frolics, took up his pencil. It was a kind of (what was called) 'Consequences', but done in the form of a novel. You have to write a passage, fold the paper over leaving one or two words visible, then pass it on to your neighbour to continue. Kipling's opening lines in one of these rounds were masterly. After fifty years I can still quote them: ' "It's a perfect Hell of a night", pouted the Duchess, unfastening her gaiters.'

On another light-hearted occasion I remember him propounding a theory that, since it was clearly impossible for one man to have written all his widely varied works, it was obvious that they must have been composed by a syndicate operating under the dubious name of Rudyard Kipling. This line of conversation was very appealing to a lad like myself, and I was keen to develop the theory in some breadth. However, some interruption came and put an end to it; but I have often thought since that someone possessed of the peculiar talent of, say, the late Ronald Knox[10] might work the idea up into a good phantasy.

So much for these happy trivialities of long ago. I am going to conclude with something quite short but more substantial; and that is a four-line eulogy in verse which Kipling wrote one Christmas for our family Prime Minister. When I spoke to you before, I alluded to it as having been framed on a wall of the library at Astley Hall, but always cursed myself for having been so foolish as never to have written it down nor got it by heart; since after my father's death it had been sold, I think to America, where so many of our Kipling letters have found their way.

It is that kindest of men, our former President, Mr Harbord,[11] whom I have to thank for procuring a photographed copy for me to keep, and for that I can't express my gratitude warmly enough. Undated, the lines are written in holograph on Astley Hall writing-paper, which, with the help of the old visitors' book, gives me authority to put the date as 1924. That politically, was the year that

Baldwin returned to power nine months after he had been defeated for the first time by Labour under Ramsay MacDonald.[12]
I'll read them.

> To him who lost and fell – who rose and won.
> Because his aim was other than men's praise –
> This for an omen that, in all things done,
> Strength shall be born of unselfseeking days.
>
> RK

I make no comment beyond saying that both the subject and the author shared the same standard of honour and always understood one another perfectly. That is why the lines are so true. Marvellous men, both.

I want you now to rise and drink with me the toast: 'TO THE UNFADING GENIUS OF RUDYARD KIPLING.'

NOTES

See p. 306, note on Baldwin. This essay is the text of a speech given at the Kipling Society Luncheon, 5 October 1971.

1. Ecclesiastical village and seat $1\frac{1}{2}$ miles north-east of Stourport, Worcestershire.

2. 'How the Leopard Got His Spots', first printed in the *Ladies' Home Journal*, Oct 1901; collected in *Just So Stories for Little Children* (1902).

3. 'The Elephant's Child', first printed in the *Ladies' Home Journal*, Apr 1900; collected in *Just So Stories* (1902).

4. During World War I (probably 1916) Lord Beaverbrook acquired control of the London *Daily Express*; in 1918 he founded the *Sunday Express*. William Maxwell Aitken, 1st Baron Beaverbrook (1879–1964), achieved distinction as a British financier, newspaper-proprietor and Cabinet minister.

5. This is the curving northern continuation of Regent Street. Until destroyed by bombs (1941), Queen's Hall was London's principal concert-hall. Promenade concerts, for the most part conducted by Sir Henry Wood from August to October over a forty-five year period, were very popular. Rudyard and Caroline Kipling were married in All Souls', Langham Place, 18 January 1892; Ambrose Poynter stood for Rudyard, Henry James for Caroline.

6. *Khan* means 'lord' or 'prince'. The title is commonly given in Central Asia or Afghanistan to rulers or officials. *Sirdar*, a Persian word, denotes a military chief, and in the late nineteenth century was given as a title to the British commander-in-chief of the Egyptian Army.

7. A horse imported from Australia, especially from New South Wales (OED).

8. Published in London and New York in 1910.

9. Richard Corbet (1582–1635), Bishop of Oxford and Norwich, wrote amiable and occasionally enthusiastic satires. 'Fairies Farewell' is characteristically

fanciful, in *Certain Elegant Poems Written by Dr Corbet, Bishop of Norwich* (1647).

10. Ronald Arbuthnot Knox (1887–1957), Roman Catholic priest and trans-lator of the Bible (completed in 1955), wrote Greek and Latin verse at Oxford that won prizes, a number of literary parodies, detective stories, and fantasies such as *Let Dons Delight* (1939).

11. As President of the Kipling Society, R. E. Harbord assumed responsibility for editing and collecting contributions to *The Reader's Guide to Rudyard Kipling's Work*, which appeared in sections between 1961 and 1972 (Canterbury: Gibbs and Sons). Author of *A Reader's Guide to Rudyard Kipling's 'Just So Stories for Little Children'* (1955), and editor of G. P. L. James's *The Royal Family Orders, Badges of Office, etc.* (1951).

12. James Ramsay MacDonald (1866–1937) began as a Fabian (1886), and helped organise the Labour Party. His opposition to the South African War and his later argument that Great Britain was wrong to enter World War I led to distortion and misinterpretation of his views. He formed an all-party government in 1932, during a financial crisis. In 1935 he supported rearmament.

Bateman's*

RUPERT CROFT-COOKE

When I was eighteen years old, Victor Neuberg,[1] the eccentric owner of a hand printing-press, published some verses of mine about Sussex and I sent a copy of the book to Rudyard Kipling. His was the Great Name in English letters and I was still a slave to superlatives.

It is not easy to explain now what he meant to my generation. We were born too late to watch his first comet-flights across the skies or to hear the jealous forebodings of eclipse when the Boer War was held to have demonstrated his archaism.

We had learned his poetry, and read his stories in childhood and although we had heard 'jingoism' and 'outworn imperialism' attributed to him, as we had heard 'Fabianism' and 'vegetarianism' shouted after Shaw, we whose boyhood was passed during the First World War were not generally a politically-minded breed and failed to see the relevance of these catcalls. We were mesmerised by his fame and his extraordinary public standing.

* *Kipling Journal*, xxx (June 1963) 5–10.

His name rarely came into our discussions or lists of 'favourite authors' as the names of Compton Mackenzie,[2] John Galsworthy,[3] Maurice Hewlett,[4] and Joseph Conrad[5] came, for he was beyond such discussion; his temples were already built, and his harshest critics had exhausted themselves.

It was not fashionable or audacious to decry him, still less to praise.

Except for Thomas Hardy, his senior by twenty-five years, he was the only living writer considered already 'a part of English literature'. He was moreover 'a part of English life' and the name of no writer since his has permeated the whole of it, has been as familiar to the near-illiterate as to the learned.

With all the media of publicity which are ours today – television, radio, the cinema and newspapers which count their circulation in millions – we cannot produce a writer with a name one half as familiar as was that of Kipling in his lifetime, though his books were never printed in cheap editions. It may not be important, it may be irrelevant to a consideration of his merits (though I do not think it is), but it is a historical fact of some interest.

We have no literary legends, no pilgrims like those who once searched Putney Common[6] for a sight of Swinburne or looked up at the window in Ebury Street[7] behind which George Moore might be standing on his Aubusson carpet, or took the train to Rye to see the home of Henry James.[8] But Bateman's, Burwash, was something of a shrine in the 1920s.

Perhaps my own hero-worship was simply that of a young man for the head of the profession he wanted to follow. It was certainly not based on any very intelligent understanding of what Kipling represented or what he had achieved. It may have had elements of snobbery, of personal ambition, of curiosity. I do not know now, but I remember the morning on which I received his acknowledgement of my book for it seemed to me the most momentous of my life.

It was a conventional letter, though there were things to be noticed about it during my countless re-examinations of it. A very small representation of a telegraph-pole and another of a railway-engine indicated telephone and station, a device common enough today but then seeming vastly original. The famous address was dye-stamped in discreetly pretty type. The letter was typewritten, but signed. It was headed *Private*, a precaution which I did not understand but vaguely appreciated.

This was its wording:

Dear Mr Croft-Cooke,

Let me thank you heartily for your *Songs of a Sussex Tramp*, specially for the Sonnet on 'Old Hastings' which I love. I envy you the beautiful printing of the volume, always excepting the linked double 'O's which seem to me to make the eye stumble.

With every good wish,
Sincerely yours,

Rudyard Kipling

I was not long in following this up with a request for an interview, since another note is dated 5 October.

I find I have a free afternoon Tuesday next (10th) and should be glad to see you if you care to come over.

An exchange of telegrams followed, in which I explained that I was teaching in a preparatory school at Sevenoaks[9] and could not reach Burwash till five, and was told by a secretary that this would be all right.

There remained four days of anticipation, and I remember them well. First I took the astonishing news to an old friend and counsellor named Douglas Blackburn,[10] a ripe-witted novelist who after a long and adventurous life, chiefly in South Africa, had found a pleasant backwater in Tonbridge,[11] where he lived by writing for the local paper. He had known me since my childhood and listened to my news with all the interest and seriousness I could ask.

'You keep these letters', were his first words. 'They'll be worth a fortune, my boy. Kipling never signs his name if he can help it. His autograph alone is rare.'

Blackburn retained his habit of exaggeration to the end of his life.

'And make a note of everything he says', he went on. 'Keep it in your mind, and write it down when you get home. Don't forget, now. It's a big privilege you've got. A big privilege. Kipling's almost a recluse. Never sees anyone. Press can't get near him.'

'Yes, I will', I promised.

'It's Sussex that's done it', he said truthfully but unflatteringly. 'The word Sussex in your title. That must have got him. He loves Sussex. You stick to Sussex when you're talking to him. Never mind Kent.'

He looked at the letters again.

'Yes, Sussex. Old Hastings. Make the most of your chance, my boy. Not many of your generation ever see him. Legendary figure. One day you'll tell your grandchildren.'

Douglas Blackburn's view of literature and men of letters was of his time. 'There were giants in the earth in those days.' A writer himself, with a dozen books behind him, one or two of them successful and well written, he saw Kipling as Tennyson's contemporaries or Thackeray's saw their laureates. He did not discuss Kipling as a critic might have done, did not mention his political bias or analyse that curious trick of 'getting his own back' on somebody or something which can be found in so much of his work. He was concerned chiefly with Kipling's place in the oligarchy – a vulgar way of looking at it, I suppose, but not an unusual one at the time, and very much my own.

I must have told everyone I knew about my appointment for the following Tuesday, particularly the customers in the private bar of the Crown Hotel.

'So you're going to see Rudyard Kipling', said Robinson, the landlord. 'He comes through Sevenoaks sometimes in his Rolls-Royce. He once stopped here for lunch.'

'You tell him', said a quiet, podgy man of forty, 'that Captain Smithers' – I forget the name – 'sends his kind regards.'

'Do you *know* him?

The man smiled.

'He'll remember me. Remind him I once gave him a cup of tea. He'll remember.'

Everyone discussed it.

'You going on that old motor-bike of yours?'

'Yes.'

'Make sure it gets you there. You keep the main Hastings road as far as Hurst Green,[12] then turn right. You can't miss it.'

I did not ask myself what I should do if I lost the way, if the motor-cycle broke down (more than a possibility), if I had a puncture, if the weather was stormy. It seemed to me the most important thing in life that I should reach Bateman's by five o'clock, yet I planned this hazardous journey without a fear, without a doubt. I still had a child's faith that nothing dire could ever happen to me.

The distance was 25 miles, but to cover this in one hour, on a motor-cycle made before the First World War, would not be easy. Signposts were 'finger-posts' and chancy things at that, while main roads were not easily distinguishable from minor ones. The main Hastings road which I had been told to follow was not then like a railway track from which it was impossible to stray, and I took at least one wrong turning. But it was just five when I reached Burwash and breathlessly asked for Bateman's. The way to it was still 'an enlarged rabbit-hole of a lane' as Kipling recalled it when, fourteen years later, he described in *Something of Myself* his first finding of 'The Very Own House'.

Bateman's is now a Kipling museum, the last shrine to be accorded to a writer after his death (unless one counts the attempt to make one of Shaw's ugly little villa), and perhaps the last that will be accorded, at least in the foreseeable future.

It seemed very large, old and noble as I approached it on my stuttering motor-cycle, a massive Elizabethan house built in grey stone with mullioned windows and warmly brick-red tiles. There were stacks of fine brick-built chimney pots and the front was broken by an obtruding porch with two storeys over it culminating in a weather-beaten stone ball at the apex. There was a flagged path leading from the wrought-iron gate to this porch while to left and right was unbroken lawn. It was growing dusk as I marched up this pathway with false audacity.

What should I say? To ring a bell and ask for Mr Rudyard Kipling would be like asking for Mr Geoffrey Chaucer or Dr Samuel Johnson. Or, in view of the house's architecture, for Sir Philip Sidney. The aura around the name was such that I really did hesitate. I felt I couldn't say 'Mr Kipling' as I might say 'Mr Watkinson' or 'Mr Rogers'. But of course I did, asking for the man who had written and invited me, not RUDYARD KIPLING.

In the moment I met him the two fused. Other conflicting ikons fused. At fifty-seven, with his vast bushy eyebrows greying, his thick glasses and his bald pate, he attracted all my adolescent reverence towards a father-figure, yet the little legs in plus-fours, the shortness, and something impish which instantly appeared, wiped out my awe and shyness, and I began to gabble of my journey, of the old motor-cycle, of the mistaken route.

'Yes,' he said, 'the Sussex man does not tell you the way. He doesn't like being asked questions, for one thing. He doesn't like admitting that he doesn't know, for another.'

I did not, as Douglas Blackburn had bidden me, make notes when I reached home. What need could there be? As if I should *ever* forget one word! A great deal I have remembered but more is forgotten, perhaps because it was small talk.

Sitting in a room near the front door Kipling spoke fondly of motoring in the early days and the hazards of the first cars, for he had motored since the turn of the century.

'I hear you have a Rolls-Royce now', I said.

'It's the only car I can afford.' Those words I swear to, and he probably used them to others. Cars were still bought as carriages had been, to last as many years as possible, and undeniably a Rolls-Royce lasted longest.

Then Mrs Kipling appeared and we went to a room on the right of the front-door to sit round a refectory table for tea, a concession, I imagine, to a hungry boy who had come so far.

Several biographers of Kipling have pawkily suggested that he was dominated by his wife and seen him striding across the Sussex downs in search of solitude and independence. Clearly my one afternoon in his home as a boy gives me no opinion about this, but when I came a quarter of a century later, to read everything then written about Kipling before writing a critical study of his prose for the English Novelists series, I could find nothing to substantiate the suggestion. Mrs Kipling seemed to me that day a gentle motherly person, with dignity but without condescension, who put me – too much, I fear – at my ease and encouraged me to chatter.

She sat at the head of the table, Kipling was on her right and I on her left, and when their daughter arrived, cheerful, hungry and in tweeds, she sat beside me. The table was very tall and I have an impression of Kipling sitting up to it like a small boy, only his head and shoulders showing, and of Mrs Kipling talking to us or making me talk as though we had both just come in from school.

I brought out my message. Captain Smithers asked to be remembered to them. They would recall a cup of tea he had given then.

Miraculously they both knew at once.

'He was so kind', said Mrs Kipling. 'Do thank him for his message. You see, he was in charge of the cemetery where our son was buried. When we went to find the grave he was very helpful and how thankful we were for that cup of tea.'

It was Mrs Kipling who turned the conversation to my book and asked about the Vine Press. To which, loyal to Victor Neuberg, I answered with great enthusiasm that it was a remarkable Sussex venture, that great books would come from it, that Neuberg himself was a fine poet.

'He says you're a minor poet, sir, who has written one major poem', I piped across the table.

It was Mrs Kipling who asked, smiling, which poem that was.

' "The Mary Gloster" ', I said triumphantly, but no one was to be drawn.

There was home-made blackberry jam for tea, and piles of home-made cakes. From politeness or not, my three hosts ate nearly as much as I. When it was over there came the great hour – Kipling took me up to his study.

This was on the first-floor, a large room, as it seems in retrospect, book-lined to the ceiling. I remember Kipling, all energy and smiles, climbing a set of library steps to reach books from upper shelves. The grey bushes of eyebrow, the domed head, the thick lenses of his spectacles and the Great Name should have made him an awesome person, but with supreme tact he talked like a fellow adolescent, was enthusiastic or condemnatory of writers of the past, as though after a study tea at school we were smoking illicit cigarettes over a discussion of 'favourite authors'. Few men of fifty-seven could have done it; fewer would have bothered.

'Now read me something you've written', he said, and using the particular manner then popular for poetry (before the BBC let actors and skilled elocutionists change the trick) I intoned some verses.

In return he read me something which I have never since been able to find, so that I have come to doubt its existence – a purple patch from Chaucer. It was not from the *Canterbury Tales*, I think; it had the cadences and catch-in-the-throat of 'Tintern Abbey' or a Keats ode, an authentically purple, almost Tennysonian stanza – and from Chaucer. Oh yes, the years, and the circumstances, the man who read and the wondering boy who listened may have combined to create that sighing and ecstatic music, but I am determined not to think so.

More concrete was a page of Chaucer's own manuscript, a little of the *Wife of Bath's Tale*, framed between two pieces of glass and having a handle like a large hand-mirror which I was allowed to pick up, to hold, to examine.

A bright fire burned and we sat beside it to talk of schools. Passionate friendships among boys were dismissed as evanescent and of no ugly significance.

'Watch young bullocks in a field', said Kipling.

Wilde – 'No, I've never cared for his work. Too scented'.

Bunyan – 'Go home and read him. Read the *Pilgrim's Progress* half a dozen times before you try to write prose.'

He said nothing, he could be persuaded to say nothing, about his own work, and small wonder, for apart from a natural disinclination for everything autobiographical he could not trust me, as he had shown by the word *Private* on his letter. He was, I think, a suspicious man in matters of personal publicity, of the Press and general gossip. Starting as a journalist himself, he distrusted anything which he thought prying. He had been caught badly on several occasions, as he later revealed in *Something of Myself*. It was, as Douglas Blackburn had said, surprising that he should have let me come to see him at all.

But having done so, he was generous. He gave me that full hour without stint – having made it clear that he would turn me out at seven o'clock. He gave me, moreover, two pieces of advice, cunningly introduced as light conversation, which I conscientiously treasured.

'Never look over your shoulder at the other man. Paddle your own canoe and don't worry about anyone passing you. Keep going in your own time. If you're going to do anything you'll do it; if not, watching other succeed only embitters failure. And failure in writing shouldn't be bitter.'

I realised soberly that Something was being said. None of the more advanced advice to writers which came later in his autobiography was given to me. Mine were beginners' admonitions.

'You'll get a lot of criticism written and spoken, some of it honest, some not, some careful, a good deal thoughtless. But remember this. You and only you who are being criticised will know what is valuable, what is helpful, whether it is praise or blame. Every now and then someone will say a thing which stops you in your tracks. "He's right", you'll say, and be the better for it.'

Elementary, perhaps, but now incalculably valuable. I may have slightly blurred the wording, but since before sleeping I committed the two little exhortations to memory any variation is slight and unimportant.

Kipling came down to the front door and switched on the light in the porch, the Drunkard's Relief, he called it, and I saw him standing in its light as I waved from the gate.

The motor-cycle would not start, and I nearly killed myself in pushing it up the hill to the village, where a blacksmith–motor-mechanic (a common calling then) attended to it, and I rode away.

NOTES

Novelist, playwright, biographer, Rupert Croft-Cooke (1903–79) wrote on a wide variety of subjects: food and wine, gypsies, circuses, Oscar Wilde, and Rudyard Kipling. He served in the Intelligence Corps during World War II, and commanded the 3rd Gurkha Rifles (1943).

1. Victor Benjamin Neuberg (b. 1883), author of *A Green Garland* (1908), *Triumph of Pan* (1910), *Swift Wings* (1921), *Songs of the Groves*; editor of *Larkspur* and other volumes; and a publisher who encouraged younger writers.

2. Mackenzie (1883–1972) was noted for novels set in exotic locales. See *Carnival* (1912) and *Sinister Street* (1913).

3. Playwright and novelist (1867–1933), close friend of Joseph Conrad, and winner of the Nobel Prize for Literature (1932).

4. Maurice Henry Hewlett (1861–1923) considered himself primarily a poet, though he wrote many Italian and historical romances, stories about modern life, and personal and critical essays.

5. Conrad lived from 1857 to 1924.

6. Algernon Charles Swinburne (1879–1909) lived his final years at 11 Putney Hill Road, with the novelist and critic Theodore Watts-Dunton.

7. A street that runs between Lower Belgrave Street and the Pimlico Road. Basically middle-class in character and outward appearance. At various times the residence of Harold Nicolson and Victoria Sackville-West, George Meredith, George Moore, Noël Coward, Margaret Oliphant, and other writers, artists and musicians.

8. Town in East Sussex; one of the Cinque Ports. Henry James lived in West Street from 1898 until his death in 1916.

9. Town in Kent, 20 miles south-south-east of London.

10. Author of numerous stories and articles dealing with South Africa; author of *Prinsloo of Prinslooslorp*; *Richard Hartley, Prospector*; *A Burgher Quixote*; *Leaven, a Black and White Story*; and *Love Muti*.

11. Town in Kent, on the River Medway some 25 miles south-south-east of London.

12. A village in East Sussex, 7 miles north of Battle.

More 'Old Bookman Days'*

ARTHUR BARTLETT MAURICE

A memorable day was one spent with Rudyard Kipling at Bateman's, Burwash. It was 1 June 1920. I was directed to take the morning train down from Charing Cross Station to Etchingham,[1] where the Kipling motor-car was to meet me. I remember that a few months before 'Tark'[2] and I had been speculating about the personal Kipling. We pictured a wizened, prematurely old man, burned out in the fire of early achievement. The Kipling I found looked almost boyish in his sport clothes, and there was the vigour of youth in his action. I did not go to interview him. I cannot conceive of anyone interviewing Kipling. Like Theodore Roosevelt, he did all the interviewing.

After the first formality had worn off Mr Kipling asked that everything that he might say be held confidential. When I assured him that it would he talked fully and freely. The promise I made has been always kept and always will be. But there is one story that may be freely told. It concerns the writing of the poem 'France',[3] and Kipling's amazing gift of prophecy. 'France', picturing the British lion and Gallic cock side by side holding the Western front, contains such lines as

We were schooled for dear life's sake to know each other's
   blade.
What can Blood and Iron make more than we have made?
We have learned by keenest use to know each other's mind.
What shall Blood and Iron loose that we cannot bind?
We who swept each other's coast, sacked each other's home,
Since the sword of Brennus clashed on the scales at Rome
Listen, count and close again, wheeling girth to girth,
In the linked and steadfast guard set for peace on earth!

* *The Bookman*, LXX (Sep 1929) 64.

I told Mr Kipling that I had had an argument and a bet as to the time that the poem had been written. I had claimed that it had appeared before the outbreak of war. 'You win', he said and went on to tell me of the poem's origin. The President of the French Republic[4] was to visit London and Mr Kipling was invited to write a poem for the occasion. He recalled that a few months earlier he had been dining at a French officers' mess. Sitting next to him was a French colonel who insisted upon the imminence of war. 'It is coming. It is certain to come and come soon. The question is, what will England do?' 'Then,' said Mr Kipling, 'I made the plunge. "We are going to take over your left wing."' With the memory of that talk with the French colonel, 'France' was born.

NOTES

Arthur Bartlett Maurice (1873–1946) was a prolific writer, taking as subject-matter Paris, *Uncle Tom's Cabin*, Poe, Dickens, O. Henry, Prohibition, Booth Tarkington and Mark Twain. He was particularly fascinated by New York City as a background for popular fiction, and by the history of illustration and caricature. He also translated several works from French literature.

   1. A village in East Sussex, 7 miles north of Battle.

   2. Booth Tarkington, American novelist and dramatist (1869–1946).

   3. First printed as a leaflet in 1913, and collected in *France at War* (1915).

   4. Raymond Nicolas Landry Poincaré (1860–1934), President of France from 1913 to 1920.

M. André Maurois on the Englishman of Today*

During the war we came to know the Englishman with his remarkable character and qualities; we feared to find this character altered in the new generation, but after studying them carefully we find our fears to be imaginary. A little group of anarchical intellectuals may seem very different sort of men from Kipling's ideal, but what does a small group of three or four thousand

* *Cornhill Magazine*, LXVIII (Jan 1930) 16.

intellectuals matter to England? Kipling himself is not mistaken. I saw him last summer in his lovely simple country house, and he spoke serenely to me of these young Englishmen. He knows that many of them, and some of the most intelligent, do not follow him any more. 'But', he said with a smile, 'it is best they should not. Young men must find themselves. Young blood must run its course and every dog must have his day.' That smile of Kipling's was full of intelligence and humour, but also of an almost religious force. Kipling is indulgent, as men who believe are apt to be, for he has great faith in England and I think he is right. If he judges by appearances and by her outward difficulties, a superficial observer may feel some anxiety as to the future of England. But when one knows her better, one sees that she is solid, rich in moral and material resources and that she has already survived more difficult trials. And for us this is fortunate, we who are her friends and who are ever more convinced that it is in maintaining our intimate understanding and affectionate relations with England that lie the salvation of the Western world and the secret of keeping the Peace.

NOTE

French biographer, novelist and essayist, André Maurois (1885–1967) wrote lives of Shelley, Byron, Disraeli, Chateaubriand, Washington, George Sand, Hugo and Proust. His memoirs, in two volumes, were translated in 1942 and 1970.

Impressions of Rudyard Kipling (1)*

HARRY FURNISS

Rudyard Kipling owed something of his early success in England to the mystery by which he was surrounded. His fame was great, and preceded him from India. Like Disraeli, he did not seek the limelight.

* *Strand Magazine*, LXV (Mar 1923) 225–8.

When I first arrived in London I lived for a year or two in a private hotel in Thavie's Inn.[1] My hostess, a charming lady, was of very artistic tastes, and among her guests I met many interesting people. Those whom I recollect most clearly were a Mr and Mrs Kipling, from Lahore. Mrs Kipling was, I believe, a connection of Sir Edward Burne-Jones – and a most fascinating and witty conversationalist. Her descriptions of India, her views on art, were delightfully instructive to a youth of nineteen. With beautiful eyes and a charming expression, I thought her the most fascinating of ladies. She was the mother of Rudyard Kipling. I remember one day Mrs Kipling showing me with pride a photograph of her precocious son, then a boy of eight or nine, standing on a chair.

A characteristic of Kipling that never fails to arouse my admiration is his courage. He has no timidity. He writes of the world as he finds it. I, too, have seen a good deal of the world. I, too, like to describe with pen and pencil men and women as I find them. And I feel certain that this information gives no offence – for how should it? – when no offence is intended.

But there is always the danger of being misunderstood – as witness the case of Kipling himself. Some seven or eight years ago I was in the States when Kipling's outspoken criticism and withering sarcasm had given great offence.

Whilst having lunch with a prominent, clever, genial Irish journalist and editor, who was, however, sparsely endowed by Nature with good looks, for his eyes were minute, his nose was short, his face was round and his complexion tinged with yellow, his stature small and his build extremely corpulent, I happened to mention Kipling.

My editorial acquaintance rose, and placing his hands on the table in front of him, as if to make a speech, stuck his nose in the air and remarked with much dignity, 'My dear sir, do not mention that man's name in my presence. He had the impertinence to call New York two miles of pig-trough!' . . .

'But you read his books?' I ventured to ask.

'Sir, I take my hat off to him as a poet and an author – but as a critic – No!'

A member of the Press Gallery in the House of Commons, whose name one may safely conjecture will not go down to posterity, once said to me, 'Gladstone and I are very much alike. We are both great eaters and great sleepers.'

In the same way I might conclude Kipling and I are very much alike. We both have good memories. Kipling's memory for detail is astounding. At least, I gather it must be so, from an incident which happened at a banquet given in memory of the great novelist, Thackeray, in the Temple. Thackeray, it may be mentioned, was a member of the Temple. And this was the most representative gathering of celebrities connected with the Law, with Literature, Art, and Science. I presume that I was invited because I had lately completed the Centenary Edition of Thackeray (named after me),[2] and as a compliment to my work for the drawings and preface that I had supplied.

On that never-to-be-forgotten occasion I found myself sand-wiched between two legal luminaries. One of my neighbours said that on his way to the Great Hall he passed the tents in which the annual flower-shows had taken place.[3] He observed, to his great astonishment, in the grounds a swarm of bees. He declared it to be a most extraordinary occurrence.

'I have never seen bees in the Temple before,' he remarked, ' and I am puzzled to know how, and by what means, they got there.'

Kipling, who was seated opposite, leaned forward and said, 'I think that I can tell you something concerning that very swarm. If you look up the *Bee-lover's Gazette*'[4] (I am not certain if I have the correct name, but it was certainly something very like that) 'of July two years ago, on the last page, half way down the second column, you will find a paragraph about a barrister in the Temple who keeps bees. No doubt the swarm you saw this evening belongs to the same man.'

I once wrote an article on the subject of 'How Workers Work', in which I said, 'Perhaps no man has, more literally, taken off his coat to work than Rudyard Kipling. A friend of mine, who saw a good deal of him in Africa during the Boer War, and who for a short time assisted him in the journal published by war correspondents, tell me that Kipling was a most wonderful worker. With plenty of paper and ink before him, his pipe alight, he would get an idea, and then, if writing verse, a tune to help out the idea, accompanying himself by tapping the table with his fingers; once started, the whole theme was in his mind, the rhythm perfect, the result marvellous.'

My first personal meeting with Rudyard Kipling took place a quarter of a century after I met his parents, and he had become famous. I happened to be in the train travelling up to London from Sussex, in which county we both were – and still are – living. I introduced myself to him by asking after his parents, and he responded with charming enthusiasm. I may at once say that, in all my journeys round the world, a more delightful travelling-companion than the great author and poet I have never met. I had drawn Kipling many times from photographs, but I had never seen him in life before, except for that very fleeting glimpse at the Thackeray anniversary. It was not his bushy eyebrows, nor the glasses, nor the moustache, nor all these features together that made me certain at first glance it was Kipling. Recent portraits had led me to expect a much older and more worn man; the feature I knew could only be Kipling's was the chin with the split in the centre – a prominent chin signifying strength.

We touched on many topics – at least, I touched and Kipling talked, and what a talker he was! Crisp as his prose, incisive as his verse, amusing as his fancies, inexhaustible as his pen. Here was the man, not to be approached intellectually, pouring out ideas and impressions in a fresh, vigorous stream which one never finds in the jaded clubman, no matter how clever he may be. Kipling's exclusiveness is his strength. His mind, like a stream that has trickled peacefully over the pebbles in the fresh, open country, is naturally different from the heated, artificial outpouring of the town wit. This simile reminds me of Kipling's raptures over the picturesque. 'Ye gods, what scenery one enjoys in Southern France!' (He had just returned from a visit there.) 'Did you ever visit . . . ?' (The name has escaped my memory.) 'No? Then you must. It is a dead village on the top of a wonderful plateau – every house, every deserted mansion, is a picture, and when I looked over the rock and found crustations which I always thought was the work of the devil – in other words, the jerry-builder[5] – I found the wind – the wind alone had made these.

'You know, when I go to a gaff[6] – which I seldom do – I always take more interest in the scenery than in the actors. I do not think scene-painters are made enough of. It is a great art.'

We then discussed scene-painting, and I told him some of the tricks of the trade and gave it as my opinion that the stage-carpenter had displaced the artist with real trees and real water.

'That reminds me', Kipling broke in. 'You knew Irving well. I didn't, but I felt what a great man he was if only by one incident. I was present at a performance at the Lyceum[7] – Tennyson's *Cup*,[8] I think – and Irving,[9] in his peculiar, jerky, impulsive manner, accidentally pulled up a small tree by the roots. There was a titter. Any other actor would have been at a loss to know what to do, but not Irving. He quickly *planted it again*, and went on with the play.

'Beerbohm Tree[10] is a wonderful man', he continued. 'I heard that a few evenings ago he recited Hamlet's soliloquy, "To be or not to be", as if Falstaff was speaking it. There is a theory, which I have always felt to be a true one, that the only character in Shakespeare who understood Hamlet, though he never met him, was Falstaff. The two characters are exact – only Falstaff is fat. Forget his fatness and, as Falstaff, recite *Hamlet*, and you will see that there is not the length of this cigarette between them.'

This theory was too novel to follow, so we switched off to Thackeray. I asked him point-blank what he thought of Thackeray. He raised his eyes and hands in admiration. 'Thackeray? A great master! Say what they like, he was great! There is a lot of meat in Thackeray. One need not read his tirades to the reader – that is an Early Victorian style of writing that may weary one nowadays. Skip those, and what everlasting pleasure there is in his reading.

'Dickens! There was a craftsman – young writers nowadays may belittle him, but one and all may learn – perhaps unconsciously – from Dickens. He was good in every line, descriptive, dramatic, pathetic. Epigram, short story, everything he had at his finger-ends. By the way, did you ever notice one peculiarity about Dickens? He never had any light in his scenes. Everything is dark. His horizons are low, his interiors so dark – one candle in a room – that a generation hence the artist will not know how to illustrate his darkness at all. Still, like the London he loved, we have to put up with the darkness and love him still.'

At the time I was illustrating the Centenary Edition of Thackeray I again travelled from the country to London with Kipling. He was interested when I told him that I had some of the drawings with me.

'What have you made of Becky Sharp?' he asked. I showed him. 'That is not what I thought Becky to be like', he remarked. 'I believed her to be a short-nosed, dark little thing.'

To which I replied that she certainly was not the Becky whom Thackeray drew with his pencil, but my idea of the Becky Sharp whom he drew with his pen. In his usual careless way as an artist he gave an utterly false impression of his own most famous character; and actresses, artists, and everyone else have followed him in this erroneous representation.

'To begin with, Becky was not altogether English; her mother was French. Her features could not have been those of her drunken father – she was attractive, pale, sandy-haired, with very large eyes, and she was Jewish, and therefore certainly had not a short nose. She was wicked, and this I have tried to show in the drawing of her eyes. I have always observed that the wickedest eye in woman is the light-grey iris and the dark pupil.'

'I never heard that before', broke in Kipling; 'dark pupil and light-grey iris! – that is new to me, by Jove! So that was Becky, was it?'

We, by a coincidence, journeyed back from London in the same carriage that afternoon, and Kipling informed me that he had had a most enjoyable lunch at the Athenaeum Club that day. There happened to be sitting at his table a number of literary acquaintances, and he brought Becky Sharp into the conversation, and ventilated my theory of her as his own. 'And what is more, I left them at it!' he added.

NOTES

Harry Furniss (1854–1925) made a considerable reputation for himself as a literary gossip, and as a master of quick sketches and caricatures. Among a number of books for which he provided illustrations was Sir Walter Besant's *All in a Garden Fair: The Simple Story of Three Boys and a Girl* (1884), a book that Kipling much enjoyed. Furniss wrote *Australian Sketches Made on Tour* (1902), *Book of Dickens Illustrations* (1910), *The By Ways and Queer Ways of Boxing* (1921) and *Confessions of a Caricaturist* (1901).

1. One of the nine Inns of Chancery to which students of law, prior to the seventeenth century, went before going on to an Inn of Court. Thavie's Inn was sold by the benchers in 1769, and no longer kept its legal character. The Inns of Chancery were located along Chancery Lane, which leads north from Fleet Street to High Holborn. Thavie's Inn now exists only as the name of a modern building.

2. Macmillan published the twenty volumes of the Harry Furniss Centenary Edition in 1911. Furniss contributed 'artist's prefaces', evaluating Thackeray's accomplishments in drawing and illustrating.

3. Paper Buildings formed the western boundary of the 'Great Garden', which was the scene of the 'great and growing Flower Show, which is one of the most popular and pleasing of the social functions of the London season' – Cecil Headlam, *The Inns of Court* (London: A. and C. Black, 1909) p. 94.

4. *The Bee-keepers' Gazette*, in fact.

5. A shoddy, flimsy, or cheap workman.

6. Slang for a public place of amusement, and in particular a low class of theatre or music-hall.

7. A distinguished theatre. The Lyceum was founded in 1765, remodelled in 1794 and 1815, destroyed by fire in 1830, rebuilt in 1834, and managed by Sir Henry Irving from 1878. John Gielgud's *Hamlet* (1939) was the last play produced there.

8. Produced in 1881.

9. Sir Henry Irving (1838–1905), originally named John Henry Brodribb;

famous for his acting in *The Bells* (1871–2), *Richelieu* (1873), *Hamlet* (1874), an elaborate production of *Romeo and Juliet* (1882–3) and *Henry VIII* (1892); Tennyson's *Becket* (1893) proved to be his last role on the stage (1905). He was the first actor to be knighted.

10. Sir Herbert Beerbohm Tree (1852–1917), actor–manager, appeared in over fifty plays, and was the lessee and manager of the Haymarket Theatre, London (1887–97). His elaborate productions of Shakespeare, and his acting of the role of Mark Antony in the forum scene of *Julius Caesar*, were much discussed.

Impressions of Rudyard Kipling (2)*

E. P. KINSELLA

When I knew that I was to meet Rudyard Kipling I praised my luck exceedingly. Many writers compel a willing admiration of their work. A very few – the princes of story-telling – command the reader's eager worship for the life and colour and magic they put into the printed page. For me, as for many others, Kipling was of those few.

I was to work with him, and that seemed better still.

The commission to work on the technical side of the film of a Kipling story, 'The Gate of a Hundred Sorrows',[1] came through my old friend Randolph Lewis, the American scenario expert. I was to do a poster for the film, make models under Kipling's supervision, sketches of native costumes and the like, according to his directions.

I have a memory of being a little nervous at our first meeting. I need not have been. Kipling gave me one sustained glance – I shall never be able to imagine him without those big glinting spectacles – and decided that I would do. From then on it was strenuous work: work that under Kipling's unwearying enthusiasm for the job in hand became in my view strenuous and delightful play. Kipling had the gift of making it seem like that to me. It was a hurrying playtime with the work never for an instant out of sight. Everything had to be

* *Strand Magazine*, LXV (Mar 1923) 228–31.

not only right, but just right. The let it go doctrine of 'That'll do' was no manner of use to Kipling – and no manner of use to me after my first hour in his company.

'I'll tell you the secret of success, Kinsella', he said once. 'It's always to do a little better than the next man – and to give good measure.'

From beginning to end I suppose there were close on 140 models and sketches done for the use and guidance of the producers of the films. There was no single speck in all the dust of detail Kipling did not help and improve, from the exact way of tying a character's sash to the exact pattern of the Mohammedan fretwork decorating a window in Lahore. With fair reason I consider myself a quick thinker – I still hope I am right; but if I am, then you must find some wholly new and ten-powered adjective for the astonishing speed with which Kipling grasps, surrounds, and settles any point of the work in hand. His swiftness was a lasting and joyful wonder. Randolph Lewis christened him the Little Master. Working for him, I had taken on a new part in life. I had become (although, again, I hold to it that I am a quick thinker) the man-trying-to-catch-up-with-Kipling. And I shall never wish for a better part.

A friend asked me for my impressions of the man.

A little man, top-hat, Astrakhan collar, the top light glinting on those big glasses. Always those glinting glasses.

That won't do, and ordinary language will not do. I register Rudyard Kipling now, as I registered him very early in our meetings, as a twelve-cylinder life-machine with every cylinder working, and the spirit of the man always in life and flame.

We met at the South Kensington Museum, where the gods of India live, and where Kipling was a man at home. Comment, knowledge, command, flow from him in a running current as he finds, in case after case, something I must note down for 'The Gate of a Hundred Sorrows'[2] or the 'Without Benefit of Clergy' films. I hardly halt by any case. I wait rather like a sprinter at the start, all ready to dash on to the next case, busy with sketch-book and pencil all the time. I am the man catching up.

'Get that, Kinsella. She'd wear a cap like that – a coquettish cap, they'd think it there. The feminine is the same all over the world – she'd wear it just as a woman might wear it in France – jauntily set over one eye. And she'd be looking out under the lashes.'

I make a rapid sketch of the native cap, I look up, and am surprised he is not there. He is already at a case farther on, beckoning me and pointing out something at the same time. 'These are the Hindu drums – you'll have to get these. They look like an hour-glass, pigskins on both ends. And the rhythm of their music sounds like the heart-beats of humanity. And here's something else. Wouldn't it be a good idea if little Tota had a bow and arrow to play with on the roof of Holden's house? I should get one down on paper, I think, Kinsella. Here, I'll show you what the bow and arrow ought to look like!'

For the first time I was too slow. Kipling had taken my sketch-book from my hand and was carefully (but swiftly, of course – always swiftly) drawing the thing for himself. A moment later, by the model of a famous tomb, he was making another sketch, to explain exactly the way in which a character would carry the money in his belt.

You remember 'Without Benefit of Clergy', the story which begins with the native woman's prayer to Holden, Holden who loves her.

'But if it be a girl?'

'Lord of my life, it cannot be! I know God will give us a son – a man-child that shall grow into a man . . . .'

There comes a son, Tota, the wonderful man-child, and Holden and the girl he loves make paradise of the house and the man-child's laughter. There come darkness and the rains, and Tota dies. His mother, Ameera, dies, and laughter goes for ever. All life is darkness now to Holden, and he dare not look upon the house that was paradise. He sends a man with money for the mother of Ameera –

Kipling dropped upon his knees to show us exactly (always exactly) how the messenger would take the money from his belt, to hand it over. He would, of course, deduct for himself dustoorie, 'that commission or percentage on the money passing in any cash transaction which in India, with or without any acknowledgment or permission, sticks to the fingers of the agent of payment'.

And as he told us, 'just how', on his knees, he acted the whole thing.

Did I say that on this occasion no notice of Kipling's visit had been given to the officials of the place? Because of this there followed also a young and anxious policeman. Unnoticed by any of us for a long time, he must have been highly suspicious of the speed and eagerness of the little man in the top-hat and the Astrakhan coat. Randolph Lewis in the rear carried a potentially iniquitous bag. I imagine quiet men are mostly the visitors to South Kensington, men who stand in some reverence before the cases, browsing among memory or knowledge, or both. We three were – to the watchful policeman – strange strangers. Whatever we were, whoever we were, who thus oddly mixed the properties of one big bag, one sketch-book, and one Astrakhan coat, most emphatically we did not browse.

Possibly the wondering policeman visualised a sudden smashing of the glass of a case, a sudden bringing into action of Lewis's bag. He followed, he watched, he wondered – and at last I saw him peering round the corner of a big case we had used, sketched, and passed. I took in his amazement, his suspicion, his young honesty, and I spoke him fair, as I pointed to Kipling, a South Kensington mile ahead.

'It's all right. That is Mr Kipling', I whispered; and the policeman answered, 'Who's he?'

Upon our next visit to South Kensington it was a different tale. There were frock-coats, a guard of reception, a host of pained regrets that we had not let them know beforehand of Kipling's visit. But I shall keep best in mind that glorious first visit, when we travelled express, until a halt was sounded, and I saw in that tranquil moment the little man with the dancing eyes standing serene and masterful among the gods of India.

I journeyed in noble company round South Kensington, but there was much more than this for me. I journeyed to the India Kipling knows in the light of the bits of talk he flashed in the intervals of work with him. There were models to be done of courtyards, wells, gates, houses, and with many of them these little illuminations came.

This was the tree where the Soldiers Three held council together and told their yarns. Here was a model of the city of Lahore. I made the very window-seat, with the tiny cushions, where Holden sat and looked out over the city and prayed fiercely for the happiness of his tiny son. In this case were the turbans, all types of turbans – Kipling gave the history of each, and the method of tying and wearing it. He talked of the temple, the model of which next claimed us.

'I scraped the dirt away from my stick, and found it was built of solid silver. In India, beside a beautiful building, you will see an ugly derelict hut. Nobody troubles to destroy it. Nothing matters. Perhaps a man meant to build there. He got as far as the foundations and then abandoned his idea, and went away and forgot all about it.'

To Kipling virtue is the doing of the job. A master of craft, that urge to get the very best out of the work in hand displays itself wonderfully in his instructions to me for drawing the poster of 'The Gate of a Hundred Sorrows'. Nothing must be shadowed or scamped.

'Take especial care that Anne does not look like the repentant Magdalene. On no account put the crucifix on her breast. She stole it, so it is in her hand. Her moral status is exactly that of the penitent thief. Her face is turned towards Ethel, and it is your business, even in the coarse work of a poster, to get something of its clouded expression.

'Mother Maturin is not thin, but a voluptuous, honey-coloured Fate. The arm holding up her chin is heavily braceleted, as also is the relaxed right arm, which should rest on her right knee. Her legs are covered to the ankle with deep red or green drapery, and her feet, which are light-coloured and shapely, carry red or green native slippers.

'The outline of the smoke-cloud itself touches the overhanging stone above the gate, in the middle, then curving down on either side. I want every gradation in the smoke that you can give, and above all I want the interlacing lines of wreaths of smoke seen edgewise. All the mystery of the symbolism of the play should be hinted at in that same smoke, which is densest and deepest just above Ethel's head, since it is the visible symbol of the weight of the sins which she takes upon her head.

'On second thoughts, it would be best to keep both of Ethel's hands down by her side, as the present attitude is too like a commonplace blessing, whereas her whole attitude is that of a soul under the weight of an accepted burden. Spirit though she is, the first and last note of Ethel Stronnard's figure is *strength*. You would do wrong to put her in a full white spirit-light. I suggest some variant of violet, or orange-violet, as more effective.'

I have not quoted these instructions in full. But I must give the last few words.

'The rest is for you to work up.'

All the models went to Los Angeles, and there, based upon the models, the scenes of the story were built up. That Kipling was satisfied with the result, with my work, delighted me. Above that, it will always delight me to remember that maxim of his I have already given: 'The secret of success is to do a little better than the next fellow, and to give good measure.'

NOTES

E. P. Kinsella, like Furniss, was a caricaturist and illustrator, as in the drawings he provided for H. F. Maltby's play, *Help Yourself!* (1926).

1. First printed in the *Civil and Military Gazette*, 26 Sep 1884; collected in *Plain Tales from the Hills* (1888).

2. First published in *Macmillan's Magazine*, June 1890, and *Harper's Weekly*, 7 and 14 June 1890; collected in *The Courting of Dinah Shadd and Other Stories* (1890).

Kipling's Reaction to a Young Man's Criticism *

BEVERLEY NICHOLS

Rudyard Kipling is a fine example of a great man who will forgive almost everything to youth. He certainly forgave me as charmingly as it was possible to do so.

It happened during lunch. I felt very guilty when they said that Rudyard Kipling was coming, because two years before, when still at Oxford, I had written a letter to the *Morning Post* on the subject of 'Our Modern Youth', in which there were a great many violent (and rather silly) remarks levelled against anybody who had the misfortune to be over forty. The letter attacked, with sublime indifference, such diverse subjects as militarism, old age, imperialism, prime ministers and incidentally Kipling, whom I had never read, but who seemed to sum up a great many aggressive tendencies. 'Where', I asked, in the peroration, 'will you find the spirit of the age? Not in the flamboyant insolence of Rudyard Kipling, not in the . . . etc.'

Not one of my best works, that letter. But it was written in a hammock, on a hot summer's day, with flies buzzing round, and certainly without the thought that perhaps, one day, the writer would meet the man whom he had attacked.

* *25: Being a Young Man's Candid Recollections of his Elders and Betters* (London: Jonathan Cape, 1926; New York: George H. Doran, 1926) pp. 189–91.

However, when Kipling was announced, he came straight up to me (where I was hiding in a corner) and said, 'You're the young man who was so rude to me in the *Morning Post*, aren't you?'

I admitted that this was so. 'I'm awfully sorry . . . ' I began.

'Sorry? What for?' said Kipling. 'I used to be much ruder to people when I was your age. The only thing that I should be sorry for was that you didn't make it worse.'

I heaved a sigh of relief.

'Besides,' said Kipling, 'that was a jolly good phrase – flamboyant insolence – I liked it.'

And then he began to talk about literary style with a gusto that is more often found in amateurs than in celebrities.

Kipling did not strike one, in the very least, as 'literary'. If one had not seen his face caricatured in a hundred newspapers, one would gather that he was a successful surgeon or a prosperous architect. Especially does he convey the surgeon, with his keen bright eyes, his more-than-bedside manner, and the strong, capable hands, that push out eagerly from the white cuffs as though they were about to carve something.

Carving, too, is a phrase that might be applied to his prose. He hacks out his sentences, cuts up his paragraphs, snips at his descriptions.

I was struck, even at the beginning, with his positively en-cyclopaedic knowledge of subjects about which he might well have pleaded justifiable ignorance. Drugs, for example. Somebody mentioned anaesthetics, and that led to a wider discussion of all drugs that partially or wholly remove consciousness. Kipling suddenly broke into the conversation, held it and dominated it, illustrating everything he said with the most apposite examples. He told me that when he was in India, as a young man, he had experimented in taking a very potent drug which even the natives can only imbibe in small quantities. 'It laid me out completely,' he said, 'and I didn't dream a bit, as I had hoped. I woke up, with a splitting headache, but fortunately I knew the cure – hot milk, as much of it as you can drink. If ever you find yourself in that condition in India, you put your last dollar on hot milk. It's the only thing that will pull you round.'

NOTE

Beverley Nichols (b. 1899), a successful author and composer, has written on a wide variety of topics: cats, psychical research, gardens and garden shows, India, people eminent in literature, art and politics; and even wrote the official handbook for the County Borough of Brighton. His plays, novels, romances for children and mysteries constitute a formidable bibliography. See *All I Could Never Be: Some Recollections* (1950).

Rudyard Kipling – a Biographical Sketch*

ANICE PAGE COOPER

Numerous as the anecdotes are the stories of the sprightly inscriptions that Kipling has written in the books of his friends. Brander Matthews[1] treasures one in playful mood that makes his copy of *Many Inventions*[2] a joy to any true bibliophile. To begin with, the volume is bound by Mr Cobden-Sanderson,[3] the distinguished bookbinder, who refuses to waste his skill upon works which do not seem to him to be worthy of sumptuous attire. It is rarely that he consents to bind the books of contemporary authors, but he took pleasure in dressing *Many Inventions* in a back of blue morocco, sides of harmoniously marbled paper and vellum corners. Mr Matthews was so delighted with the book that he asked Kipling to autograph it. Kipling wrote in reply that the blank pages in front of the text were very tempting, so he wrote in all of them. On one was a parody of Browning, on another a parody of James Whitcomb Riley in such perfect dialect that Howells was ready to accept it as the actual work of the Hoosier lyrist, and on a third the following quatrain:

> See my literary pants:
> I am bound in crushed levants.
> Brander Matthews did it, and a
> Very handsome thing of Branda.

NOTES

Page Cooper (1891–1958) was a popular writer on such topics as dogs, horses and hospital life. She wrote about writers with a large audience such as Du Bose

* *Around the World with Kipling*, ed. Irvin S. Cobb (New York: Doubleday, 1926) p. 37.

Heyward and Faith Baldwin. Her book on Kipling appeared in 1926, and *Heritage of Fire: The Story of Richard Wagner's Granddaughter*, written in collaboration with Friedelind Wagner, in 1945. Her anthology *The Boudoir Companion* came out in 1938.

1. See p. 141, note on Brander Matthews.

2. First printed in 1893, the volume has fourteen stories and two poems.

3. Thomas James Cobden-Sanderson (1890–1922) invented the phrase 'arts and crafts', and, developing further the traditions established by William Morris and the Burne-Jones family, ran the Doves Bindery in Hammersmith and (after 1898) the Doves Press, which specialised in fine printing.

Six Hours with Rudyard Kipling*

ARTHUR GORDON

The year was 1935, the month was June, the English weather was blue and gold. The world was young, and so was I. But, driving down from Oxford in the old Sunbeam I had borrowed for the occasion, I felt my assurance deserting me.

The great man was almost a recluse now, and it was said that he did not care for Americans. Through a mutual friend I had managed to secure permission to visit him. Now as I neared the little village of Burwash, where he lived, I began to experience something like stage-fright. And when I found the sombre seventeenth-century house and saw my host walking down to the gate to meet me, I grew so flustered that I hardly knew whether to shake hands or turn and run.

He was so small! The crown of the floppy hat he wore was not much higher than my shoulder, and I doubt if he weighed 120 pounds. His skin was dark for an Englishman's; his moustache was almost white. His eyebrows were as thick and tangled as marsh grass, but behind the gold-rimmed glasses his eyes were as bright as a terrier's. He was sixty-nine.

He saw instantly how ill at ease I was. 'Come in, come in', he said

* *Kipling Journal*, xxxiv (June 1967) 5–8.

companionably, opening the gate. 'I was just going to inspect my navy.' He led me, speechless, to a pond at the end of the garden, and there was the 'navy': a 6-foot skiff with hand-cranked paddle wheels. 'You can be the engine-room', he said. 'I'll be the passenger-list.'

I was so agitated that I cranked too hard. The paddle-wheel broke and there I was, marooned in the middle of a fishpond with Rudyard Kipling. He began to laugh, and so did I, and the ice was broken.

A gardener finally rescued us with a long rake. By then my host had me talking. There was something about him that drove the shyness out of you, a kind of understanding that went deeper than words and set up an instantaneous closeness. It was odd: we couldn't have been more different. He was British; I was American. He was near the end of an illustrious road; I was at the beginning of an obscure one. He had had years of ill-health and pain; I was untouched by either. He knew nothing about me – there was nothing to know. I knew all about him, and so to me he was not just a fragile little man in a toy boat. He was Kim and Fuzzy Wuzzy and Gunga Din. He was Danny Deever and the Elephant's Child. He was the dawn coming up like thunder on the road to Mandalay; he was the rough laughter of the barrack-room, the chatter of the bazaar and the great organ tones of 'Recessional'. To me he was, quite simply, a miracle, and no doubt this showed in my dazzled eyes, and he felt it.

I had had an ulterior motive in coming, of course, I wanted to meet him for himself, but I was also a puzzled and unsure young man. I had in my pocket a letter offering me a job as instructor in an American university. I didn't really want to be a teacher; I knew I didn't have the selflessness or the patience. What I wanted to be, ultimately, was a writer. But the teaching job was the only offer I had, and, at home, the dead hand of the Depression still lay heavy on the land. Should I play it safe, and say yes to the offer?

What I wanted desperately was for someone of great wisdom and experience in the field of letters to tell me what to do. But I knew this was a preposterous responsibility to thrust upon a stranger. And so I waited, hoping that somehow the heavens would open and the miracle of certainty would descend upon me.

While I waited, he talked. And, as he talked, I began to forget about my problems. He tossed words into the air, and they flashed like swords. He spoke of his friendship with Cecil Rhodes, through whose generosity I had gone to Oxford. 'They say we were both imperialists', said Kipling a little grimly. 'Well, maybe we were. The word is out of fashion now, and some Englishmen are weak enough to be ashamed of it. I'm not.' He questioned me almost sharply about some poets of prominence: T. S. Eliot, Gertrude Stein, E. E. Cummings.[1] I said I thought they were good. 'Do you?' he said guilelessly. 'Quote me a few lines.'

I sat there, helpless, and he laughed. 'You see,' he said, 'that's the trouble with verse that doesn't rhyme. But let's not be too harsh where poets are concerned. They have to live in no-man's-land, halfway between dreams and reality.'

'Like Mowgli', I said impulsively, thinking of the brown-skinned boy torn between village and jungle. He gave me a look with his blue eyes. 'Like most of us', he said.

He talked of ambition, of how long it took fully to master any art or craft. And of secondary ambitions: the more you had, he said, the more fully you lived. 'I always wanted to build or buy a 400-ton brig,' he said reflectively, 'and sail her round the world. Never did. Now, I suppose, it's too late.' He lit a cigarette and looked at me through the smoke. 'Do the things you really want to do if you possibly can. Don't wait for circumstances to be exactly right. You'll find that they never are.'

'My other unrealised ambition', he went on, 'was to be an archaeologist. For sheer, gem-studded romance, no other job can touch it.' We returned to his study, a large square room lined with bookcases on two sides. There were his desk, his chair, an enormous waste-basket and his pens – the kind you dip in ink. At right-angles to the fireplace was a small sofa. 'I lie there,' he said with a smile, 'and wait for my daemon to tell me what to do.'

'Daemon?'

He shrugged. 'Intuition. Subconcious. Whatever you want to call it.'

'Can you always hear him?'

'No', he said slowly. 'Not always. But I learned long ago that it's best to wait until you do. When your daemon says nothing, he usually means no.'

Mrs Kipling called us to lunch, and afterwards I felt I should take my leave. But Kipling would not hear of it. 'I'm still full of talk', he said. 'You've eaten my salt, so now you must be my audience.'

So we talked. Or rather, he talked while I made superhuman efforts to remember everything. He had a way of thrusting a harsh truth at you and then, in the next breath, beguiling you into a wry acceptance of it. 'If you're endowed', he said at one point, 'with any significant energies or talent, you may as well resign yourself to the fact that throughout your life you will be carrying coat-tail riders who will try to exploit you. But instead of fretting about this you'd better thank God for the qualities that attract the parasites, and not waste time trying to shake them off.'

We talked of friendship; he thought young ones were best and lasted longest. 'When you're young', he said, 'you're not afraid to give yourself away. You offer warmth and vitality and sympathy without thinking. Later on, you begin to weigh what you give.' I said, diffidently, that he was giving me a lot, and his eyes twinkled. 'A fair exchange. You're giving me attention. That's a form of affection, you know.'

Looking back, I think he knew that in my innocence I was eager to love everything and please everybody, and he was trying to warn me not to lose my own identity in the process. Time after time he came back to this theme. 'The individual has always had to struggle to keep from being overwhelmed by the tribe. To be your own man is a hard business. If you try it, you'll be lonely often, and sometimes frightened. But no price is too high to pay for the privilege of owning yourself.'

Suddenly the shadows were long on the grass. When I stood up to go, I remembered the letter in my pocket and the advice I had thought I wanted. But now there was nothing to ask. Do the things you really want to do . . . Don't wait for circumstances to be exactly right . . . When your daemon says nothing, he usually means no . . . No price is too high to pay for the privilege of owning yourself. I knew, now, that I could refuse the teaching job and wait for my daemon to speak clearly to me.

We walked to the gate, where my host held out his hand. 'Thank you', he said. 'You've done me good.'

The thought that I could have done anything for him was beyond my grasp. I thanked him and climbed into the old Sunbeam. I looked back once. He was still standing there in his floppy hat, a great little man who forgot his own illness and his own problems and spent a whole day trying to help a troubled and self-conscious boy from across the sea.

He had a gift for young friendships, all right. He gave me much more than advice. He gave me a little bit of himself to carry away. After all these years, I feel the warmth of it still.

NOTES

Gordon (b. 1912) was a Rhodes Scholar, Managing Editor of *Good Housekeeping* (1938–1946), Editor of *Cosmopolitan* (1946–8), and a roving editor of *Guideposts* from 1955 on. He fought in the US Army Air Force during World War II, and contributed to the text of *American Heritage Book of Flight* (1960); co-authored a book on Norman Vincent Peale (1958); and wrote a highly-praised novel, *Reprisal* (1950), a story about race hatred recorded by a Northern journalist.

1. Thomas Stearns Eliot (1888–1965); Gertrude Stein (1874–1946); Edward Estlin Cummings (1894–1962).

Poets' Corner*

Rudyard Kipling died at 12.10 a.m. on 18 January 1936. With the idea of going to the South of France for his health, he had come up to London on 9 January, and fell ill at Brown's Hotel on the night of 12 January. He was taken to the Woolavington Ward of the Middlesex Hospital at 8 a.m. on 13 January, and an operation for gastric ulcer was performed an hour later by Mr A. E. Webb-Johnson.[1] After a slight rally, peritonitis set in, and the end came on the following Saturday morning. The body lay in state in the mortuary chapel of the hospital, with a Union Jack as pall over the coffin, until the cremation at Golder's Green on the evening of 20 January. On the morning of 23 January the casket containing the ashes, draped with the Union Jack, was buried in Poets' Corner.

A great tribute to Mr Kipling was shown in the messages received by Mrs Kipling from the Royal Family in the midst of their own anxiety. The Queen telegraphed: 'The King and I are grieved to hear of the death this morning of Mr Kipling. We shall mourn him not only as a great national poet, but as a personal friend of many years. Please accept our heartfelt sympathy.' The Prince of Wales (King Edward VIII) sent a telegram: 'Please accept my sincere sympathy in the sad loss you have sustained by the death of your distinguished husband.' The Duke of Connaught's[2] words were, 'Deepest sympathy in your sad loss.'

The service was performed by the Dean of Westminster[3] and the

* Unsigned report in *Kipling Journal*, no. 37 (Mar 1936) pp. 2–4.

Abbey clergy. The funeral service included J. B. Dykes's[4] setting of the hymn, 'God of Our Fathers' (better known as 'Recessional'); the Blessing, specially composed for the occasion, was given by the Dean: 'In thankfulness to Almighty God for the life and work of one who has been allowed to speak as a prophet to many generations of men, his own generation and those which are yet to come – unto God's gracious mercy and protection we deliver him. The Lord bless him and keep him, and the blessing of God Almighty be upon you now and always.'

The pall-bearers were: the Prime Minister, Mr Stanley Baldwin (first cousin); Admiral of the Fleet Sir Roger Keyes;[5] Field-marshal Sir A. Montgomery-Massingberd;[6] Professor J. W. Mackail;[7] Mr H. A. Gwynne (Editor, *Morning Post*);[8] Sir Fabian Ware;[9] Mr A. B. Ramsay;[10] and Mr A. P. Watt (Mr Kipling's literary agent). Among the family present were: Mrs Kipling, with her son-in-law and daughter, Captain and Mrs George Bambridge; Mrs Stanley Baldwin; Miss Betty Baldwin[11] and Mr Oliver Baldwin;[12] Mr A. W. Baldwin; Miss Florence Macdonald;[13] and Mrs Thirkell, Miss Cecily Nicholson (Mr Kipling's secretary) was with the family.

The Kipling Society was represented by: Mr G. C. Beresford ('M'Turk'); Mr J. H. C. Brooking (Founder);[14] Mr S. A. Courtauld;[15] Lady Cunynghame;[16] Major-general L. C. Dunsterville ('Stalky' – President); Sir Francis Goodenough;[17] Lieutenant-general Sir George MacMunn (Hon. Treasurer and Chairman of Council);[18] and many others.

The foreign ambassadors and ministers present were: the French Ambassador;[19] the Brazilian Ambassador;[20] the Belgian Ambassador;[21] the Italian Ambassador;[22] the Netherlands Minister;[23] the Danish Minister;[24] the Finnish Minister.[25]

The High Commissioner for Canada;[26] Mr U. C. Duffy, representing the High Commissioner for Australia;[27] the Agent General for Victoria.[28]

Among those present were: the Lord Chancellor and Viscountess Hailsham;[29] the Chancellor of the Exchequer[30] and Mrs Neville Chamberlain; Mr A. Duff Cooper,[31] Secretary for War; Lord Eustace Percy;[32] Lord Lloyd;[33] Lord and Lady Rennell;[34] Lord Beaverbrook;[35] Sir William Rothenstein;[36] Sir Frederick Macmillan;[37] Sir Michael O'Dwyer;[38] Mr and Mrs L. S. Amery;[39] Mr R. D. Blumenfeld;[40] Mr Laurence Binyon;[41] Dr Archibald Fleming;[42] Mr Alfred Noyes;[43] Mr Gilbert Frankau;[44] Mr R. P.

Hodder-Williams;[45] Mr Ian Hay; Mr E. V. Lucas;[46] Mr Francis Toye;[47] Lady Tree[48] and Miss Neilson-Terry;[49] and General Sir Ian Hamilton[50] with fourteen veterans of the South African War.

The following were represented: the Archbishop of Canterbury;[51] the Secretary of State for the Colonies;[52] the Army Council; the Imperial War Graves Commission; the Boy Scouts Association; Messrs Doubleday Doran and Co.; the Irish Guards; the Royal Society of St George; Sir Josiah Stamp;[53] the Imperial Service College; the British Empire League; the Society of Authors; the Dickens Fellowship; the Globe Mermaid Shakespearian Association; the Athenaeum; the Authors' Lodge of Freemasons; the English Verse Speaking Association; and the London Library.

This is a very condensed list of those who attended Kipling's funeral; we have merely tried to give members an idea of the esteem in which he was held by various people and interests. Neither will our space allow us to publish a list of the many floral tributes that were sent. Mention however, must be made of two: a workman on Mr Kipling's property at Burwash, knowing that his late master loved three English trees – the oak, the ash and the thorn – made a wreath from the leaves of these three, which was placed upon the grave in the Abbey; another wreath was from the companions of his schooldays, the Old Boys of the United Services College.

NOTES

1. Alfred Edward Webb-Johnson (1880–1958) was a distinguished surgeon, serving both Queen Mary and King George V (during his last illness). Dean of Middlesex Hospital.

2. Arthur William Patrick Albert, Duke of Connaught and Strathearn, third son of Queen Victoria (1850–1942). Fought in Egyptian War (1882) and Bengal (1886). He became a field-marshal in 1902; presented King Edward VII at the coronation durbar in Delhi (1903), and served as Governor General of Canada (1911). In 1928 he retired after sixty years in the Army. Kipling's father was employed by the Duke to decorate a room for him.

3. The Very Revd. W. Foxley Norris, KCVO, DD.

4. Published as the hymn 'God of Our Fathers' in *Hymns Ancient and Modern* (1916). 'Recessional', under its own title, has been set to music at least twenty-eight times; under the title 'God of Our Fathers', eleven times; and under the title 'Lest We Forget', nine times.

5. Roger John Brownlow Keyes, 1st Baron Keyes (1872–1945), was born in India; fought in the Boxer Rising; ran the submarine service (from 1912); was engaged in the Dardanelles campaign (1915); and helped to train commandos in World War II.

6. Sir Archibald Armar Montgomery-Massingberd (1871–1947) fought in South Africa and at the Marne.

7. Mackail (1859–1945) was a classical scholar, literary critic and poet. He studied under Benjamin Jowett at Balliol; translated Virgil and various Latin works; wrote about George Wyndham and William Morris. His wife, Margaret, was the only daughter of Sir Edward Burne-Jones. One of his children was the novelist Angela Thirkell.

8. Howell Arthur Gwynne (1865–1950), a journalist, special and war correspondent for Reuter's (1893–1904), Editor of the *Standard* (1904–11) and the *Morning Post* (1911–37); supporter of tariff-reform. Noted for his political friendships.

9. Sir Fabian Arthur Goulstone Ware (1869–1949) was an editor and a prime mover in the formation of the Imperial War Graves Commission.

10. Allan Beville Ramsay (1872–1955), Master of Magdalene College, Cambridge, from 1925. Vice-chancellor of Cambridge University (1929–51). As Lower Master of Eton College (1916–25), he once invited Kipling to read from his writings to his students.

11. Esther Louisa Baldwin (b. 1902), fourth daughter of Stanley Baldwin.

12. A close friend of Kipling until political differences separated them, Oliver Baldwin (1899–1958) was the 2nd Earl Baldwin of Bewdley. His opinion that 'Mary Postgate' was 'the wickedest short story ever written in the history of the world' (which was made public shortly after Kipling's death) stirred up a great deal of controversy. It was Oliver who discovered the true circumstances of John Kipling's death at Loos; see C. E. Carrington's *Rudyard Kipling: His Life and Work*, 2nd edn (London: Macmillan, 1978) pp. 509–10.

13. See p. 21.

14. Co-founder, in 1927, of the Kipling Society, along with Major J. H. Beith ('Ian Hay') and L. C. Dunsterville ('Stalky'), who served as the first president of the Society.

15. Samuel Courtauld (1876–1947) was an industrialist and art patron (for example, he gave money for the purchase of Van Gogh's 'Sunflowers'). His home is now the Courtauld Institute of Art.

16. Maud Albinia Margaret Selwyn married Sir Percy Francis Cunynghame (1867–1941) in 1903. He was attached to the staff of HH the Rajah of Sarawak, and retired from the post in 1909. Lady Cunynghame died in 1948.

17. Executive Chairman of the British Commercial Gas Association from 1912. Served on London War Pensions Committee (1916–1921). Hospital philanthropist, and active in the Kipling Society from its beginning.

18. Sir George Fletcher MacMunn (1869–1952), British officer, who served in India, Kashmir, South Africa and the Great War (1914–1919). A founder of the Kipling Society, and author of several books about Kipling.

19. Monsieur Charles Corbin.

20. Senhor Raul Régis de Oliveria, GBE.

21. Baron E. de Cartier de Marchienne.

22. Dino Grandi.

23. Jonkheer Maitre R. de Marees van Swinderen.

24. Count Preben F. Ahlefedt-Laurvig, GCVO.

25. G. A. Gripenberg.

26. The Hon. Vincent Massey.

27. Duffy was the assistant secretary, representing the Rt Hon. S. M. Bruce, PC, CH, MC, MP, the High Commissioner for Australia.

28. The Hon. Richard Linton.

29. Douglas McGarel Hogg, 1st Viscount Hailsham (1872–1950), was invited by Bonar Law to become Attorney General (1922); Baldwin retained him in this office (1923). Secretary of State for War (1931), and Lord Chancellor under Baldwin (1935).

30. Arthur Neville Chamberlain held the post of Chancellor of the Exchequer from 1923 to 1924, and from 1931 to 1937.

31. Alfred Duff Cooper (1890–1954), 1st Viscount Norwich, politician and diplomat; enemy of the Munich settlement (1938), as a result of which he resigned as First Lord of the Admiralty. Ambassador to Paris, 1944–7.

32. Lord Eustace Sutherland Campbell Percy (1887–1958), Baron Percy of Newcastle, politician and educationist; President of the Board of Education and member of Privy Council (1924); helped to develop British policy toward India before resigning from the Government in 1936. Served as Vice-chancellor of the University of Durham.

33. George Ambrose Lloyd (1879–1941), intelligence officer, Governor of India (he invited Kipling to visit him, but Carrie's health prevented acceptance of the invitation), and statesman. He imprisoned Ghandi to maintain the 'rule of law'. He favoured imperial causes, Arab interests and Tory politics.

34. James Rennell Rodd (1858–1941), 1st Baron Rennell, diplomat, scholar, and associate of Burne-Jones, Wilde and Whistler in the 1880s. Ambassador to Rome, 1908–19. Author of *Homer's Ithaca* (1927). His wife was Lilias Georgina (*née* Guthrie).

35. See p. 357, n. 4.

36. Painter (1872–1945), Principal of the Royal College of Art, and official artist for the battle-front in France during World War I.

37. Publisher (1851–1936), son of Daniel, who, with his brother Alexander, founded Macmillan and Co. in 1843. Sir Frederick, interested in the New York branch (which became independent in 1890), helped to frame the Copyright Act of 1911.

38. See p. 91, note on O'Dwyer.

39. Leopold Charles Maurice Stennett Amery (1873–1955), statesman and journalist.

40. Ralph David Blumenfeld (1869–1948), an editor known as 'RDB', was sent to London by the United Press to report on Queen Victoria's Jubilee. He worked on the *New York Herald*. After 1900, he was an employee of the *Daily Mail* and of Northcliffe. Later still, he wrote for the *Daily Express*. He became a British subject in 1907.

41. Robert Laurence Binyon (1869–1943) worked in the British Museum, specialising in Chinese and Japanese art, Blake's woodcuts. and Botticelli. He knew Hopkins, Bridges and Masefield, and wrote art-histories, poems and literary criticism.

42. A Scottish minister (1863–1941), who occasionally preached before Queen Victoria and King George V in Scotland, Dr Fleming contributed numerous pieces (usually anonymous) to newspapers and magazines.

43. Noyes (1880–1958), poet, novelist and dramatist, may be most famous for 'The Barrel-Organ' ('Come down to Kew in Lilac-time'), and his strong opposition to Joyce's *Ulysses*. *The Unknown God* (1934), written after his conversion to Roman Catholicism, is directed toward agnostics.

44. Frankau (1884–1952) was a cigar-merchant, a soldier in the East Surrey

Regiment during the Great War, and a popular novelist (e.g. *Christopher Strong*, 1932).

45. Robert Percy Hodder-Williams, publisher and Chairman of Hodder and Stoughton (1927–47).

46. Edward Verrall Lucas (1868–1938), journalist, essayist and critic, author of numerous travel books, anthologies and romances, as well as a highly praised *Life of Charles Lamb* (2 vols, 1905). A contributor to *Punch*, and (after 1924) Chairman of Methuen.

47. John Francis Toye (1883–1964), music-critic of the *Morning Post* from 1925. A song-composer, and author of biographies of Verdi and Rossini.

48. Maud Holt, daughter of William Holt, married Sir Herbert Beerbohm Tree in 1883. She was a distinguished actress, famous for her portrayals of Ophelia and Lady Teazle.

49. Phyllis Neilson-Terry (b. 1892), actress. Her mother was Julia Neilson, who married Fred Terry in 1891, and worked with him in the productions of romantic-historical plays such as *The Scarlet Pimpernel* (1905).

50. See p. 134, note on Hamilton.

51. (William) Cosmo Gordon Lang, Baron Lang of Lambeth (1864–1945), became Archbishop of Canterbury in 1928.

52. The Rt Hon. J. H. Thomas, MP.

53. Sir Josiah Stamp (1880–1941), President of the British Association for the Advancement of Science (1936); Chairman of London School of Economics; wrote extensively on economics; created 1st Baron Stamp in 1938.

Epilogue: 'Twilight in the Abbey'*

Mr Frederick T. Barrett sends the following extract from a letter written to him by his sister shortly after Kipling's funeral in Westminster Abbey on 23 January 1936:

There was a miserable cluster of us, about a hundred, on the pavement outside the North Door of the Abbey – love locked out. We all lingered on for a bit, disappointed, but we could hear the strains of the organ, and there was always the hope that a place might be found for 'just one more'. While looking at the strange medley I began to play a game all to myself, finding Kipling

* Unsigned article in *Kipling Journal*, XXXII (Dec 1965) 84–5.

characters among them and thinking how he would appreciate the types assembled there to pay homage. I found the Absent-minded Beggar easily – also 'we be soldiers three, *pardonez moi, je vous en prie*', and so on, from the many sallow yellowish faces that spoke of 'far-flung outposts of Empire'. It was a lovely game, but slowly the crowd gave up hope and dwindled away, leaving a faithful eleven and finally seven. By that time I was Commander of the Keyhold and we all listened or peeped in turn.

It was all very tantalising. There was just that big iron-framed keyhold and iron-studded relentless oak door.

But looking at its iron I wondered whether it was Sussex iron and that gave me an idea for another game. I thought, 'You be glad you are Sussex-born. I'll try Dan and Una's (or rather Puck's) incantation this time.' So I began pressing the studs to 'By oak and ash and thorn'.[1] There was still the organ to beguile us and it was rather a nice game. But suddenly – and it almost gave me a fright – I was certain the door gave a slight move, behind my shoulder, very quietly and cautiously. Someone said to me, 'May I come out, please?' She came out and I stepped in.

There was still an irate verger to face and a pleading in whispers for the six behind me, but we got there. The spell had worked, you see!

We were where we shouldn't have been at all – quite a front view, as well as more than half the service. The funny coincidence, to give the last touch of embroidery to the story, is that the woman who came out was the image of Gloriana, deathly pale, slightly reddish hair, very imperious, with maid or companion in attendance, and altogether it made me feel quite uncanny.

Lovely fairy story, isn't it? But true!

I wonder I didn't fall into the Abbey. There was a surprise step down. I landed plonk on a paving-stone and it seemed only a second before I had to face the verger, who fortunately could not be over-irate in whispers. His final word to me was 'Then stay where you are.' For that I was only too thankful! And now every time I hear Kipling's 'Recessional' I think of how I gate-crashed, literally and yet by magic.

I had a clump of South down grass with me, 'Where sheep-bells tinkle as you pass',[2] and when no other horrid verger was looking, I pushed it under the oak and ash and thorn sent by the Burwash gardener. So Puck was thoroughly represented. It was next to the

French Ambassador's wreath, but we know which RK would
have appreciated most, or more!

And a few days earlier, when the news came to a schoolboy near
'sleepy Chester' that his favourite author had died, some clumsy
verses were strung together as the best tribute he could as yet
produce to the writer who had meant more than any other to a
lonely, bookish child:

> The world rolls on and many pass away –
>   Those whom we ill can spare – and such a one,
>   Kipling, has left us now: his course is done
> And this our land is poorer from today.
> For he is dead who held us all in sway
>   With magic words, words that were his alone,
>   That will not sound again now he is gone –
> Is gone, and oh! the world seems sad and gray.
> Yet in that night before mine eyes there gleam
>   A shadowy throng that being drew from thee,
> Mourning the passing of a soul supreme:
>   Mowgli and Stalky, Terence Mulvaney,
> Kim, Puck, and Jungle People swell the stream
>   That witness to thine immortality.

Finally, after the words of lesser men, Miss A. M. Punch reminds
us of the tribute paid to the memory of Rudyard Kipling by his
greatest contemporary.

In this – the centenary year of Rudyard Kipling's birth, we note
with happiness, reflections on his mastery which come to us over
the wide fields of the world from 'the masses, the under-dogs, the
men of small account', no less than from the 'great, and well-
bespoke'; fully justifying Admiral Chandler's dictum.[3]

But for the summation of our claims to Kipling's greatness, surely
we are led to the Rt Hon. Winston Churchill, CH, PC,[4] MP – his style
of that day – when on 17 November 1937 he – himself a lord of
language – proposed a toast from which we quote as follows:

We meet here tonight . . . to honour the memory of a writer, of a
man, and of a force. . . . There seems to be no gallery of human

activity which he could not enter easily and unchallenged, and which having entered, he could not illuminate with a light unexpected, piercing, enchanting, and all his own.

There have been in our own time greater poets and sages. . . . But in the glittering rank which he took by Right Divine there has never been anyone like him. No one has ever written like Kipling before, and his work has been successfully imitated by none. He was unique and irreplaceable.

NOTES

1. The final lines of 'A Tree Song' in *Puck of Pook's Hill*. Variants of the final line end each stanza. Pook often swears by Oak and Ash and Thorn in the stories.

2. Misquoted from 'A Three-part Song', which was first printed in *Strand* and *McClure's*, Oct 1906, and collected in *Puck of Pook's Hill* (1906):

> I've given my soul to the Southdown grass,
> An' sheep-bells tinkled where you pass.

3. Rear-Admiral Lloyd H. Chandler, a bibliographer, prepared an analysis of Kipling's writings (both authorised and unauthorised), with some assistance from a reluctant Kipling. The Chandler Index is now in the Library of Congress.

4. Companion of Honour, Privy Councillor.

Index

The names of authors of selections are printed in bold type.

Church of the Recessional (California), 167
'Church's One Foundation, The', 19, 139
Cincinnati, 203
City Club (Cape Town), 279, 284
City of Berlin, 94, 106
City of Peking, 173
'City of Two Creeds', 72, 84
Civil and Military Gazette (Lahore), 31, 61–3, 67, 81, 92–3, 97, 354; contributions to 'turnover' section, 65, 89, 104; description of newspaper offices, 84–7, 92–3; ethics as a journalist, 354–5; first literary efforts, 65, 72–3, 77–8, 87–8, 118, 125, 326; inexperience, 63–4; journalistic duties, 65–6, 68–70, 80, 86–8, 110; readers' attitudes toward *C. and M.*, 81; RK stops writing stories for, 101; RK's work habits, 65–6, 70–1
Civil and Military Gazette Press, 84
Civil War (US), 324
Clemens, Cyril, 239–44
Clemens, Olivia Susan, 248–9
Clemens, Samuel Longhorne (Mark Twain), 247–50
Clemens, Samuel Longhorne (Mark Twain), 153–5, 197–8, 239–42
Club, North-west Provinces, 101
Cobb, Irvin, 322
Coe, A. E., 165
Coe (reporter), 191
Coleridge, Samuel Taylor, 41, 301
Collins Street (Melbourne), 273
Collins, Wilkie, 197
Colombo (Ceylon), 60
Comedie Française, 319
'Concerning a Certain Criticism' (Conrad), 327
Confessions of a Thug, The (Taylor), 28
Connaught, Duke of, 352, 387
Conrad, Joseph, 326–30, 359
Convent of St Martha, 165
Cook, J., 165
Cook, Miss, 294
Cooper, A. Duff, 388
Cooper, Anice Page, 382–3
Cooper's Hill Engineering College, 31

Copyright Act, 125
Corbet, Richard, 355–6
Corbin, Charles (French Ambassador), 388
Costebelle Hotels (Hyeres), 285
Country Life, 243
Courtauld, S. A., 388
Craik, 125
Crane, Susy, 248
Crapaud, Jean, 334
Crashaw, Richard, 301
Cream of Reviews, 81
Crewe, Lord, 294
Croft-Cooke, Rupert, 358–66
Cronin trial, 202
Crown Hotel, 361
Cuba Street (New Zealand), 269
Cunynghame, Lady, 388
Cup, The (Tennyson), 373
Curtis, Holbrook, 258
Curzon, Lord, 154

Dante, 41
Danube, 289
Dapple Gray, 9
David Copperfield (Dickens), 10
Davies, Matthew, 274
Dawbarn, Robert H. M., 108–9
Debs, Eugene, 177
De Morgan, William, 142
'Dennis', 197
Denzil, Sir, 6
Derby, Lord, 293
'Derby scheme', 293
Detroit Free Press, 156
Devil's Peak (Cape Town), 283
Devonshire, 143
Dickens, Charles, 119, 197, 373
Dickens Fellowship, 389
Disraeli, Benjamin, 369
Distribution of Wealth, The (Carver), 307
Ditchingham, 148
Dodge, Mary Mapes, 260
Dogras, 33
Dongola, 347
Donne, John, 301
Doubleday, Frank, 155, 258, 298
Doubleday and Page, 114
Doubleday Doran and Co., 389